SEAL SURVIVAL GUIDE

SEAL SURVIVAL GUIDE

A Navy SEAL's Secrets
to Surviving Any Disaster

CADE COURTLEY

GALLERY BOOKS
New York   London   Toronto   Sydney   New Delhi

Gallery Books
A Division of Simon & Schuster, Inc.
1230 Avenue of the Americas
New York, NY 10020

Copyright © 2012 by SEAL Survival, LLC

All rights reserved, including the right to reproduce this book
or portions thereof in any form whatsoever. For information,
address Gallery Books Subsidiary Rights Department,
1230 Avenue of the Americas, New York, NY 10020.

First Gallery Books trade paperback edition December 2012

GALLERY BOOKS and colophon are registered trademarks of
Simon & Schuster, Inc.

For information about special discounts for bulk purchases,
please contact Simon & Schuster Special Sales at 1-866-506-1949
or business@simonandschuster.com.

The Simon & Schuster Speakers Bureau can bring authors to your
live event. For more information or to book an event, contact the
Simon & Schuster Speakers Bureau at 1-866-248-3049 or visit our
website at www.simonspeakers.com.

Designed by Julie Schroeder
Illustrations by Jesse Peterson

Manufactured in the United States of America

20 19 18 17 16 15 14 13 12

Library of Congress Cataloging-in-Publication Data

Courtley, Cade, 1969–
    SEAL survival guide : a Navy SEAL's secrets to surviving any disaster /
Cade Courtley.
       p.   cm.
1. Survival.   2. Disasters.   I. Title.
    GF86.C68 2012
    613.6'9—dc23   2012036842

ISBN 978-1-4516-9029-3
ISBN 978-1-4516-9030-9 (ebook)

To my teammates both here and above

Contents

Introduction

What enables someone to carry a 250-pound man up three flights of stairs while taking enemy fire or spend six sleepless days and nights running around with a fractured right leg? What allows a man to break through a door knowing full well there is someone with an assault rifle on the other side trying to kill him? How is it possible to endure continuous physical abuse and confinement in a three-by-three-foot concrete box without food for more than a week and finish with a smile? Or not only survive exhausting days and nights of subzero temperatures during a blinding blizzard but thrive, coming out harder and stronger? How does one swim seven miles in frigid, whitecapped ocean waters? What makes one voluntarily return time and time again to a war zone?

Essentially, what makes a Navy SEAL?

There are currently nine SEAL teams and approximately 2,500 active-duty U.S. Navy SEALs. President John F. Kennedy created the SEALs in 1962, announcing his plans to do so during the same historic speech in which he promised to put a man on the moon. The president wanted specialized units to handle extremely dangerous and covert operations and become the elite force for unconventional warfare techniques. Since the creation of the Navy SEALs, they have been involved in thousands of combat missions, first making their name in Vietnam. There, SEAL Teams One and Two accomplished an amazing kill ratio of 200:1. SEALs were so feared by enemy forces that they were simply known as "the men with green faces." SEALs also served in Grenada, Panama, Somalia, Bosnia, Afghanistan, and Iraq, in addition to conducting numerous highly classified operations in countries not mentioned above. Recent notable operations include freeing the hijacked captain of the *Maersk Alabama,* the rescue of American hostages in Somalia, and the killing of Osama bin Laden.

Mr. President, you got your money's worth.

"SEAL" is an acronym for "Sea, Air, Land." The idea was to forge a military unit that could operate effectively in all environments. Prior to the formation of the SEALs, there were numerous specialized military units, such as the Scouts and Raiders, formed in 1942, nine months after the attack on Pearl Harbor. These guys were trained for stealth and conducted preassault assessments of beachhead landing areas, marked targets, and did whatever it took to make a mission by other forces more successful. There were also the Naval Combat Demolition Units and the Underwater Demolition Teams (UDTs), which many remember as the classic "frogmen" of World War II. These were amphibious units that went in prior to conventional battles to clear beach obstacles, cut underwater enemy cables, or rig buoys, bridges, or enemy ships with explosives. They were responsible for blowing out fortified German gaps during the Omaha Beach landing, for example, which ultimately led to victory for the Allies. In addition, the Office of Strategic Services had a group called Operational Swimmers, which more closely resembled current SEAL operations. These men were dropped by parachute behind enemy lines for guerrilla warfare, or donned the first flexible diving masks and fins to attack by sea.

The SEALs were formed to create a military force that combined all these varying branches, capable of operating in all environments. Whether it be the Arctic tundra, the jungles of the tropics, the desert, or the ocean, SEALs are trained to adapt to any variable and carry out everything from top-secret missions to conventional warfare. SEALs perform the most dangerous and oftentimes unimaginable tasks, and they do so with uncompromising principles and resolute loyalty.

To be eligible to become a SEAL, you must be a U.S. citizen, pass a basic physical, have good eyesight, and be under twenty-eight years old. If you score well on the Armed Services Vocational Aptitude Battery test, and at a minimum swim five hundred yards in under twelve and a half minutes, do forty-two push-ups in two minutes and fifty sit-ups in two minutes, and run one and a half miles in under eleven and a half minutes (although much higher scores are required for serious consideration), then you might get a chance to attend training.

Only one out of a thousand who want to become a SEAL gets the opportunity to attend BUD/S (Basic Underwater Demolition/ SEAL Training), the twenty-six-week training process of becoming a SEAL, and of those, less than 15 percent will make it to graduation. Once trainees have completed BUD/S, the training continues with the twenty-eight-week course of advanced training called SQT (SEAL Qualification Training), which teaches them all of the skill sets they will need to officially become a Navy SEAL. The guys who thought it would be cool to be a SEAL because they saw the teams in the movies or wanted to use their SEAL status to pick up chicks last about two days. The ones who make it endure the toughest military training in the world and possess traits in common that include persistence, dedication, and tenacity; quite simply, these men are *hard*. But it's much more than that.

These new SEALs then report to one of the following SEAL teams: Teams One, Three, Five, and Seven are based in Coronado, California. SEAL Teams Two, Four, Eight, and Ten are located in Little Creek, Virginia. Once they join their team, they will spend another eighteen months training with their platoon prior to a six-month deployment. So if you are lucky enough to not get injured and make it straight through training, it will be at least thirty-one months before you are a combat-ready Navy SEAL.

As you might notice, I didn't mention SEAL Team Six, since before the bin Laden kill, this was a theoretically nonexistent unit and no one was to know of its missions or activities—it was our secret. So much for OPSEC (Operational Security). Nevertheless, to be chosen for SEAL Team Six, a SEAL must serve for six years on other teams, and then they'll have the opportunity to screen for this crew of all-stars.

When I entered BUD/S, I was determined not to quit. I convinced myself there was no backup plan. I would graduate or die trying, even if it took me nine months longer than usual to get through it, since I had broken my leg three times and suffered a fractured skull. I spent the entire six days of Hell Week running on a partially fractured right leg. To say my comfort zone was pushed with every step I took is an understatement. I did finally graduate as a lieutenant, and everything I learned and endured during training has served me well and kept me alive.

As they say in Washington, D.C.: "If we want a mission done right . . . we SEAL it."

I tell you this not to boast. Those of us who have served in the teams are hesitant to list our trials. I cite the above examples to validate that what I have to offer comes from very real and current experiences. The information in this book doesn't come from an "Internet expert" or someone "out of the game" since Vietnam. Rather, it comes from someone who has been there, done that, and truly survived.

For a Navy SEAL, achieving and maintaining maximum physical fitness is a basic job requirement. I've spent the better part of my life working hard to stay at peak physical levels for mission success, but I will never forget the strongest muscle of all—and that is the brain. It is the foundation on which everything else is built. In this book I will teach you the true secret techniques used by Navy SEALs and demonstrate how to significantly enhance your odds of survival in any situation.

The real successes and achievements attributed to SEALs are actually due to the way we have trained and conditioned our minds. It's the ability to see the real world and react to any situation without hesitation and make split-second decisions that could have global ramifications.

I am writing this book to give you the tools needed to think like a SEAL, to adapt rapidly to the unexpected, and to ensure maximum survival. If you follow the advice in this guide, you will significantly reduce your chance of becoming a mere mortality statistic when adversity strikes, and instead become one of the few who will survive.

The world we live in is truly dangerous, but the intent of this book is to empower. It will give you the tools you need to survive in almost any situation, especially the most deadly. No one needs to become a reclusive survival fanatic or live in a paranoid state. We must all be prepared and vigilant, but living scared is not living. I became a Navy SEAL to protect our country and defend our rights and freedom. Be confident in yourself and the new skills you will learn, and then go on and enjoy every day of your life.

This will take some work, but everything worthwhile does. Staying alive, I'll assume, is the goal of all of us. These are the twin promises of this book:
  A. You will learn how to gain the mental and physical abilities that will enable you to survive a crisis when the time comes.
  B. You will learn skills and techniques to give you confidence and freedom in the world now, even if you never are faced with a life-threatening situation.

It's Time to Harden Up!

Many indulge in lifestyles without discipline, preferring the path of least resistance. The overall attitude of the population is geared toward seeking self-centered comfort and convenience. Obesity is at an all-time high, and the trivial distractions that surround us, from video games to our infatuation with trash TV, seem to be designed to make us weaker as a nation, and incidentally unprepared. No matter your age or the physical condition you are in right now, this is the time to begin a new regimen and develop a mindset that will turn you into a survivor who can live with confidence and freedom in this changing world.

The world is a dangerous place and getting more so with each passing day. Yet, the United States is as soft as it's ever been. It's not a question of *if* but *when* the next man-made or natural disaster will occur. I don't say this lightly, to posture as some crackpot doomsayer, but to give you the facts. If you want to make believe that all is just fine, then keep your head in the sand and put this book down right now. You'll get nothing out of it.

The cold, hard reality is that the vast majority of people are simply not equipped to successfully deal with impending catastrophes, which will claim hundreds or even thousands of lives. In addition, you must be prepared to face personal dangers from crimes, accidents, and potentially fatal mishaps, which are increasing and will surely get worse in these perilous times.

I look forward to the day when this is no longer true. Until then, I will do everything in my power to teach you how to be a survivor and not a statistic. In this guide, I will provide a step-by-step plan for action to keep you alive during the most deadly circumstances.

When the unthinkable happens, you will have a Navy SEAL as your personal guide.

Be a survivor—not a statistic!

PART ONE

SEAL Mindset and Survival Psychology

EXPAND YOUR COMFORT ZONE

You know your current comfort zone, defined as the daily routine you do and the things that make you feel secure, content, and in control. However, most of our daily comfort-zone rituals will leave us unprepared to deal with even the smallest discomfort and will certainly render us incapable of handling an emergency or life-threatening challenge.

Challenge Your Limits and Daily Routines

Push the boundaries of your comfort zone at least once a day. There are so many opportunities to do this without attempting all at once to become an ultra-marathon runner, although this is a great goal. You must first expand your mind to the possibilities of doing certain things that you previously believed unachievable. Start with small steps and note progress by keeping track; make a list, and check off all the things you do each day to challenge yourself, both physically and mentally. Ultimately, by expanding your comfort zone you will increase both your physical and mental toughness, which are the keys to survival.

I believe that if you first focus on changing small things, you can begin the process of thinking differently, and ultimately achieve the goal of acquiring the SEAL mindset of survival, which will allow you to endure anything. You will quickly see that *doing* things differently makes you *think* differently. Observe your current routine and then start by doing simple things another way. For example, use the stairs instead of the elevator to take you up only a few floors. Climb at a reasonable pace and know that when you reach the top, you have just expanded your comfort zone. When in your car, don't fight to get the space closest to the store, but purposely look for one that will make you walk. Force yourself to meet three new people and learn at least five things about them. If you have to balance your checkbook, leave the calculator in the desk and make your brain complete this task. Open up the contact list in your phone and memorize five numbers each day. You must seek out ways to expand both mind and body. Start paying attention to how you think about things. If you expand your comfort zone in this manner, you will be better able to do the rest. If you already exercise or jog, for example, increase your distance or speed. Run that extra mile, or run it a minute faster. Do that one additional push-up. Try holding your breath for a minute, and then try two. When in the shower, after scrubbing down with the warm water you usually prefer, finish the last thirty seconds with a blast of cold water. By pushing your physical limits, you are also forcing your brain to expand its comfort boundaries, thus gradually making yourself physically and mentally tougher.

Now that I am out of the Navy and getting older every day, I continue to push my comfort zone by engaging in activities I did when I was in SEAL team, including skydiving, shooting, climbing, and long swims. Instead of doing these things in preparation for a mission, I do them not only to maintain these very perishable skills, but also to keep my mind and body sharp—I still push the comfort zone and know that this will allow me to be every bit of the warrior I used to be.

Everyone's comfort zone is different, so for some of us, expanding it means starting with drinking one less beer or forgoing dessert. Yet all of these little daily victories will bring us confidence later, especially when our lives depend on it. It's so much easier to do nothing, and it seems natural not to bother, but I tell you: These first exercises are essential in changing your mindset and eventually can be the very things that will separate the survivors from the victims.

Here is a visualization I use: I like to imagine that pushing my comfort zone daily is similar to rolling a boulder up a hill. If I let it, the rock will always want to tumble back down, and I'll have to start from the bottom again. Expanding the comfort zone on a daily basis will actually make it easier to get that boulder closer to the summit—and to our success or ultimate survival.

COMFORT ZONE CHECKLIST (all answers need to be yes):
- ❏ Did I challenge myself today?
- ❏ Did I do something positive that my mind initially didn't want to do?
- ❏ Did I do something positive that my body initially didn't want to do?
- ❏ Can I do more?

INCREASE YOUR PHYSICAL TOUGHNESS

So I'm telling you to get in shape, but here's a different motivation that should make you finally do it. Ask yourself, "Is my body at a state of readiness that will get me through whatever might come my way?" Don't like to exercise? You tell yourself there's no time, or some other excuse, and ultimately never begin. But imagine when the time comes and those whom you love depend on you. How would you feel if you were unable to drag your child, sister, or father from a burning building because you were out of shape? Imagine if you were unable to outrun a mugger or a rapist because you were too winded.

Achieve a Better State of Physical Fitness

No matter what physical condition you are in now, it can be improved. Running and swimming will improve your cardiovascular fitness and will definitely pay off if you find yourself being chased or having to run from something like a wildfire. Pull-ups, push-ups, and weight training will obviously improve your physical strength and could come in very handy if you have to remove rubble from an earthquake that has collapsed on a relative. Rock climbing or surfing will not only improve your balance but make you more comfortable with heights and being in the water, two things that are incredibly useful during a high-rise fire or flash flood. Take up some type of fighting or martial art, because not only will you will enjoy the physical fitness benefits it provides, but you won't be shocked and unprepared if you find yourself in a situation where fighting is the only option.

There are numerous training programs available that can guide you and help you achieve a better physical condition. No matter if you begin by taking a daily walk or joining a gym, your motivation is more than weight loss, per se (though that is good); you are also working to be better prepared to survive whatever may come your way. Improve your physical endurance, and it will provide the confidence that you can and will survive anything, under any circumstances. Expand your physical comfort zone, and you will become physically tough.

When I was training to go to BUD/S, I put a pull-up bar in my bedroom door. Every time I entered or exited the bedroom—ten pull-ups. Every time I went into the bathroom—twenty-five push-ups. Simple, a little masochistic, and very effective.

SEALs stress great physical fitness because it is an absolute necessity for mission success. The average person will never need to run with a hundred pounds of equipment through the desert for several days, or jump out of a plane only to have to swim three miles in the freezing ocean before making it to the designated target. Then again, maybe you will. The sailors of the ill-fated USS *Indianapolis* never thought they would have to tread shark-infested waters for  several days. Nor did the Uruguayan rugby team that survived a plane crash ever imagine that they would have to make a hundred-mile trek over snow-covered mountains to get out alive. In both cases, these brave people were able to survive not only because of their incredible mental toughness, or mindset, but also because they possessed the physical ability to do so.

SEALs say: "It's hard to stay hard—dying is easy."

PHYSICAL TOUGHNESS CHECKLIST (all answers need to be yes):
- ❏ Did I physically challenge my body today?
- ❏ Did I elevate my heart rate and breathing today?
- ❏ Did I exercise longer or faster today than yesterday?
- ❏ Will I exercise longer or faster tomorrow than I did today?

INCREASE YOUR MENTAL TOUGHNESS

How do you achieve a SEAL mindset, which is what I call **mental toughness**? For me, I reduced the goal of changing my mindset to a simple phrase that I repeated over and over during Navy SEAL training in Coronado, California: "Never quit!" It actually really simplified things for me. Instead of being mentally consumed by every nuance (cold, heat, exhaustion, stress, fear), I just kept repeating in my mind, "Never quit!"

SEAL training has remained largely unchanged for more than forty years because it simply works. It continues to produce some of the finest future warriors of any school in the military by using a very basic blueprint:

1. Break (beat) the individual down.
2. Build them back up, achieving a both physically and mentally tougher trainee.
3. Repeat . . . repeat . . . repeat.

As a senior SEAL instructor, I used to tell my students, "SEALs are formed like a sword is forged from a piece of steel—by constantly heating, hammering, and cooling by submergence in water. In the end, both weapons are ready for battle."

Attack Your Fear List

Physical toughness and mental toughness are branches of the same tree. By pushing yourself physically, you will be pushing yourself mentally, but as I said earlier, the brain is the strongest muscle in the body, and it requires an expanded workout program. Here is the quickest and most effective way to "exercise" your mental toughness, something that I call the Fear List.

Start by making a list of five things that make you nervous or scared. It could be heights, fighting, small spaces, or the water. Let's take public speaking, for example. I've seen some of the toughest guys in the world become Gummi bears when required to speak in front of a group of people. Next, create a five-minute presentation based on something you are very familiar with. Practice this several times by yourself, speaking out loud. Finally, you *must* organize a group of people, be it coworkers or an assemblage at a public event, and give your presentation. It may not be perfect, but you have just conquered a fear and in doing so made yourself mentally tougher. Continue down your Fear List, and you will see how quickly you can remove other fear-induced limits. This will give you more confidence in all other areas of your life. Remember that living in fear is not really living.

When confronting each of your fears, remember how SEALs train: Break down, build back up, and repeat. When you repeat these actions, even if you don't succeed completely the first time, the next attempt will make you mentally tougher. There are also some other simple tools for acquiring mental toughness. First off, I absolutely forbid whining or blaming others—both are completely antithetical to achieving mental toughness. For example, the next time you go into a store and there is a long checkout line, don't moan. Instead, monitor how you can control your mind and force yourself to be patient. In fact, if impatience is your weakness, then that is your personal impediment to mental toughness. Instead, let the person standing behind you get ahead of you, until your impatience has no power over you. Break, build back, and repeat. If you get a flat tire, get out of the car and fix it. If you run out of gas while driving because you didn't check your gauges or equipment, blame no one. Learn as you walk to the nearest gas station and back with a gas can in your hand, doing so without saying a word. If you get caught in the rain, remind yourself it's only water and endure it until you have an opportunity to change into dry clothes. This is how you achieve mental toughness on a daily basis.

SEALs say: "The only easy day—was yesterday."
(Because yesterday is over.)

MENTAL TOUGHNESS CHECKLIST (all answers need to be yes):
- ❏ Did I identify a fear?
- ❏ Did I make preparations to conquer this fear?
- ❏ Did I conquer this fear?
- ❏ Did I move on to my next fear?

Hell Week occurs during the first of several weeks of BUD/S training. It consists of six nonstop, hypothermia-filled, sleepless days and
nights and is the time when most of the DORs (drop on request), or
quitters, ask to go home. This training is the ultimate test of mental and physical
toughness. We were trained to suffer in silence—we may have been cold, tired,
and hurting, but nobody wanted to hear it. I will never forget when a nationally
ranked triathlete in our class, who had barely broken a sweat in the previous
weeks of training, quit on the third night of Hell Week. He decided he just didn't
want to go back into the water. As naturally gifted as he was athletically, he
had never truly been mentally pushed like he was during Hell Week. But I also
remember another member of my class, a 135-pound, skin-and-bones-looking
guy who was one of the slowest runners and barely said a word. He continued
on the rest of the week determined and made no sign that he was enduring
hardship. I later learned that he had lived his entire life being put down for his
size. Hell Week was just another week for him. That's mental toughness.

MENTAL PREPARATION

Again, the brain is the strongest muscle in the body. You've heard
stories of how combat soldiers have been shot repeatedly but were

not aware of it until the fight was over. These stories are true, and the power to do such things comes from the mind and can be tapped into by practicing mental preparation. This practice can allow you to far exceed your physical limitations. Just as you train other muscles, you can train the brain with mental-preparedness exercises—and you don't need to go to the gym to do it! It's an exercise you can do anywhere. I can't stress enough how important mental preparedness is for surviving and enduring any life-threatening situation that you could encounter. This is how you practice it.

Emergency Conditioning (EC): Make the Unknown Familiar

Using visualization techniques is a good way to practice what we call **emergency conditioning (EC).** I will highlight this phrase throughout the guide and explain the types of visualizations that are most effective in survival scenarios. It means conditioning the mind in advance of emergencies, thus producing psychological strength in times of crisis. This is also referred to as "battle-proofing" or "battle inoculation" by military personnel. Example: A soldier lying on his cot imagines a nasty firefight with the enemy, including what it will sound like and smell like, the heavy breathing, and the utter exhaustion.

If the brain imagines something in deep and vivid detail, it will become part of a person's "experience files." This visualization exercise will actually fool the brain into believing that you have already experienced this event. You can tap into these files at will by hitting the play button that starts the "movie" of what you have already visualized and planned. It will seem more or less familiar if ever you are confronted with a similar experience. This internal battle-proofing gives you an incredible advantage.

Visualization: Make a Movie in Your Mind

No matter if you are going to work or are in a mall, boarding a plane, or anywhere else, look around and take mental notes of the particulars of the place—try to describe the exact details of where you are. This is the setting for your **mental movie.**

Now, imagine what you would do in this fixed environment if

something were to go wrong. In this book, I will explain the specifics for each situation, but for now, remember this key step in changing your mindset to one that puts you in **SEAL mode.** In your mental movie, play out various scenarios from start to finish. Begin by imagining the most likely scenario that you may find yourself in, focusing on what to do during a life-or-death situation, such as a home invasion, a fire at work, or being lost in the mountains.

When I was a platoon commander, after receiving a "tasking" (mission request), this is how I would do my entire mission planning: I would visualize every detail, starting with my men, the equipment, the time of day, and the weather, and slowly start *my* movie. I would hit pause or even rewind when I came to a place that I saw as a flaw or obstacle to success. I would play out all the various contingencies in my head until I could visualize any number of versions of events that might take place, working through every possibility. I would often rewind to make a correction, such as add or change equipment or alter an action. I would then continue forward to a point where ultimately my mental movie was a successful mission from start to finish—one from which all my guys would come back safe!

SEALs say: "Plan for success and train for failure."
The movies we see on the big screen about Special Ops make it all seem flawless. However, more often than not, our best plans went out the window once the bullets started to fly. This is when the training and diligence during our mental-preparedness and visualization phases paid off. They give you backup plans to deal with any contingency.

Rehearsal: Act Out Your Plan

To take this a step further, you can actually practice and rehearse what you have visualized. This is essentially what fire drills accomplish in schools and why airline personnel try to show passengers emergency procedures at the beginning of every flight. In your home, you should rehearse and teach your children what to do in the event of a house fire. Most kids respond better when given explicit rules to follow, and doing so will not only give your kids specific things to do during such an event, it will also reduce their fear; they will be more confident in an emergency and their usefulness to the general safety of the family will be increased. For example, to prepare for a power failure, you could turn off the lights in your home to practice how to navigate in darkness or how to get to designated evacuation exits. Rehearse with your family how to respond to a variety of dangerous situations, such as a home invasion. Make sure everyone knows the plan for each scenario from start to finish. The more you practice, the easier it will be.

Obviously, there are limitations to how far you can take this rehearsal. Please do not light a fire in your kitchen to practice escaping your house, or run down the street yelling "Rape!"

This pre-emergency technique will not only enable you to implement your visualization but will also begin to train your muscles, allowing you to physically perform without forethought in a controlled environment. If in your "movie" you have yourself doing a backward somersault, the rehearsal nixes that idea as something unrealistic. Throughout the book, each scenario I discuss requires various rehearsal drills that can be practiced and used to improve muscle memory and response time.

Muscle Memory

By repeatedly practicing your emergency procedures, you are also creating **muscle memory.** Of course, the muscles do not literally have the ability to store memories, but your brain does. It knows (via a complex system of neurological circuitry) what you want the muscles to do the more you practice the same action time and again. After you

learned to ride a bike as a kid, you never forgot how to do it. It's the same if you learned how to swing a tennis racket or hit a baseball over the fence. The more you practiced those activities, the better you got, as if your muscles remembered on their own how to respond. Rehearsing various skills needed to survive helps improve muscle memory. If you really want to bring it up a notch, you need to repeat the same action 2,500 times before it becomes so ingrained that you can do it without even thinking about it. Athletes know this, as do those who practice fighting and forms of martial arts. The thousands of punches, kicks, and combinations they execute when in a fight happen automatically.

In SEAL team, muscle memory was in full effect when it came to using our weapons, be it the thousands of times we changed magazines in our rifles or drew our handguns from the holsters and fired them. There was never a need to look; my hands instinctively went there and did what they were supposed to do. It felt like I was born with the weapons.

You should practice the various self-defense techniques I will demonstrate in this book, such as the correct way to throw a punch to immobilize an assailant or use your elbows to ward off an attacker. Gaining that extra second could very well be what enables you to survive.

By practicing emergency conditioning, visualization, and rehearsal techniques, you essentially do the following:

- Minimize fear of the unknown by preconditioning your mind (emergency conditioning).
- Make unimaginable stressful scenarios more familiar (visualization).
- Increase your capability and gain confidence (rehearsal).
- Practice how to remain calm under pressure (rehearsal).

For a SEAL, one of the requirements is to go through SERE (Survive, Evade, Resist, Escape), or POW school. This training includes an extremely realistic imprisonment scenario following several days of trying to evade capture without food, water, or sleep. Mental and physical abuses, including the now-infamous waterboarding, were all part of the training. I gained a few bruises and lost over twenty-two pounds. My girlfriend didn't even recognize me when I was done. It was challenging, but nowhere near as challenging as what actual POWs face.

SERE school is a classic example of fear of the unknown transforming into confidence. High-risk training performed in a controlled setting will give you the best chance at success when actually confronted with fear in an uncontrolled environment.

Create a Trigger

One of the last things you need to do as part of creating mental preparedness is develop what I call your **trigger.** In order to do this, you must dig deep and identify the single most important thing in the world to you and make a mental portrait, so to speak, of this image. This is what you will use to ignite many of the essential qualities needed to survive. This trigger is the thing that makes you want to live, no matter what comes your way. The most effective trigger will be different for everyone. For some, the trigger will be the image of their child, whom they want to be there for and whom they want to see grow into a man or woman. For others, the trigger image could be elderly parents who need them.

Your trigger image can change as priorities in your life change. When I was going through BUD/S, my trigger was seeing myself walking across the stage at graduation and looking out at family and friends as I was handed my certificate of completion—that image made me endure. But once I got to a SEAL team and took on the incredible responsibility of leading men into life-threatening situations, my trigger was the image of all my men returning from a mission unharmed. I was not going to attend any of my guys' funerals—not on my watch—and that made me pull my trigger and do whatever needed to be done to keep my men alive.

Your trigger could be an aspirational one—i.e., thinking that nothing is going to rob you of your life before you achieve your goal. It's as powerful as a protective trigger, such as saving the life of a loved one or protecting a member of your team. Both work, as long as you take the time to make this an extremely vivid visualization. Let it burn into the files of your mind. You must be able to say, "I will live and endure anything for this."

This image or visualized goal is now your trigger. You will use this most important memory file as the ultimate motivation to get you through anything life throws at you. But to maintain the effectiveness of your trigger, you should save it for only the direst situations.

Life or death . . . **Pull that trigger!**

Violence of Action

In the SEALs, we use the phrase **violence of action.** It simply means that we apply complete and unrestricted use of speed, strength, surprise, and aggression to achieve total dominance against an enemy or an adversarial situation. When the trigger is pulled and violence of action is employed, you are telling your mind and body, "*I am unstoppable.*"

You don't have to be a SEAL to implement violence of action. If your trigger is strong enough, tell yourself, "What I do in the next thirty seconds will determine whether I will live or die." Then it will happen, and the violence of action will be an unexpected advantage for success in many situations.

I know it is difficult for many people to imagine their own death, so try to understand how important the concept of violence of action is by dissecting your trigger. What if even the slightest hesitation or that 1 percent less than total effort causes you to fail? What if the death of a loved one results from the one second that you paused or the less-than-full-strength tackle you made? Then imagine an hour later as you are contemplating what has happened and realize that you didn't fully commit to the event. Make sure you never find yourself in this position. When the trigger is pulled, the full concentrated and coordinated effort of mind and body can transform a ninety-pound elderly woman into a tiger.

Situational Awareness

In military-speak, **situational awareness** is defined as the ability to identify, process, and comprehend the critical elements of information about what is happening to the team with regard to a mission. More simply, it's being aware of what is going on around you.

During CQC (close-quarters combat), which is a technique used for hostage rescue and for raids, as team leader I had to be aware, for example, of multiple teams who were all moving in numerous directions in a building and all assigned to various floors. I had to make sure we were simultaneously engaging targets while being certain that no one was ever in an adjacent room in which a bullet could penetrate the wall, hitting one of us. In this extreme example of situational awareness, I had to know what was happening to the troops on the exterior of the target building, who could have been engaging enemy fire, while at the same time coordinating the use of our air assets and artillery to help suppress enemies advancing on our position.

Because I know the importance of situational awareness during battle, I must admit I get annoyed by the vast number of people who go about their lives without paying even the faintest attention to where they are or what's happening around them. It puts them and the general security of society at risk. These are the very people who most often get victimized or end up on the casualty list. The next time you go to a crowded shopping mall or airport, you will be amazed to observe how many people seem to be oblivious to their environment, insulated in their own world. As we will see, airports and malls, in particular, are two places where you should be absolutely vigilant and aware of your surroundings.

Of course, there are environments that require different levels of situational awareness. If you're at home or at a resort, you should fully enjoy the peace and relative security these places afford. As you will learn, these places can be made safe and allow us to relax and enjoy life. On the other hand, airports, the streets of a foreign country, or crowded stadium events, for example, are not the environments in which to take a mental vacation. You owe it to yourself to stay alert.

Just like visualization, situational awareness drills can be practiced anywhere. Make it a game you play using the following checklist:

SITUATIONAL AWARENESS CHECKLIST
- ❏ Try to guess what individuals around you are thinking or doing.
- ❏ Look for odd behavior or things that seem out of place.
- ❏ Determine where you'd go if you had to seek immediate cover from an explosion or gunshots.
- ❏ Find the two closest exits.
- ❏ Determine whether someone is following you or taking an unusual interest in you.

Imagine this scenario: You see a guy at a shopping mall wearing a heavy coat, holding a cigarette with two inches of ash on the end of it, and he's not inhaling. He continues to look over his right shoulder at another guy fifty feet away with a similar heavy coat. It is 90 degrees outside. If you practice even the slightest measure of situational awareness, this scene should set off alarms in your head. In terms of honing your situational awareness, you may find it helpful to think of yourself as trying to note variances against the baseline, or what is normal.

Composure Under Pressure

Medical experts tell us that daily stress should be minimized. They advise us to find ways to reduce it to achieve better health. However, the stress we experience when confronted with a serious and very real life-threatening situation is something entirely different. Physiologically, a part of the brain called the hypothalamus triggers the release of stress-response hormones, including adrenaline, into the bloodstream. Another stress-response hormone is the steroid-like cortisol, which is produced in the cortex of the adrenal glands. This hormone increases energy and metabolic efficiency and helps regulate blood pressure.

Simultaneously, blood is being diverted away from the brain and skin to the muscles to maximize the chances of survival. Your brain now virtually has "tunnel vision," focusing on nothing but doing what it must to survive. You hear stories about people in desperate situations with superhuman strength. That is all attributable to the body's stress response.

SEALs say: "The more you sweat in training, the less you bleed in combat."

This is where all the physical and mental preparation pays off. The body is helping by releasing hormones, and if we know how to utilize this natural stress response, we can remain calm under pressure and rise to the occasion during any life-threatening situation. You will simply fall back to the level of preparation and training you have achieved.

In the SEALs we would go to great lengths to make training as realistic as possible, using live ammunition, extreme weather, and no sleep. At the end of a long day of training, when I felt like I was getting less than the maximum output from my guys, I decided to add a four-mile run in the sand and make everyone swim past the surf zone in the cold winter waters of the Pacific. The waves were huge, and we sat out there shivering our asses off until the last man joined the group. I made sure I was always the first one in the water and the last one out.

Although heightened stress levels are a natural reaction to emergency situations, it is very important to manage these levels. If they are allowed to elevate too rapidly, your body will quickly go from a ready-to-respond mode to a worthless state called "lockup."

Combat Breathing

One of the best stress-managing skills is called **combat breathing.** This is simply a four-second inhalation followed by a four-second exhalation. In addition to properly regulating the body's oxygen and CO_2 levels, it will also decrease the heart rate and help clear the mind. And because it is such a basic technique that requires only breathing and counting, it will reduce stress and sharpen focus.

Checklists

Another formula for training your mind to respond quickly is to reduce actions to a **checklist.** Under great stress the mind works best when it has a step-by-step plan for action. Checklists catch mistakes, and it's easier to remember what to do when information is broken down into one-line ideas and organized in a way that's conducive to immediate recall. Before missions, I used a series of checklists that I went over multiple times. Airline pilots do the same thing before each flight, even if it seems redundant. You will best survive all the scenarios discussed in this book when you remember to utilize this checklist format.

Here are the basics of a checklist for dealing with many of the survival topics I will discuss in this book, when time is something you don't have the luxury of, but action must immediately be taken.

IMMEDIATE ACTIONS CHECKLIST
1. Remove yourself from immediate danger—get off the X.
2. Take a few seconds to assess the situation.
3. Make a self-assessment, including checking for your own injuries and what clothing, food, water, and equipment you have available.

4. Use the Rule of Three (see page 23). Formulate a game plan by making a decision. Foster group cohesion by assigning individuals responsibility.

5. Live or die. Pull the trigger! This is your *mission!*

On one particular mission, there were ten things that needed to happen in a very specific order or my men were going to die. I had a "play list" strapped to my forearm, like the ones most quarterbacks use. It was great, especially during the utter chaos that ensued, to look down at my forearm and go, "Snipers—check; doors breached—check; entry teams in—check; helos inbound—check; kiss my ass, Tom Brady—check."

The Mechanics of Survival

Humans have three acute stress responses when confronted with a potentially life-threatening situation: fight, flight, and freeze. These survival tools are found in all species, from spiders and cockroaches to primates and human beings. The best response will depend on the situation. However, to freeze in a life-or-death moment is rarely a desirable reaction. A deer that stares at the headlights gets hit by the car.

You may react with fight or flight while others freeze. If so, be a leader, step up, and get them in gear. Simple verbal commands to someone who is in the freeze state, like *"Move!"* may save their life. Again, step up and be a leader in this situation.

From Freeze to Fight

I recently came upon an intersection where a pedestrian had just been run over by a car. A small crowd had formed by the time I approached the seemingly lifeless, bleeding body. They were all just staring—frozen. I immediately pointed at individuals and gave them very simple tasks: "You—call 911." "You—stop that traffic." "You—stop that traffic." "You—get me a shirt to stop the bleeding." They all set about doing their tasks as I worked on the injured pedestrian. He left the scene breathing and with a pulse. The onlookers rose to the occasion and transformed into action mode. We all have the ability to use our natural response hormones to do good and save lives. That day I was very proud of this group of strangers who all pulled together to help a man survive.

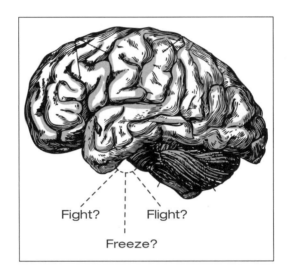

Fight? | Flight?

Freeze?

I mention this to show how to get people, and yourself, out of the "freeze" mode, which is the reaction many who have never practiced any of the survival methods explained above get locked into. Depending on the circumstances, flight is needed when you see that outrunning an attacker is possible. However, if you find yourself in a situation where the only appropriate response is to fight, make it count. Remember your trigger and pull it!

When you find yourself in a life-threatening situation, decisions are going to have to be made. Make the right decisions, and you live; make the wrong ones, and you die. Some must be made immediately—like whether to fight or flee. Others will provide the luxury of contemplation for a few minutes to several hours, given the situation. I will discuss various scenarios in this book and how best to respond with the mindset of a SEAL. By practicing the various techniques explained above, you will be given a great advantage. Your self-confidence, motivation, preparedness, and mindset will all come together, and you will do what is needed.

SEALs say: "Whatever you do in training, you will do under stress."

USE THE RULE OF THREE

I will never forget one of the earliest and best pieces of advice I got from Warrant Officer R. when I was in training. Yelling in my face, he drove home a very important point: "The worst decision is no decision. Now make a call!" I carried that with me throughout my career and had several opportunities to use it, including recently in Iraq, when I was confronted with the decision to stay, flee, or fight. I had only a minute to decide, and based on variables like whether I was outgunned, whether I had the necessary speed, the possibility of causing an international incident, and the threat of torture, I am happy I made the right choice. It was the only time that "stay and reason" worked.

Warrant Officer R.'s advice is absolutely true and essential in many life-threatening situations. So, once you are out of immediate danger—and only then—you can use something called the **Rule of Three** decision-making process to help you know what to do next.

Come up with three—and only three—possible options or courses of action. Look at the pros and cons of each option. Honestly weigh factors like risk, your ability to accomplish each option, and whether your plan is realistic. This will give structure to your thinking process in extreme circumstances. Then, without debating and rethinking each of your options, make the call and choose the one your gut tells you is the best. When life and death comes down to mere moments, second-guessing yourself will be your death knell. Instead, and most importantly, be confident in your decision and proceed. You can change or adjust later, but this survival decision is now your *mission*. You will accomplish it!

LONG-HAUL SURVIVAL

Some survival situations are going to require an approach very different from one you would use during a mall shooting or a mugging. Instead of taking minutes or hours, the situation might play out over a period of weeks or months, such as being lost at sea. If you find yourself in a long-lasting survival scenario, all the rules still apply. However, you need to readjust your mindset and decision-making when confronted with the challenge of long-haul survival. You'll need to modify certain priorities while still applying mental and physical toughness to endure and survive. You must place yourself not only physically but, even more so, mentally into an efficient mode. Save your strength and resources; conserve your energy and shift into low gear. Stay positive, but say to yourself, "I may be out here a long time." Just remember your entire mission is survival, as long as that mission takes.

SEALs say: "Becoming a Navy SEAL is 100% physical and 100% mental."

Mind Shift

To better illustrate this, imagine the difference between running one lap around a track and running to the next town. Imagine sitting down for Thanksgiving dinner, then imagine making that same plate of food last for twenty days or feed twenty people. Long-haul survival requires not only a particular mindset, but a **mind shift.** The example I like to use is that of a mountain goat, or for you off-roaders, four-wheel low gear. You need to think about gains in inches as you crawl up that mountain, or closer to safety/rescue. These inches become little victories. It's the one more breath, the one more step, the one more mile, the one more day, the one more sunrise. And the sum of these little victories is your survival.

Let's say you are in a scenario that will require you to walk a hundred miles to safety. To most people reading that sentence, this will feel like an impossible task. Now let's make it more mentally feasible. At a very reasonable pace, you should be able to walk three to four miles in a couple of hours. This will leave you plenty of time with the remainder of the day to eat, drink, and sleep. If you walk only this distance, you will be able to complete this trek in about thirty days. This is a very realistic scenario where each day will bring you closer to your goal: survival.

I often think about what it must have taken for John McCain and the other POWs in the Hanoi Hilton in Vietnam to endure daily physical and mental torture for over seven years. Think about the sum of the pain. Contemplate their situation, and six days on a raft in the middle of the ocean sounds pretty nice.

LONG-HAUL SURVIVAL CHECKLIST
- ❏ Stay busy.
- ❏ Set clear objectives.
- ❏ Savor little victories.
- ❏ Maintain group cohesion.
- ❏ Assign individual responsibilities.
- ❏ Worry about others' needs.
- ❏ Focus on the mission, the mission, the mission.

One of the advantages of being an officer in the SEALs was that I always had all eyes on me, which helped me remain at my best. I didn't have time to think about how absolutely miserable I felt or how physically difficult the situation seemed. I had decisions to make, and they had to be the right calls. If I showed any weakness (such as evidencing the effects of being cold, tired, or nervous), it would trickle down and poison the men and the mission. You will see how you, too, can follow these same rules and take charge during a crisis.

PART TWO

Survival Scenarios

ABANDON SHIP

Ships sink every day. The moment you step aboard a boat or anything else designed to carry you on water, you must consider the possibility of its going down. Anything that floats, from a cruise ship to a canoe, can sink. Tens of thousands of boats go under every year, and at least four large ships sink every week.

As with most life-threatening situations, an accident at sea happens quickly, and if a ship starts to take on water, there will be no time to find out where basic survival gear is kept. Oddly enough, most ship sinkings (nearly 64 percent) take place within sight of a dock or land. However, 34 percent of sunk vessels go down because of breaches in the hull (the boat's bottom), more often when very far out at sea. Hulls can get damaged from striking an object, for example, or from the failure of an underwater gasket or of an engine mount. But once a hole forms under the waterline, the clock of impending disaster goes into overdrive. A two-inch hole that is only three feet below the surface will allow as much as 138 gallons of water to come rushing in per minute. Even the smallest breach will usually rip open the hole further due to mounting pressure, thus allowing even more and more water in at proportionally unstoppable rates.

During the last five years, one hundred million people took vacations on cruise ships. In the U.S. alone, approximately seventy-five million people partake in recreational boating activities per year. Obviously, there is a difference between the sinking of a commercial cruise ship and a personal watercraft; however, the tools and mindset required to survive are the same. Chances of surviving at sea or in open water if forced to abandon ship are not good, so the decision of whether to leave a vessel in distress is extremely important.

**NEVER HESITATE TO ASK QUESTIONS
THAT COULD SAVE YOUR LIFE**

I have noticed time and again how many people are reluctant to get the information they need because they feel socially awkward doing so. SEALs don't use the word "embarrassment," especially when we need to get the facts to do the job correctly the first time. Everyone appreciates a leader, and knowledge and information are primary requirements of becoming one. Don't let the fear of what others think of you become an impediment for survival.

Situational Awareness: What to Do When Boarding a Ship or Boat

When you board a boat, ferry, or cruise ship, the very first thing you must do is take a visual inventory or do a situational awareness drill.

1. First, locate safety equipment and evacuation routes.
   a. On commercial vessels, signs indicating the location of life vests or life preservers are usually stamped or stenciled on walls. The devices could be under seats or stored above. On a cruise ship, they may be in your cabin. I can't stress enough that when you are traveling internationally, particularly in poorer countries, the safety standards we have come to expect in the United States are not always adhered to.
   b. Look to see where lifeboats or rafts are located. What type of survival equipment do they have? How many people are they designed to carry? Are there enough?
   c. Know where all exits are located; preferably know at least two that are in opposite directions. This is especially important if you are inside the ship. Know how to find your way out, and how to find the bow (front)

of the ship and the direction of the stern (back). The stern is usually where engines are located and where most fires occur.

2. If you don't see what you're looking for, or want more information, walk around and do what SEALs call an **AFAM,** or **area familiarization.** This is an integral part of situational awareness. Ask the crew if there are life vests, for example, even if you have to use pantomiming sign language to communicate, or show a picture of such items you retrieved from (or preloaded onto) your smart phone.

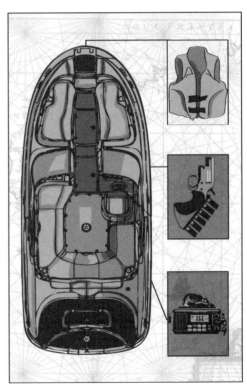

3. Generally, you want to find a seat, cabin, or comfortable place to situate yourself as close to the water-line as possible. This will minimize the distance you have to travel if abandoning ship is necessary.

4. Rehearse evacuating from your cabin or any location on or within the ship. Remember particular features that will help you locate life-boat stations or the bow of the ship. Keep in mind that you may be required to evacuate with little or no visibility.

5. If you go out on a recreational boat, ask where the life jackets are stored. Ensure that there is at least one for every passenger and that they are the correct size. Additionally,

familiarize yourself with radio and electronic equipment. A good skipper, even a buddy operating a twenty-foot sailboat or fishing boat, knows about safety. They will appreciate having another person along who knows where survival gear is stored and how to get at it in the event that a boating accident or mishap occurs.

What to Do When a Ship Is Taking On Water

The scenario of a ship taking on water can be reduced to two questions:

1. Do we stay, reasonably believing that we can keep the vessel afloat? Follow-up questions: If there is a fire, can you extinguish it? Do you have the tools and ability to either stop the leak or remove the water faster than it's flowing in? All of these actions are incredibly dangerous and will require a very high degree of skill.
2. Do we risk possible drowning, exposure (hypothermia or heatstroke), dehydration, and starvation on the open water?

Can the Leak Be Stopped?

As mentioned previously, water is such a powerful force that you will have limited time to determine if a breach can be plugged. On a commercial ship, it is unlikely that you will be given the opportunity to decide if the hull breach, or other cause of a leak, can be contained and the ship saved. On smaller boats, you might be able to assess the damage and employ bilge pumps and even bailing buckets that could give you a chance to keep the boat afloat. Abandoning ship is the last option, but in many situations there may not be much of a choice.

On recreational fiberglass boats, it might be good to have a packet of fiber mesh (which looks like sheets of sandpaper) and tubes of silicone or marine caulking, which can slow smaller leaks and allow bilge pumps or bucket-bailing to be effective. For boats with wooden hulls, fabric from clothing can be fashioned into a patch and applied over the breach with pitch or roofing cement, although it is best to attempt this repair on the exterior of the vessel, if seas permit. For metal hulls, there are cold-weld products available. Depending on the boat you have, these items should be kept aboard for such emergencies.

In 1947, when Norwegian explorer Thor Heyerdal crossed the Pacific Ocean in a balsa-log raft, he used banana leaves to plug leaks. Any marine emergency comes down to acquiring the SEAL mindset of survival: Do not panic, think clearly, and act decisively.

Abandoning Ship

The call to abandon ship, which, by definition, means to intentionally and permanently give up and leave a vessel that has sustained a disaster that is beyond control, is a serious one. However, if you make that decision, or if this is the call made by the crew of a commercial vessel, there is no time for second-guessing and hesitation. Survival in this situation, as during many disasters, depends on your ability to organize your actions into an order of priorities.

For instance, you must decide if it is worth returning to your cabin if your life vest is there, or instead forgo it and begin an alternate plan. Worsening circumstances may warrant heading to the bow, even without a life vest, or toward lifeboat stations, or at least toward a part of a ship away from fire, smoke, or the rush of incoming water.

Pull the Trigger

This is when the skills that you practiced in the mindset preparedness section, and the small daily drills you did to make yourself harder, will ensure your survival. If you tell yourself you are going to die, chances are you will. Your mission is to survive.

If you are inside the ship, get up to the deck. If you are on the deck of the ship, get to a lifeboat or raft, or get to a location of greatest safety. Again, this may sound oversimplified, but in this extremely terrifying situation, you must calm yourself and move with purpose.

Remember, I discussed how fast water can fill the interior of a boat or ship; for this reason, you need to make your way upward and outward. You want to get to the deck of the ship and work toward being as close to the waterline as possible. But if the ship is listing or leaning port (left), for example, then you go in the opposite direction. Since you made a situational assessment when you boarded and rehearsed your evacuation, you should remember details that will allow you to get your bearings even when the ship is lopsided.

Mayday

At some point it is important to alert the outside world—*anyone you can reach*—to give the status of your vessel, your intentions, and most importantly your current position. But if you aren't able to give a GPS or radar position, utilize bearings and the distance of landmarks to help rescuers know the location of the boat or that the ship is going down. Mayday calls are always repeated three times and at a minimum give the following:

1. Who you are.
2. Where you are.
3. What you plan to do.

The mayday call is a universally accepted distress signal that implies that a vessel is in "grave and imminent danger." As with many nautical phrases, the exact origin of the phrase is not totally verifiable, but it probably stems from the French command "*m'aider,*" meaning "help me." ("SOS" was used when telegraphy was the only means of communication. The letters stand for "Save Our Ship.")

In U.S. waters, channel 16 communicates directly with the Coast Guard and with other nearby boats. Most recreational boats over twenty feet in length are equipped with VHF marine radio. Information communicated via radio will allow rescue crews to calculate wind and currents to help find you and gives an invaluable point of reference. If you are on a cruise ship, for example, and are within cell phone range, call 911, or call anyone you know. Even if you only leave a message on a voice mail, this can later be used to pinpoint the coordinates of where you were when you were last able to make a call.

Going into the Water

The most important action to take at this point is to do whatever you need to do to avoid drowning. Expect chaos in the form of screaming and panic.

Once the decision is made to enter the water, you should first attempt to do so in a life raft or boat. Your priority is to get away from the sinking vessel as quickly as possible. A large, sinking ship will create a powerful downward suction that has the ability to pull you under if you are in the vicinity. Help others out the best you can, given the situation.

If you are unable to get to a life raft or boat and have to enter the water by yourself:

1. Put on several layers of clothing. This will provide thermal protection against the cooler water temperature; additionally, the clothes will help you float and stay buoyant due to the air trapped within.
2. Place your life vest on the outside of your clothes.
3. Collect any survival items you can find, like water, small foods, or a flashlight and signaling devices. If you feel you may have a problem floating with the items you have collected, you can always wrap them in an extra life vest or even place them in a plastic storage container like Tupperware.
4. Find a clear landing zone in the water you are getting ready to enter. If you have the opportunity to enter upwind and avoid any potential smoke, do so.
5. Place your feet and knees together, cross your arms over your chest, and tuck your chin. Go!

As a general rule, *never* dive headfirst. Doing so risks greater injury to your face, head, and neck. Given that you don't know what's in the water, it's better if you allow your legs to absorb the blow, and therefore increase your chances of surviving the initial jump. Keep your feet and knees together to protect your femoral arteries, which can cause rapid bleed-out if cut.

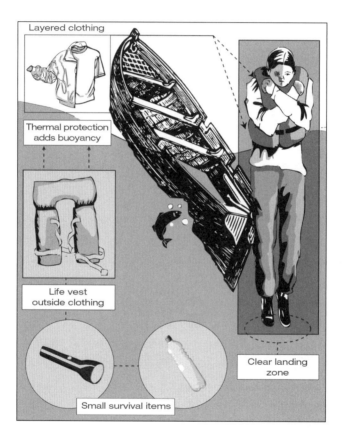

Layered clothing

Thermal protection adds buoyancy

Life vest outside clothing

Small survival items

Clear landing zone

6. Get clear of the sinking vessel. Swim to a lifeboat or anything else that may be floating.
7. If there is fuel in the water, stay clear of it! If it is burning, avoid or swim under it. (This may require you to briefly

remove your life vest—either toss it to a clear section of water ahead of you or drag it behind you, utilizing the straps or any line you may find.)

WHAT WENT WRONG?

In January 2012, the Italian cruise ship *Costa Concordia* hit an underwater rock outcropping that breached the hull. The ship was in 150 feet of water and sank within 1,000 feet of the shore. Yet thirty-nine people died. Survivors related how the crew delayed reporting the severity of the situation and even told passengers to return to their cabins. Those who ignored these instructions and made it to the deck lived. In this situation, the passengers had lost faith in the crew. If you are in a similar situation, use your survival tools and follow your instincts. If the crew, instead, seems prepared and diligent, become a leader to those around you and try to keep everyone calm. Even if you are in the line to board a lifeboat, don't let chaos set in, as this will lessen your chances of survival.

ACTIVE SHOOTER

Malls, markets, and schools—we expect to go to these places to stroll, shop, relax, or learn in environments that are relatively secure. One of our great freedoms is to go about our daily lives without fear. However, think about the 1999 Columbine High School shooting that killed fifteen, or the 2005 Tacoma, Washington, mall shooting that wounded seven, or the 2007 Westroads Mall incident in Omaha, Nebraska, with nine dead, or the Virginia Tech massacre in that same year when thirty-two died, or the 2011 slaughter of sixty-nine innocents at a Norwegian youth camp.

THE JULY 2012 MASS SHOOTING AT THE CENTURY MOVIE THEATER IN AURORA, COLORADO

Over 300 people went to see a midnight screening of the film *The Dark Knight Rises*. Of those, fifty-eight were wounded and twelve never left the theater.

I am aware of the vast and varying opinions regarding guns and gun control. That said, imagine if just one person in the theater that night had had the required training and was carrying a properly permitted concealed weapon. This senseless horror happened in my own backyard, so forgive me for playing armchair quarterback and taking the scenario one step further: I'm at the theater when James Holmes opens fire. Two seconds later I'm returning accurate fire toward the muzzle flashes. You don't have to be a Navy SEAL to do this, you just have to step up—wouldn't it have been some shock to this killer if he found the "video game" he was playing in his mind started shooting back? GAME OVER.

Some will argue that more guns would cause more devastation. Well, it doesn't get much more devastating than a psycho with over one hundred and fifty rounds shooting at a mass of innocent people at point-blank range.

Given all these incidents, one thing can be said about the people who do this: they are similar only in their intent to kill. Their motivation to commit these acts might be a personal vendetta, or to further a political or religious agenda, or some psychological disorder—so stay alert, because the shooter could be anyone, anywhere.

The paramilitary or trench coat garb that is often used to conceal weaponry, of course, is not by any means the preferred look of an "active shooter." The Virginia Tech murderer wore a maroon hoodie and a gray hat. The Norwegian shooter donned a police uniform. He actually called out to the fleeing students, identifying himself as a police officer. He then gunned down those who ran in his direction believing they were heading to safety.

Police and SWAT (Special Weapons and Tactics) divisions of law enforcement units refer to this crime while it's under way as an "active-shooter incident." In most cases, the perpetrators of these attacks pick "soft targets," with the full intention of having unrestricted access and time to claim as many victims as possible before they are captured or gunned down. A "soft target" generally refers to any public place where there are large groups of people (predominantly young adults, women, and children) and little or no security, such as malls, markets, and schools. These targets are unprepared for defense against individuals with massive firepower who have the sole intent to kill and cause mayhem.

Examining the psychology of these assailants might lead to the ability to spot such personality types before they get a chance to carry out their murderous schemes, but this won't help you to survive if you happen to be involved in an active-shooter incident. Once these shooters are engaged, reasoning with them or attempting to talk them into surrender is frequently fruitless.

Despite the above list of carnage, many prefer to live by the "this won't happen to me" way of thinking. Unfortunately, those people are usually among the list of the latest victims on the nightly news. *Step up—be prepared!*

Response Time

Ten minutes and thirty seconds—that's the national average time it takes a police officer to show up at the scene after a high-priority 911 call is received. In the Virginia Tech shooting, for example, thirty-two people were already dead within minutes, and the police weren't even notified until fifteen minutes after it began. In many larger cities, including Los Angeles and New York, there are full-time officers assigned to SWAT operations. Yet, statistically, it takes them approximately twenty to thirty minutes to get to the scene. In smaller municipalities, it's often the case that officers who are regularly assigned to other departments are trained for active-shooter incidents. It can take forty-five minutes or longer for these units to respond. Nearly 99 percent of the time, these critical situations are handled by regular patrol officers before SWAT ever gets there. This is why it is your response time and what you do that really count.

Situational Awareness: Exits, Cover, People

When you're going to a mall or market, or even during your first days of class at a new school, make a mental note of **exits**. Have at least three options, preferably in three different directions. This could be as obvious as a double-door entry or as desperate as a second-floor window with a ten-foot drop onto pavement. Second, observe the whereabouts of any large items or objects that seem sturdy enough to provide **cover**, if needed, and file this information. In some malls, for example, there may be a lounge area with furniture, or sculptures, or columns that are placed at regular intervals. In a school, are the desks bolted to the floor? Do the windows open? Filled bookshelves in a library or the cooking and dishwashing equipment in a cafeteria will provide very good cover. Third, look around at the **people** you pass while in public places or when you're among crowds. If you're at a mall, pay special attention to individuals who don't seem to have the demeanor of the average shopper, and to individuals carrying large bags, such as duffel bags, or wearing unseasonably heavy clothing. Keep an eye on people who seem particularly nervous or who are sweating. Watch individuals wearing military-style boots or clothes that seem out of place. Many times, these shooters imagine themselves as members of some type of militia or are military imitators, and

could be wearing army boots or fatigues, though they are clearly identifiable as someone not on active duty.

SITUATIONAL AWARENESS CHECKLIST for entry of a soft target:
- ❏ Find your exits.
- ❏ Locate places or objects that could serve as your nearest
  cover.
- ❏ Observe individuals who are dressed strangely, acting
  abnormally, or carrying something suspicious.
- ❏ Trust your gut.

Once a Shooting Begins

People who have never heard the sound of gunfire often compare it to
the sound of a car backfiring or a loud firecracker. But the discharge
of a firearm in a closed environment, such as a mall or a classroom, is
distinct and will leave no question that an assault of a deadly nature
has begun. And as your ears begin to ring, you must understand that
what you do in the first few seconds of this event will determine if you
live or die. Some think that gunfire produces the smell of burning sul-
fur or gunpowder, like the odor at a fireworks display. However, mod-

ern ammo uses smokeless powder and is virtually odorless. Of all your senses, initially trust your ears in this scenario—the sound of gunfire is unmistakable.

REVERSE 911

Many cities are now using Reverse 911, a mass notification system to text information about an emergency in progress. In an active-shooter incident, students and parents would be alerted via text message, sent from local law enforcement. Students would be specifically instructed to lock the doors, turn off lights, lie on the ground, and stay put. Check to see if your local area, or those places you're visiting, have this set up and opt in to make sure you get the information you need.

Step 1: Get Off the X

You must remove yourself from the immediate vicinity of the source of the gunfire, which is referred to as the **kill zone** or the **X**, and do so without hesitation. In tactical terms, it's essential to get out of the line of fire during any lethal encounter or if engaged in a self-defense shooting incident. Simply put, you must do whatever it takes to get clear of the kill zone and find **cover** if you expect to have any chance of survival or retaliation. If you survive the first ten seconds of this type of ambush, you have a much better chance of making it out alive.

FIGHT, FLIGHT, FREEZE

In many shootings, bystanders who freeze are added to the casualty toll. Do not freeze or burrow in—react and move immediately.

In order to get off the X, move! When a shooting occurs in a public place, the natural and initial response is to use the flight instinct, but you must do it with forethought. Nevertheless, you must move! There is little time to think, but it's best to make your flight a calculated one, so you don't turn yourself into a more visible and attractive running target. By scrambling in panic, you could end up going nowhere worthwhile, or even going closer to the line of fire. This flight must be for the purpose of getting clear of danger—off the X—and not flagging your position. Usually, you'll instinctively move in a route away from the shooter, preferably in a direction that is opposite from his or her focus.

Hitting the floor and lying flat is usually the first thing people do instinctively, but don't just cover your head and hope for the best. You must begin moving immediately while staying low. If you are able to dive for one of the objects you earlier identified as cover, make that move now. Get to your cover while staying as low as possible, and do it with maximum purpose.

HOW TO TELL WHERE GUNFIRE IS COMING FROM

In a closed environment, and depending upon the proximity of the shooter, you cannot trust your ears to determine the direction of gunfire. Gunfire will cause a deafening echo, and you might be hearing what the bullet has hit rather than where it came from. Since smokeless gunpowder is used in modern ammunition, the best way to determine the shooter's location is to look for muzzle flashes. These emanate only from the weapon and clearly tell you to move in the opposite direction.

MOVEMENT TECHNIQUES

Generally you will use the **low crawl** method, which involves pushing with your toes and pulling with your fingers, inch by inch if necessary, keeping you flat to the floor and out of range.

When you see the opportunity, you might use what's called the **high crawl**, lifting your belly only inches from the floor and moving on your knees and elbows.

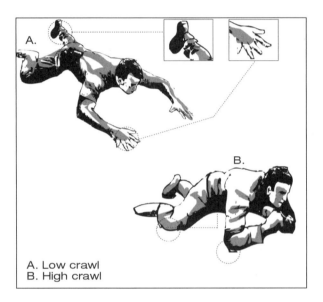

A. Low crawl
B. High crawl

COVER VS. CONCEALMENT

Cover is defined as something that will stop bullets, such as a concrete wall or a large potted plant. Concealment may hide you, but it will not stop bullets. For example, if you're outdoors, a rock is cover, while in contrast, a bush offers concealment. In a shopping mall, a rack of clothing could be used for concealment. Whatever you choose as cover or concealment, avoid bunching up with too many people. In these circumstances, people huddled together will create a larger and more attractive target; a single bullet can penetrate several people.

Cover | Concealment

GET FARTHER FROM THE X

After you've found initial cover, you'll want to still continue to move *away* from the shooter, going from cover to cover. Make a visualization of the path you will take; this will help you to set your mind to achieving small goals or little victories, as each move takes you farther from the X. For example, you see a potted plant fifteen feet away. Your goal is to make it to that point, and thus you gain one more little victory in the overall plan to escape. Once you make it to that secure cover, you follow your path, determined to get to the next goal point. At first, get between covers by making small bounds. As you gain distance from the shooter, you can increase the distance you travel between covers. You must start by low-crawling, but note that the farther away from the shooter you are, the faster you can move, until even sprinting if the situation warrants it. With assault rifles having a maximum effective range of six hundred meters, or six football fields, and with sniper rifles even hitting targets much farther, you should always remember that if you can hear gunfire, you can be shot. You must continue to act with maximum purpose and calculated caution.

BULLET PENETRATION

The three most common weapons used in an active-shooter situation are a handgun with nine-millimeter rounds; an AK-47, or similar weapon, which uses a 7.62 x 39 millimeter round; or a twelve-gauge shotgun with 00 buckshot. Bricks, concrete, medium-to-large trees, or several layers of wooden boards will stop all of the above rounds from penetrating. However, the typical wall of a house or apartment (made of plywood, two-by-four-inch studs, and drywall) will not. Neither will the aluminum body of a car. In a mall, for example, the usual potted plants have concrete containers that will effectively stop the aforementioned ammunition. A mailbox will not. In SEAL team, when we needed to take cover behind a vehicle, we tucked behind the wheels. The tires at the front end of the car are better, since the engine block and axles provide additional fortification and make it a good cover.

DECOYS

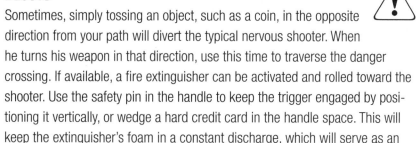

Sometimes, simply tossing an object, such as a coin, in the opposite direction from your path will divert the typical nervous shooter. When he turns his weapon in that direction, use this time to traverse the danger crossing. If available, a fire extinguisher can be activated and rolled toward the shooter. Use the safety pin in the handle to keep the trigger engaged by positioning it vertically, or wedge a hard credit card in the handle space. This will keep the extinguisher's foam in a constant discharge, which will serve as an excellent smoke screen.

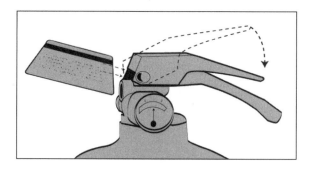

Smoke screen

Danger crossing

DANGER CROSSINGS

Even when places have numerous objects that afford cover or conceal-ment, your escape route will often have open spaces, like hallways, that must be crossed. These junctions, while you are still in the line of fire, are called "danger crossings." If you come upon a danger crossing, take a moment to discern a pattern in the shooting and try to move when there is a pause in the gunfire. This will generally happen when the weapon is being reloaded, and it will give you a few seconds to move without taking fire. While preparing your body to make this move, use the combat breathing technique we discussed earlier. You can do this—now you have the skills!

MOVING IN A SHOOTING ENVIRONMENT

You have cleared the kill zone, but there is still a good chance that you'll be shot at. Maintain a lower profile (slightly hunched over, with your weight over the balls of your feet). Continue to move from cover to cover. Utilize shadows or "dead space" areas that are obstructed from view. The **sniper walk** is a good technique when stealth while moving from the X is required. This is done by staying in a crouched position with the body kept low and using heel-to-toe steps.

Stay a foot off the walls. When a bullet hits and ricochets off a wall, it tends to travel down the wall within approximately six inches of it. If you are against the wall, you will get hit.

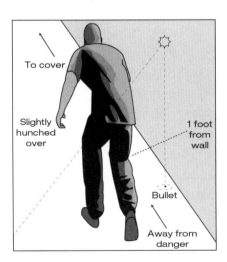

Once you have successfully cleared the kill zone, you need to quickly decide the best way to either gain the greatest distance from the shooter or ultimately exit the building. Now, remember where you saw the main exits. Fire-exit doors in many public buildings are required by law to be at the rear of the building, or at the back of each store in malls.

Continue to move, but take no chances because the shooter could be following you. Put as many obstacles between you and danger as you can—for example, close doors as you go or tumble merchandise to the ground, making it harder for the shooter to trail you if that is their intention.

If, and only if, you feel that you are at a location of relative, short-term safety, gather yourself. When you are in a defensive position that is well hidden and away from the site of the shooting, take a moment to calm yourself and keep your mind alert. Now is the time for the next phase of survival.

Step 2: Regroup and Regain Focus

You'll naturally think, "What the hell just happened?" But don't ponder this. It will not be of immediate help to wonder about the assailant's motives. Regain focus through your combat breathing. Recall the image you made as your trigger and focus. The calmer you are, the better equipped you'll be to outthink your assailant.

Step 3: Self-Assessment

Once you've regained your clarity, now is the time for a secondary type of situational awareness: the self-assessment. First check yourself for wounds. If you have made it this far, you are probably not critically injured. Existent breathing and a heartbeat rule out serious injuries, but many times, in great stress, people will be injured and not know it. Do a quick head-to-toe self-assessment, paying particular attention to bleeding and fractures, and treat yourself, if required. If you can, take a quick drink of water.

Next take an inventory of the resources that you still have at hand that could help you further. Is there anything that can break a window, for example, or something to act as a portable shield? Is there a vending machine or a water cooler nearby so you can get some nourishment? You have just been through strenuous physical activity and could require significantly more effort until you are safe. Things to consider:

- Clothing: Remove excess or brightly colored clothing, and accessories you don't need (coat, purse, shiny jewelry, etc.).
- Equipment: Look around for anything that could . . .
  - help you escape
  - help transport the injured (see Part Four, "Survival Medicine," page 305)
  - serve as a weapon (see "Improvised Weapons," page 301)

During a training evolution* I was run over by a boat operated by Navy personnel who weren't paying attention and veered from their normal course. They obviously didn't know that they even hit me, but nevertheless, I took the full force of the collision to my head while I was in heavy surf. I have never been hit that hard in my life. When I resurfaced and saw the blood coming from my ear, I decided it was time to swim to shore. Once I got to the beach, I felt fine and was more concerned with giving the boat driver the universal sign for FU than anything else. It wasn't until I had regained consciousness an hour later in the ER that I was informed that I had sustained a fractured skull and a subdural hematoma (bleeding brain), the source of the blood coming out of my ear. Thank God for the cold water, or I would have lost consciousness way before hitting the beach. It wasn't my time.

*"Training evolution" might seem like a strange term, but that's what we call various phases we go through to become a SEAL. In a sense, it is true to the meaning of the word "evolution": We are transformed from our previous selves and evolve into warriors.

Step 4: Develop a Game Plan

Success in warfare often comes down to the side that knows their battlefield better. If a mall or school turns into a battlefield, knowledge of the environment will be a great advantage. If you are in a familiar environment, such as the office building where you work, where your previously acquired situational awareness provides knowledge of the exits, this is the time to figure out where you are. During your time getting off the X, you may find yourself in a place somewhat different than expected yet still familiar in general. Most buildings and stores use repetitive construction, such as repeating floor plans. You can make a representation of your logistics on the floor in front of you by using items to diagram the area. If you are in an unfamiliar place, like a mall, and your smart phone still works, get a map from the website, or use evacuation placards or signs posted on walls to get your bearings.

MAKE A DECISION USING THE RULE OF THREE

Make a decision as to the next course of action, choosing the best of the three plans you can conceive. There isn't time to second-guess yourself or for debate. Pick what seems like the best of the three options and then act decisively.

In the case of an active shooter, for example, your three options might be:

1. Head to the nearest exit.
2. Run to the highest level and attempt rescue from the roof.
3. Set an ambush, recover a weapon, and shoot your way out.

If you're able to, call 911. Give police as much **HUMINT (human intelligence)** as possible, including: who you are, what's happening and where, how many shooters and their physical description, which types of weapons are being used, and any special gear, such as body armor, that you observed. Describe the shooter's skill level, ethnicity, language, accent, body movements—anything that may be helpful.

As mentioned above regarding police response, don't wait for help.

You might be dead before the cavalry gets there. In making your decision to evacuate, choose the most discreet way out and the one most likely to limit your chances of meeting the shooter again. Your goal now is evacuation. However, remember that the safest evacuation route may not be the most direct. The best exit may not be the closest one.

MOVING AS A GROUP

If you find yourself among a group of other survivors, it's now your job to assign responsibilities. This will focus individuals who are likely still in a serious panic mode. Maintain group cohesion by displaying a sense of purpose and by offering a reasonable game plan. Remind people: "We're in this together, and we're going to get out of this together."

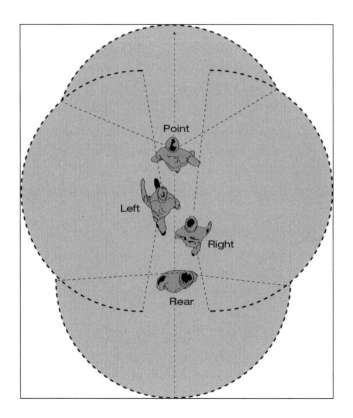

Your group has now become a small unit and can benefit from using standard, small-unit tactics and techniques employed by the military. Usually, but again depending upon the scenario, it's better to move in single file, where each person has a couple of feet or an arm's length of separation. Assign a person on the line to scout out areas that you plan to travel to during your evacuation. By using all eyes, the group maintains **360 degrees of awareness.** The leader, or the one in point position, is responsible for the front 180 degrees—or from nine o'clock to three o'clock, with twelve o'clock always being the direction of travel. The second person covers the left, the third covers the right, and so on. The last person in line scopes out the rear to alert the group of any indication that the shooter is following them. If you are in the rear, don't walk backward; you will undoubtedly trip and fall. Instead, every three or four steps stop momentarily and spin back. Then continue moving forward. The last person will be responsible for the 180 degrees of the rear view (from three o'clock to nine o'clock). This method allows you to know what could be coming at you and gives you the extra seconds needed to react.

Step 5: Live or Die

Sometimes, the only way out is to fight. There will be times when your course of action might be limited to taking on the shooter. As cold-blooded and mechanical as these shooters seem, especially with firepower in their hands, they are expecting to eventually come against some intervention or police confrontation. This oftentimes will lead to overconfidence or recklessness and brazen actions. The 1997 shoot-out at a North Hollywood bank is an excellent example. Two heavily armed men robbed a bank, and when they confronted police upon exiting the bank, they expended two thousand rounds of ammunition before they were finally gunned down, despite believing they were invincible. It's best to try to capitalize on a shooter's lack of discipline or training when trying to plan an attack.

When I die, let it be on my feet, with a white-hot smoking rifle, empty mags, and bloody knuckles. —Cade Courtley

---

HOW TO SET AN AMBUSH

The best ambush is one in which your target ends up in the exact location you want them in, essentially walking right into your trap. Put yourself in a hidden position that the shooter must pass by. This is known as the "strike zone." Obviously, surprise is the key to a successful ambush. Additionally, you will increase the odds of your success with a weapon. (See "Improvised Weapons," page 301.)

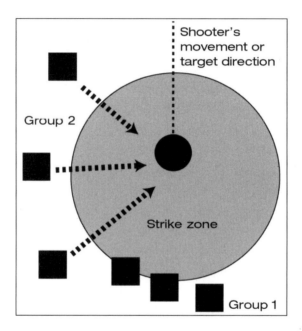

Types of ambushes

- **Ambush with multiple people:** This is the ideal form of ambush. You have greater numbers and are able to strike from multiple positions simultaneously. Just remember that with multiple people, the odds of hurting one of your own increase. Make sure that you direct those in your party to remain at preestablished set points in the ambush to avoid causalities from what is referred to as "friendly fire."

- **L ambush:** One group sets up to lure the shooter toward them, while the other group, to the right or left, is prepared to engage once the shooter enters the strike zone.

I can't emphasize enough the necessity of violence of action for an ambush to be effective. If you must face the shooter and it comes down to either his going down or your dying, this is "pull the trigger" time, and you can and will put every ounce of your being into defeating the enemy. Survival is your *mission*! (See "Fighting," page 146, for more on how to approach an attack.)

ACTIVE SHOOTER NEUTRALIZED

If the ambush is successful and the shooter is dead, good; the mad dog is done. If the shooter is alive, then make sure to bind and gag them.

Never assume this is the only shooter or that the incident is now over!

1. Stop and listen; do you hear any more gunfire?

2. Does the shooter you took down have a radio? If they do, there is someone else they must have been communicating with.

3. Attempt to get further information regarding the number and location of other shooters from the assailant using any effective form of coercion. Yes, I mean torture. This person was trying to kill you and other innocents; I would use whatever means necessary to know whether he or she is acting alone.

4. Immediately inform the police of your status and pass on any useful information.

Again, never assume an active-shooter situation is over until law enforcement declares it to be over. Strip any and all equipment the shooter may have for your own use. Take weapons, ammo, and body armor. Any communication equipment will be especially useful. It will not only enable you to monitor what the other shooters are doing, but it will give you the opportunity to jam their communication with each other.

HOW TO JAM OR "HOT-MIKE"

To jam most walkie-talkies or radio devices, press and hold down the transmit button. On most radios, this will not allow anyone else to transmit, thus jamming the transmission and removing the shooter's ability to communicate with any partners.

ALLOCATION OF RESOURCES

Divvy up the weapons and equipment you have taken from the shooter and give them to those most experienced and capable of using them. If there is only one weapon or set of body armor, give it to the point man, because he or she is up front and the one most likely to encounter the next shooter.

Step 6: Encountering Law Enforcement

If you're successful and you make it out alive, you surely don't want police to think you are one of the assailants; you don't want to die from this form of **friendly fire.** As in the military, law enforcement officers are taught to look at people's hands first. If your hands are free of weapons, then you aren't considered a shooting threat. So when you are about to exit and think there is a high probability of encountering law enforcement, you must empty your hands. Put all weapons on the ground and away from you. Place hands high in the air and yell out, "Friendlies—we are unarmed." Keep repeating this, and do so loudly. Do exactly as you are instructed to do at this point; there will be time for them to realize that you are the survivors once police have you in a nonthreatening posture.

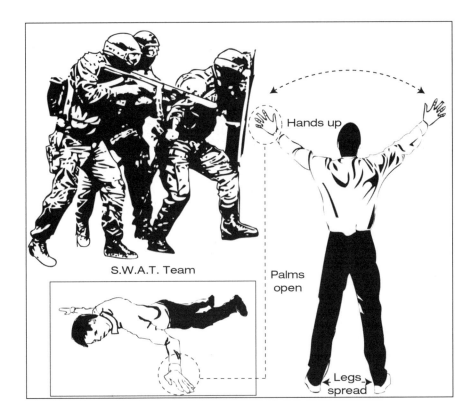

S.W.A.T. Team

Hands up

Palms open

Legs spread

ACTIVE SHOOTER CHECKLIST

1. Get off the X. Remove yourself from immediate danger.
2. Regroup and regain focus.
3. Perform a self-assessment for injuries and resources.
4. Form your game plan. Make a decision, keep the group cohesive, and assign individuals responsibility.
5. Live or die. Pull the trigger! This is your *mission*!
6. Make sure you safely encounter law enforcement.

AIRPLANE CRASH

Airline travel is now a common occurrence, with an estimated two billion people worldwide flying every year. When you enter an aircraft, you literally turn your life over to the mechanical integrity of the aircraft and to the pilot's skills. However, preparedness, rehearsal and reenactment, and the SEAL mindset can enhance your odds of survival in the event of a crash. Although airplanes are widely considered the safest way to travel, they do occasionally go down. While it seems hard to believe sometimes, there is always a chance you can survive an airplane crash, and how you approach the act of air travel can increase your odds of survival.

The two main threats to you on an airplane (aside from hijacking and terrorism, which we'll save for a later section) are the impact of the plane against something, and post-impact conditions, mainly fires, fuel combustion, and smoke inhalation. It is estimated that 30 percent of those who have died in airplane accidents were lucky enough to survive the crash but failed to respond properly after.

Preflight Preparation

When SEALs plan for a mission, be it in the Arctic, the tropics, an urban setting, or the desert, a critical part of our success is the uniform and gear we wear and use. In tactical planning, this is grouped with overall equipment. Nevertheless, the choice is made on the basis of functionality. The military has learned over the years that clothing, footwear, and other accessories provided to a soldier are important elements of the planning phase. This is

also something to consider in your daily routines—are you dressed to handle an emergency?

When traveling by airplane, think less about looking fashionable or professional and more about what would serve you best if something were to go wrong. This applies to both men and women.

- Always wear long pants and long-sleeved shirts or blouses made of less flammable material (such as 100 percent polyester, nylon, wool, or silk) and avoid more combustible fabrics (such as cotton, cotton-polyester blends, rayon, or acrylic). This will act as a layer of protection for your skin should a fire occur, and prevent you from sustaining cuts or lacerations caused by debris that might impede your escape.

- Avoid wearing sandals, open-toe shoes, or high heels. You may want to wear sandals to get yourself in vacation mode, for example, or high heels to look stylish; however, these types of shoes will hinder you should you need to climb through burning wreckage or debris, broken glass, or flammable liquids. In fact, high heels have to be removed before going down inflatable evacuation slides, wasting precious seconds during an escape.

- Have a handkerchief or some other cloth you can cover your mouth with in case of a smoke or noxious-fume event. This won't always be enough, but it may buy you precious seconds.

WHERE TO SIT

Book a seat with emergency evacuation in mind. In examining the statistics of airline crashes compiled by the Federal Aviation Administration, the greatest number of survivors are among those who were seated toward the back of the aircraft. First class may have the most comfortable seats and allow you to be the first on and the first to disembark during nonemergency situations, but these seats are not statistically the safest. In fact, passengers seated closer to the tail have an estimated 40 percent higher survival rate. In addition, seats closest to the exit doors are preferable. If you survive the initial impact, you want to be in a position to get out of the aircraft as quickly as possible.

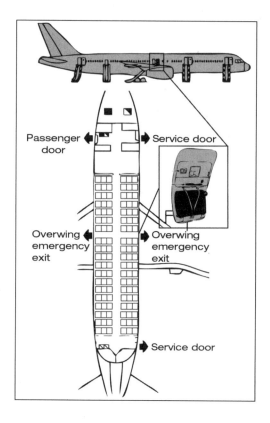

The one thing that has killed more SEALs than anything else (by a wide margin) is helicopters. I often thought it was the most dangerous part of the job: many men crammed into a small space, flying around in something that has a ton of moving parts and shouldn't really work. Then it must slow down, giant target that it is, when it's most vulnerable, during takeoff and landing. Unfortunately, it is a necessity of war.

GATHERING INTELLIGENCE

In the military, we have no choice in boarding the aircraft to which we are assigned. However, in the civilian world, many people spend considerable time researching the ratings of a hotel, for example, but gather no intelligence on the aircraft that will get them there. To enhance your chances of survival, include in your travel plans, well in advance of the flight, research information about the safety record of the plane you are ticketed to take.

Some commercial airlines keep planes in service for more than forty years. You can check the mechanical data and safety records of any plane. The Federal Aviation Administration maintains incident reports for all aircraft. You can find detailed records by knowing the aircraft's identification, or "N," numbers, which are found near the tail of every plane. You can request the N-number of the plane when you book a ticket. If you go to the FAA website (http://www.faa.gov/), the N-number will tell you the age of the plane and many other invaluable details.

Situational Awareness on the Plane

From the time you enter the plane your situational awareness should be extremely high. Be aware of the following:

- ❏ The condition of the plane.
- ❏ The condition of the pilots and flight crew.
- ❏ Your fellow passengers: Does anyone seem unusually nervous, uncomfortable, or out of place?
- ❏ Where are your two closest escape routes? Say it to yourself: "Back, four rows, right." Or "Forward, three rows, left." Repeat it several times.

Start your mental movie in real time by observing every exit as you pass it. Once you get to your seat, immediately find your two closest exits. If you're sitting in an exit row, study the door and make sure you know how to open it. Learn the door's particular operating procedures carefully. In normal circumstances, the flight attendant will open the door, but if the attendants are dead or injured, you'll need to do it.

Be ready. Whenever the plane is below ten thousand feet, which is normally the first five and last ten minutes of the flight (although this time could be longer if the plane is kept in an extended midair holding pattern near the destination airport), you should be in full alert mode. This is when pilot error, mechanical failures, and varying environmental factors, from wind shear to birds, cause crashes. During takeoff and landing, be fully prepared to respond quickly to any emergency condition.

Impact: Brace Yourself!

Let's face it: There's not much that you can do here but be alert. Throughout the flight, but especially during takeoff and landing, keep your seat belt securely fastened. The seat belt should be placed as low as possible, at the upper part of your pelvis, and not across your stomach.

The slightest slack in the seat belt—even a centimeter too loose— will increase the G-force your body will be subjected to during a crash. This is a lesson every new SEAL has to learn the hard way when doing a "map of the earth" low-level approach for insertion on a target. Since "map of the earth" basically means you are riding a roller coaster at treetop level, *believe me,* you don't want any slack in that belt.

If the crew has issued a crash alert, or you just know your plane is going down, brace yourself. The primary function of a proper brace position is simply to place yourself firmly against whatever is in front of you, such that when the sudden deceleration causes you to be thrown forward, you're already in contact with whatever it is you would hit. In a plane, you want to brace against the seat in front of you. If the plane has a video screen, don't brace against that surface. Rather, position your head above or below it. (Lower is generally better.)

The secondary function of a brace position is to stop your limbs and head from flailing about and hitting things during the violent motion of the crash. You want to wrap your head in your arms, tightly clasping your hands and fingers together. If you have a pillow, blanket, or other potential padding handy, use it as a cushion between you and any nearby hard surfaces that you may strike during impact.

The reason you always see flight attendants making sure that all seats are in an upright position during landing and takeoff is to limit casualties and additional injury upon impact. There are two ways to practice and prepare to brace yourself properly.

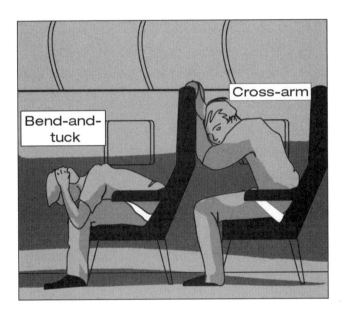

THE CROSS-ARM BRACE POSITION
Grab the back of the seat in front of you with one hand. Then cross the other hand over the first hand to also grab the back of the seat. Place your head in the compacted triangle that you have created with crossed hands. This method is better than lacing your fingers and covering your head, but this is only effective if the seat in front of you is close enough to reach without loosening your seat belt.

THE BEND-AND-TUCK BRACE POSITION
If the seat in front of you is out of reach or you have a bulkhead before you, then lean forward. Place your chest to your thighs, and put

your head between your knees. Reach down with your hands and grab each opposite ankle, or place your hands behind your head to protect the back of your neck.

For both bracing methods, make sure your feet remain flat on the floor and farther back than your knees. You'll need your feet to be intact and be the least likely body part to sustain injury in order to aid in your swift evacuation.

Postimpact

Congratulations! You survived the impact . . . but it ain't over until it's over. Remember: If the plane has crash-landed and is somewhat intact, more die from the aftermath, primarily from fire and smoke inhalation, than from the impact.

PULL THE TRIGGER—GET OUT!

Time is now of the utmost essence. If there is fire or smoke, you will probably have no more than two minutes to save your life. You must now draw on the situational awareness you practiced while entering the plane. Remember, the plane could be lopsided or even upside down. The emergency lighting may not be working. But if you counted the rows of seats from the exit door, for example, you have a plan for escape and know the direction you need to go. In general, fuel is stored in the vicinity of the wings or toward the rear of the craft. The best way to escape fire is by moving toward the front portion of the plane.

LIFE BEFORE PROPERTY, ALWAYS

Do not try to get your laptop, purse, or bags in the storage bin. As common-sensical as this sounds, people do this frequently. It not only loses time but makes climbing over seats, or whatever is needed to get out, more cumbersome. However, if the crash landing occurred in water, then make all efforts to retrieve the life vest under your seat.

FINDING THE BEST EXIT

Unfortunately, the closest exit may not be the best. It could be blocked with debris or be where a fire awaits outside. Exit doors are usually placed in tandem, opposite each other, with one on each side of the airplane. If you see one as more dangerous, then cross over and make for the exit door on the other side.

Once you reach the exit door, do not shove others out of your way. An orderly evacuation will create less confusion and save more lives. Urge those around you to remain calm and keep a line in order, if possible. However, do not allow delay caused by a passenger who is locked up with shock, or "frozen," to block the exit route. These people need to be physically pushed down an inflated slide, for example. When you make it to the front of the exit line, immediately disembark the plane. Do not wait for the person in front of you to clear the slide before taking your turn. Do not sit on the edge of the door and gently lever yourself onto the slide; you are not a child trying a playground chute for the first time. Do not pause, but continue moving through the door, jumping out and onto the slide. You've pulled the trigger, so act!

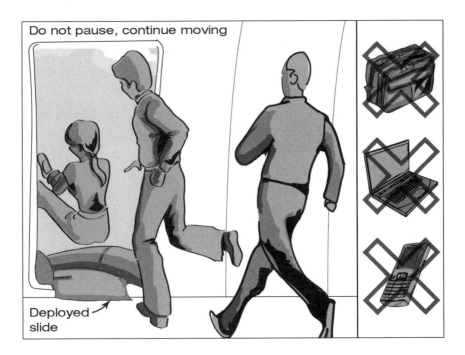

Do not pause, continue moving

Deployed slide

What to Do Once You're Out

If you are in water, then the survival tactics discussed in "Abandon Ship" (page 29) will be of value, though you should swim as far away from the airplane as you can. If it's a crash on land, which occurs more often, then move swiftly away from the plane. Secondary explosions are likely. You want to gain the greatest possible distance, preferably at least five hundred feet upwind, and wait there. If your crash landing was in a remote area, then remain in the vicinity of the plane, for this is the first place that rescuers will search for survivors. Call out, gather other survivors, and render any assistance you can until rescuers arrive. If rescue is prolonged, remain at the site as long as you can; however, improvise ways to signal your location. For example, keep a fire going, and use wet timber and leaves, which create more smoke. Or hang cloth or white shirts from high tree branches to aid in your rescue.

ANIMAL ATTACK

Dog Attacks

For many of us who own dogs, the term "man's best friend" couldn't be more accurate. The degree of loyalty dogs have toward humans is unparalleled in this world. But, as it is with any animal that has teeth, sometimes man's best friend becomes his worst enemy.

I am a true believer in the phrase "There are no bad dogs, just bad owners." The majority of dog attacks occur because of a lack of containment or inadequate training. Unfortunately, since there will probably never be any shortage of bad owners, dog attacks will continue to occur, and in some instances turn into life-threatening situations. Due to the large population of dogs in America—seventy-two million— the dog is classified as the most dangerous nonhuman mammal in our midst. During a ten-year study period, pit bull–type dogs were accountable for more than 60 percent of all fatalities, and Rottweilers caused more than 10 percent of known deaths. In fact, insurance companies will often raise a homeowner's premium if any of the following dogs, regardless of the dog's individual temperament, are known to be on the property: Akitas, Alaskan malamutes, bulldogs, mastiffs, chows, Dobermans, German shepherds, huskies, presa canarios, Rottweilers, and Staffordshire terriers, better known as pit bulls.

In 2010, there were thirty-four fatal dog attacks in the U.S. More than 350,000 dog-bite victims are seen in emergency rooms every year. Approximately 800,000 victims annually receive some form of medical attention related to dog bites.

DOGS AND CHILDREN

Someone is bitten by a dog every seventy-five seconds. And more than 80 percent of the time, it's a child that gets attacked. Due to our familiarity with and love of dogs, many forget that dogs originated from a species of wolves, most likely the small East Asian wolf, about ten thousand years ago. Unlike wild animals that usually try to avoid encounters with humans, dogs have long since lost their fear of people. Yet, regardless of centuries of domestication, dogs are still guided by their genetically ingrained survival instincts. They follow a dominant leader and remain territorial, loyally devoted to the pack. Nearly all canine species, including dogs, abide by a pack rule of hierarchy and dominance. Children are rarely considered leaders to be feared or followed, primarily since they are comparatively smaller than adults and often the same size as many of the aggressive dog breeds. When we consider dogs not as pets but as potential threats to our lives and the lives of our children, it must be remembered that any breed of dog can be potentially unpredictable. The habits and peculiarities of dogs, or of any hazardous animal, should be sized up the way we would do for any adversary, to be used as an advantage during a survival scenario.

STAND YOUR GROUND OR RUN?

I advise you not to run from a dog, but as with all survival scenarios, there are exceptions. If, for example, you see two guard dogs racing toward you at full speed, none of the tactics below will be effective. Dogs can't climb. So if you have the time to get to high ground, like up into a tree, on top of a Dumpster, or over a fence, do it. That one extra push-up you did and the effort you made to expand your comfort zone can turn a dangerous dog encounter into nothing more than a close call.

HOW TO AVOID A DOG ATTACK

First off, never purposely aggravate or tease a dog. Also note that dogs that are regularly chained and confined are usually more aggressive and should be avoided. It's unwise to assume that only certain breeds are dangerous. Just about any dog can cause injury.

1. When approached by a potentially dangerous dog, don't look it in the eye, because it may consider this a threat to its hierarchical status. In addition, do not smile, since the dog only sees your teeth and could consider this a threat. Generally, you don't want to overreact to the dog and let it think you are fearful, nor do you want to seem threatening from the start.

2. Observe the animal's body language. A growl or bared teeth is obviously a sign of aggression. But a more subtle thing to observe is the position of the dog's head. If a dog has its head held high or low, it is not usually in an aggressive mode. If the head is even with its body, then it is preparing to attack or fight.

3. Be alert so you can react quickly if events change. At first, stand firm, remain calm, and do not move suddenly. Do not run, as this will activate the dog's prey-chasing instinct. It is best to turn sideways so that you are not directly facing

the dog. This will display that you are nonthreatening; still, watch intently with a peripheral view.

4. If the dog is still approaching, loud commands, such as "Down! Stay!" could make it pause. But don't point your finger or expose your hands.

5. You must control your fear. At this point, you are assuming a nonthreatening posture to avoid an unwanted fight.

6. Gradually back away from the animal, making no sudden movements or changes in posture. Once a sufficient gap has been established, get to a place out of the sight line of the animal.

7. If the dog attacks, follow the actions in the "What to do when attacked" list below.

MENTAL TOUGHNESS

The principles of a SEAL's mindset and rules of engagement are equally applicable in dealing with animals as in dealing with human foes. When under threat, staying cool and assessing the situation to avoid a fight is also a way to win.

WHAT TO DO WHEN ATTACKED

Now that the dog has picked a fight, you will do everything you can to gain immediate control and subdue the animal. When a dog bites, it does not merely chomp down and go but rather digs in and grips, shaking its head and tearing flesh. You want to protect your face, throat, and chest. If it is going to bite, you want it to attack the thickest flesh of your outer legs, again protecting the more vulnerable areas of the groin and inner thighs. This will also give you an opportunity to attack the dog's more vulnerable parts.

1. Try to limit dog bites to areas of your body that have thicker skin. Even better, if you have time, wrap a jacket or

extra layers of cloth around your arm and offer that to the attacking dog.

Keep head out of biting/scratching range

2. If the dog has you in its grip, turn on the animal and drop your full weight onto its body. Slam your knees, or crash down with your elbows, directly onto the dog's body. Try to land on its ribs, which break easily, and strike at its head, especially at the back of the neck or at the base of the skull. While avoiding its teeth, wrap your forearm around its throat, thus controlling its ability to bite you more.

3. You can also reach for the dog's hind legs and lift them off the ground. The dog will immediately lose its ability to maneuver and bite you further.

4. Use a towel, coat, or shirt to cover the dog's head, which often subdues it quickly.

5. If available, a blast of cold water from a hose, or even a bucket of cold water thrown into its face, will disorient the dog enough to allow escape.

6. If you are attacked by multiple dogs, don't try to subdue each dog with your body weight, as you would during an

attack from a single dog. Dogs work in packs, and this will make you more vulnerable. Instead, attempt to strike at each approaching dog's nose or eyes, or grab one of their limbs. If the dog pack senses a more formidable adversary from the onset, the dog pack's instinct will often make them back off and retreat.

A fight with a dog is much like a knife fight—he who bleeds least wins!

MUSCLE MEMORY

It takes many repetitions for any action to become "memorized" by the muscles. One exercise you might try in order to be better prepared for a dog attack is to practice the above maneuvers on your own dog, if you own a medium-size to large breed. Of course, you will not use the force applied to an attacking dog, but you can incorporate how to turn and move correctly during your normal playtime with your pet.

AFTER THE ATTACK

1. Once the dog stops its attempt to bite, back away slowly.
2. Call the police or the local animal control unit.
3. Find out who owns the dog. You need to get documents pertaining to the inoculations it has received, specifically against rabies.
4. Seek medical attention for your wounds. Dog bites tear the skin and often require stitches. In addition, a dog's mouth, contrary to popular myth, has a lot of bacteria that can cause serious illness if a wound is unattended.

During mission planning, we had intelligence concerning dogs that might impede our goal and were part of the target's contingencies. The exact method used to neutralize aggressive dogs in the field is classified information. However, Special Ops has some really incredible dogs. In fact, during the raid to kill Osama bin Laden, the highly trained men of SEAL Team Six had with them a uniquely trained dog as part of the mission. SEAL canines are not your standard bomb-sniffing dogs. The dog on the bin Laden mission was specially trained to jump from planes and rappel from helicopters while attached to its handler. The dog wore ballistic body armor, had a head-mounted infrared (night-vision) camera, and wore earpieces to take commands from the handler. The dog also had reinforced teeth, capped with titanium. I would not want to try the techniques this book recommends on this dog. Thank God he's on our side.

Bear Attacks

There are approximately 550,000 North American black bears roaming the forests of the lower fifty states at the present time. The chance of encountering a bear is increasing. As their natural habitat shrinks and their population grows, bears are losing their fear of humans. They are also acquiring a taste for our foods and garbage. In general, bears will want to avoid a fight and will only attack when:

- Scared, startled, or cornered.
- Very hungry or disturbed while eating.
- Injured or sick.
- Protecting their cubs.

If you go out into the woods or live near bear country, it's important to know the characteristics of each of the three different species of bear you may come across.

BLACK BEARS

These are the smallest bears, but the males can still weigh nearly 400 pounds, while the females average about 300 pounds. They are swift, reaching speeds of 35 mph, and they are good climbers. Many black bears are identifiable by a light patch on their chests and light-colored snouts.

1. Despite their size and strength, bears would rather not have a conflict. If you are in black bear country and suspect they are close by, make noise. Bang pots, blow a whistle, or shout out. This will usually get them to clear out before you approach. You don't want to surprise a bear by walking stealthily through the forest. If you spot a bear that doesn't see you, especially if it's rummaging through a park garbage can or eating, give it a wide berth.

2. If camping, make sure your foodstuffs are well away from where your tents are set up. Or suspend food supplies in a

satchel tied to a thin branch that bears cannot reach. Dogs and pets also attract bears to your camp, so most pets should be left home.

3. You should always carry bear-repellent spray. This is basically a concentrated pepper spray but is supersized and highly compressed to reach greater distances. The active ingredient is a chemical called oleoresin capsicum. Bear sprays are designed to wear in a holster and should not be buried deep in your backpack.

   There are some drawbacks to bear spray: If you shoot it at the bear from too far a range, you'll only make it angrier. Some recommend spraying the bear when it's about forty feet away, but that is too risky, since the repellent could disperse and not affect the bear. Wait, wait, wait, and then spray the bear when you know that the full force of the repellent will be most effective. You have to stand firm and get the spray fully in its face. Also, many people spray it prematurely and are downwind, causing them to blind themselves with the bear spray. Despite varying opinions, if used properly, bear sprays do work and should be an essential survival tool when entering bear country.

4. If you come face-to-face with a black bear, don't run or try to climb a tree. As mentioned earlier, black bears will out-climb you, and you'll be trapped. Instead, keep a calm demeanor. Stand as tall and squared off as possible to show your size. Be loud and forceful in your voice. Give the bear an escape route, a way out of the encounter. Wave your arms and show that the bear may lose if it decides to attack. A bear will test you and make a false start to see if you will run. Here is where your mental preparedness comes into use. You have rehearsed and know what to do in a bear encounter. However, while standing still during the initial bluff or charge, you must have your bear spray readied and pointed like a gun, firmly in your grip.

BROWN BEARS

Brown bears, including the subspecies of grizzly and Kodiak bears, average 500 to 800 pounds, but can weigh up to 1,700 pounds, thus making them among the largest land predators on the planet. Commonly they are medium to dark brown, with distinct shoulder humps. If you are attacked by a brown bear, you may need to use different survival techniques than you would with a black bear.

1. Use the previously discussed tactics of avoiding the bear and attempting to use a bear-repellent spray. However, these animals are larger and much more unpredictable than black bears.

2. If the bear continues to come at you, immediately fall to the ground and cover your head and your neck with your hands. You also want to get into a fetal position to protect your stomach. Tuck your knees into your chin and don't move a muscle.

3. Then, even as nervous as you'll likely be, play dead. For grizzlies, most attacks on humans are for the purpose of neutralizing a potential threat. If you seem as if you just died of fright, then chances are they will leave you alone. The bear may push at you or see if you move, but if you can remain dead calm during this assault, you may very well live to talk about it. When it comes to outrunning or wrestling a grizzly, your chances of winning are remote. It's not fun, but the bear will often linger nearby for as much as twenty minutes. At this time, attempt to conceal your hyperventilation and control your body so you're in a state of complete stillness.

4. In the event that you must try to ward off an attacking brown bear, go for its nose or eyes. It will be difficult to avoid its powerful paws and sharp claws, but this is your only option. The bear's nose and eyes are its most vulnerable points, and if you can inflict a blow to these areas, you could get a chance to flee.

POLAR BEARS

If you are in regions where polar bears roam, there is a limited chance of surviving a face-to-face encounter if you are unarmed. The best advice is to stay clear and avoid polar bears at all costs. If you play dead with a polar bear, it will eat you. Bear spray might work, and if it comes down to hand-to-hand combat, again go for the nose and eyes. However, if you try to outrun a polar bear on the ice, it will catch you quickly. A polar bear has sandpaper-like paws that make it proficient in running and not slipping on frozen surfaces.

Mountain Lion Attacks

The mountain lion, also known as puma or cougar, is the only long-tailed wildcat in North America. They live for upwards of twelve years and can weigh as much as 160 pounds. They are primarily nocturnal and secretive, and their diet is composed mostly of deer and elk. Your chances of seeing a mountain lion in the wild are slim, but you should always be aware of an animal that can leap upwards of eighteen vertical feet and feeds on meat. Do the following things to avoid a mountain lion attack:

1. Travel in groups and make a lot of noise. Lions will go out of their way to avoid confrontation.
2. If you do come upon a lion, face it and appear as large as possible by raising your arms or holding objects like an open coat.
3. Give the lion an escape route. If necessary, throw rocks or tree limbs at it to move it along.
4. Back away slowly but continue to face the lion. Don't run, as this will only stimulate its chase response.
5. If you are attacked, stay on your feet and fight. Lions have been known to retreat when their prey fights back.
6. If a lion manages to attack and has you in its grip, strike and jam a stick or rock at its eyes and nose, which might loosen its hold and give you an opportunity to escape.

One of the SEALs (who shall remain nameless) whom I had the honor of working with in my first platoon at SEAL Team Two was the victim of a wild-animal attack. Imagine this—the guy had spent the better part of twenty years in some of the most hostile places on the planet. He survived countless combat situations in addition to walking away from three—that's right, three—helicopter crashes. And then, he almost got killed by a deer while jogging in Germany. He was on a forest trail when he came face-to-face with a huge antlered stag standing on its hind legs, with hooves up, ready to fight, as they do during mating season to protect their turf. WTF?

AUTO ACCIDENT

There are more than 200 million vehicles in the United States, many heading in any number of directions at this given moment, and all operated by individuals with varying degrees of alertness and skill. The chances of getting into a car accident at least once in your life are estimated to be more than 95 percent—essentially it's not a matter of *if* but *when* you'll be in an accident. Approximately 43,000 Americans are killed on our nation's roadways every year, and another 100,000 become permanently disabled due to car accidents. So what is the single best thing you can do to increase your chances of walking away from an automobile accident?

Wear Your Seat Belt

Even if the death rate due to automobile accidents is so high, cars are actually much safer than ever before. For example, in the 1950s, when there were a third as many cars on the road, more than 32,000 car-related fatalities occurred each year. The retractable seat belt was invented in the 1940s and offered as an option on cars only during the 1950s. In the United States, auto manufacturers were not required to put them in all cars until 1968. It wasn't until the nineties that most states passed laws requiring drivers to wear one.

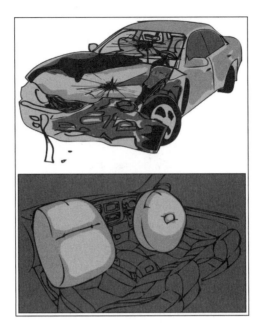

Most deaths from auto accidents result from injuries sustained when the body is slammed against the steering wheel, for example, or dashboard. Seat belts prevent death from internal injuries that happen when the car is stopped suddenly during an accident, and when the driver or passengers are subjected to impact.

There are a number of seat belt designs, but all should be strapped low around your hips. Make sure the shoulder strap crosses over your chest diagonally and that it is as snug as you can have it while maintaining maneuverability.

The work I did in Iraq involved a lot of high-speed driving. We rarely wore seat belts because the idea of having to quickly evacuate the car and getting caught up in the seat belt was a nightmare. Hell, with all of the gear we wore it was hard enough to get out as it was. But when I learned that the leading cause of injury in the crew I was working with was automobile-related accidents, I went against the "trapped" fear and started making my men strap in anytime the speed of the vehicle was over 35 mph. It paid off and saved lives.

Other Safety Features and Precautions

I absolutely love classic cars, but I now understand why traffic fatalities are at an all-time low. Many of these older cars had only lap belts, seats without head support, hard steering wheels with protruding steering columns, narrow pedals, and no air bags.

Air bag technology was invented to protect astronauts when early spacecraft were designed to crash-land back to Earth. The first car air bag was invented in 1968 and installed in some government vehicles in 1973. Air bags became a standard-issue feature in cars in 1990, but not until 1999 were both cars and light trucks required to install both driver and passenger-side air bags. An air bag senses impact and sudden deceleration and inflates at a speed of 200 mph, as fast as a shell fired from a sawed-off shotgun. This millisecond in which an air bag is deployed has decreased the risk of dying during a front-end collision by 30 percent. Do not disable your air bag, and have its functionality checked periodically.

Air Bag Precautions

The early-model air bags were so strong that some actually caused decapitation if they malfunctioned. They are still powerful but are far more sensor-regulated. However, a small child in the passenger seat should be placed so that his or her seat is as far back as it can be from the dashboard. Because accidents aren't planned and an air bag is deployed on impact, I recommend driving with your hands at the **four o'clock and eight o'clock positions** on the steering wheel, rather than the standard two and ten. This will provide a clear path for the bag to release without sending your arms and hands into your face. Do not place any object on top of the air bag enclosure, or you may end up eating it. Keep your head back against the headrest but loosen your shoulders.

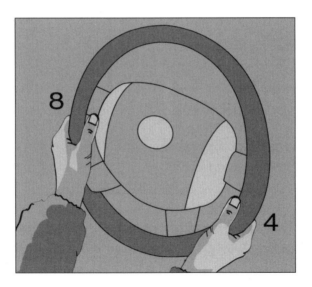

Newton's Law

An object in motion will stay in motion. This is why the addition of the chest belt and headrest have been so successful in reducing injuries and fatalities. The belt keeps your entire body firmly in the seat, while a properly adjusted headrest (middle of the headrest even with the middle of the back of your head) will eliminate whiplash. When you get in an accident and stop abruptly, things like your head, books, cell phone, golf clubs, and such don't realize this and keep moving. Anything loose lying about the car can become a deadly projectile and cause injury. For example, don't keep a baseball bat in the area of the back window, or it will turn into a club upon impact and possibly kill you. Stow all stuff under the seat, or in the trunk, or in wheel-well areas.

SEALs say: "Take care of your gear and it will take care of you."

Vehicle Maintenance

The vehicle you get into every day is one important piece of "gear." It's actually amazing the abuse most vehicles go through and yet keep running despite our lack of regular maintenance. Make a checklist of items that need to be maintained and serviced on your vehicle, and follow it. You can greatly decrease the chances of an auto accident by simply maintaining your vehicle. Pay particular attention to the condition of your brakes and tires. The extra thousand miles you are trying to get out of your tires could mean the difference between avoiding an accident and being the cause of it.

Common Sense Is Rarely Common

You've heard the advice about driving defensively, but it's no mere cliché. In some foreign countries there seem to be no traffic laws. People drive at crazy speeds, on the wrong side of the road, and think of traffic signs as only suggestions. Not to mention after spending the majority of your life driving on the right side of the road, it takes a lot of focus to tell your brain and muscles to drive and stay on the left side in countries where this is required. The death rates from car accidents in these countries are astronomically higher than in the United States. In America, many traffic signs were installed only after fatalities occurred at that site, so their presence is a warning to you to obey the rules. If it's raining, you don't need to go 60 mph just because the speed limit allows it. Adjust to environmental conditions—you don't want to be among this year's car causalities or become permanently handicapped due to your own carelessness.

Focus

The car is a powerful machine that can injure or kill. I couldn't imagine texting or talking on my cell phone while I was cleaning my rifle, but nowadays people eat while driving, shave, put on their makeup—and even watch TV. In this wonderful age of electronics, there is a spike of accidents resulting from multitasking while driving, attributable primarily to distractions. Texting and e-mailing while you should be keeping your focus on the road are the latest causes of fatal car crashes.

The Accident: Avoid and Minimize

Again, driving is something that requires a high degree of situational awareness. Observe the road, looking for things that could end up causing an accident. Drive defensively from the moment you start your engine until you turn it off (see "Road Rage: Defensive and Evasive Driving," page 266). As an avid motorcyclist, I am constantly trying to anticipate what the drivers around me will do next. Keep your head on a swivel. Watch for cars ahead, and look for pedestrians, trying to anticipate their next move. It's recommended to keep two car lengths behind the vehicle ahead of you, which will provide enough time to brake and react to the unexpected. If you notice a distracted driver, stay extra clear. Also, many of the people driving rented moving trucks are inexperienced in handling these oversized vehicles and should be given a wide berth. If you see a car that has just parked, be prepared for the driver to fling open the door without looking. Be particularly watchful of kids playing on the sidewalk, for if they start to chase a ball, chances are they will not check for oncoming traffic.

If all efforts have failed and a crash is imminent, maintain your composure. You must try to respond with decisive maneuvers, but you must do so as smoothly as possible.

1. Brace your hands on the wheel in the four o'clock and eight o'clock positions to allow the air bag to deploy without being obstructed by your hands and arms. Put your head back against the headrest and relax your body.
2. Try to slow your vehicle as much as possible, especially if you are veering toward a tree or a concrete barrier.
   - Braking: There are certain techniques to braking that are proven to keep maximum control. Primarily, if you slam the brakes, you will lose control. Antilock brakes have an antilock brake system (ABS) computer chip that regulates brake fluid and prevents the brakes from freezing up if pressed firmly. If your car lacks antilock brakes, then pumping the brake pedal will prevent lockup and allow you to retain control. Slammed brakes cause your car to skid, leaving you to lose control and making the result of the accident far more likely to be even less favorable.
3. Use the front of your car. The way new cars are designed, hitting something head-on offers more protection than taking a blow from the side. The side panels of cars are usually less fortified.
4. Steer smoothly. Just as you don't want to jam the breaks, you don't want to jerk the steering wheel quickly (even if driving at normal speeds). This will cause the vehicle to skid and oftentimes spin in the opposite direction.
   - If the car begins to skid, your instincts will falsely tell you to turn the steering wheel in the opposite direction. In fact, it's best to turn the wheel toward the direction of the skid to regain control.
5. Sometimes you may need to accelerate while you steer or weave out of range of an oncoming car to avoid an accident.

Tire Blowouts

If you are dealing with a blowout or get a flat while driving, do not slam on the brakes. Let off the gas and allow your car to gradually decelerate on its own while steering at a slight angle toward the shoulder of the road you are on.

Postaccident

After the accident, if you are conscious, you want to exit the vehicle quickly. However, assess the area in which the accident occurred. For example, you do not want to step out into oncoming traffic. If the air bag deployed, the interior of the car will be filled with talcum powder. When the air bags deploy, a small explosive charge ignites two chemicals that react to form the nitrogen that is used to fill the air bag. The smell of that chemical reaction is unfamiliar to most, and that, combined with the talcum powder filling the car's interior, causes many people to think the car is on fire. That usually isn't the case. If the car is truly on fire, the smoke will most likely be dark and oily. Remain calm and go into combat breathing. If you can leave the car, chances are your injuries are not life-threatening. Even if you find yourself trapped within the vehicle, you must still retain your wits; try to stay conscious by telling yourself that you can endure and that help will arrive shortly. No matter the pain, know that feeling anything is a good sign. You are alive.

BIOCHEMICAL ATTACK

In 1995, in Tokyo, Japan, a religious group released sarin, a deadly nerve gas, on several lines of the Tokyo metro during rush hour. Crowds fled packed subways, gagged, vomited, and collapsed on the streets during the chemical attack, which killed twelve people and caused thousands of severe injuries. The same group had used the nerve gas a year before. Sarin was released from trucks, targeting a neighborhood where judges lived who were about to pass a verdict in a real estate case that was not favorable to the sect. Eight died from that incident. For the Tokyo metro operation, small pouches of sarin were dropped and punctured by sharpened umbrella tips.

The use of biological and chemical weapons is nothing new to warfare. In the 1300s, invading Tartars used a form of biotoxin when besieging cites. They gathered bodies infected with bubonic plague and catapulted the corpses over the walls of enemy fortresses. In 1972, an ecoterrorist group called RISE tried to disperse microbial pathogens using crop-dusting aircraft. Biological and chemical attacks use various toxic agents to cause massive casualties, and although they are often dispersed differently, survival methods for both scenarios are similar.

Biological toxins are designed to spread pathogens that cause disease, while in chemical warfare liquids or gases are employed that are meant to cause the body to malfunction rapidly. In any regard, such attacks are considered highly probable to occur in the United States in the near future. As mentioned, disbursement methods vary, but experts agree that in order for these biochemical agents to be effective and cause massive contamination, the agent must be something that is quickly absorbed by the skin or inhaled, or something ingested that lacks taste, color, or smell.

Early Signs

Here is another incident when situational awareness is of paramount importance. The earlier that biological toxins or chemical agents are detected, the better your odds of survival. As mentioned, in situational awareness exercises, you note variances against the baseline, or what is normal. To detect biochemical attacks, you need to pay attention to oddities or unusual things in the environment.

Chemical agents will frequently give signs of exposure within minutes or hours. They are generally liquids, often aerosolized, and most have a unique odor and color. Biological agents usually have no odor or color and can be in either liquid or powder form.

Biopathogens introduced into water supplies, for example, can take days to be noticed. For instance, when anthrax, often delivered in powder form, is used it generally takes two to five days before symptoms appear.

Some examples of possible preattack warning signs:

- Surfaces covered with an oily substance.

- Liquid sprays dispersing from unlikely areas.

- The presence of vapor clouds. These could appear as unusually low-lying clouds or as a colored fog that is unrelated to weather. You could see clouds of dust suspended over an area and drifting in a manner unlike any natural occurrence.

- A large number of birds, fish, or small animals suddenly found dead.

- An odor that seems out of place but isn't necessarily foul smelling. You may smell something similar to almonds or peach kernels, or fresh-cut grass or hay. If you are on a farm, this may be normal, but in a city, for example, a sudden smell of mowed lawn drifting through the streets should be cause for alarm.

- Trucks spraying or dispersing mist, or low-flying, crop-dusting-type aircraft in unusual areas or without pre-announcement. For example, mosquito-spraying trucks and their nightly routes are announced and made public.

- Someone entering a building or public transportation, like a stadium or a subway car, for example, dressed unusually (such as a person wearing a long-sleeved shirt or overcoat in the summertime). If you see someone wearing breathing-protection equipment, particularly in areas where large numbers of people are gathered, then treat the suspect as a potential disperser of toxins. If his breathing equipment is already in place, chances are the toxins have already been released. Rapidly leave the area and notify police.

- Multiple people nearby suddenly vomiting, convulsing, having difficulty breathing, or acting confused and disoriented. This means a chemical attack has already begun.

How to Protect Yourself and Escape

The quicker-acting chemical toxins are designed to cause an immediate inhalation hazard. On the other hand, many chemicals of this nature also break down and lose potency rapidly when exposed to the sun, diluted with water, or dissipated in high winds. However, you will not know the difference at the time, so reacting quickly and gaining distance from a biological or chemical agent is the key to survival. The next decisions you make will be the difference between living and dying.

1. Unlike professional firefighters or those of us in the teams, you are not likely to have protective gear on hand, so you'll have to make do.
   - Take maximum effort to cover your mouth and nose. Use your shirt, a coat sleeve, a handkerchief—even a plastic shopping bag will provide some form of protection.
   - Minimize exposure to all body parts by covering arms and legs, tucking your pants into your socks, and raising your collar, and most importantly check that any cut or abrasion is thoroughly bandaged. If you are wearing shorts or a dress, try to find anything to cover your legs—plastic garbage bags, a blanket, the fabric stripped from an umbrella—even newspapers will minimize exposure.
2. Get off the X. Attempt to figure out where the toxic agent is emanating from by noting any of the unusual signs mentioned above, and move as far away as possible without passing through the contaminated area. When evacuating the area, make sure you move *upwind,* or *into the wind.* Downwind a greater concentration of toxins will be heading in that direction, carried by natural air currents.

Quickly assess the direction of the wind by holding out a piece of thin paper, looking for a flag, or watching how trash in the street is tumbling. The only time you would not move upwind is when you know for certain the source of the disbursement, which always dictates moving in the opposite direction.

3. During flight, resist the temptation to take deep breaths to smell if the air is "all clear." Wear protective breathing apparatus or keep your mouth and nose covered for as long as possible.

Wind direction

IMPROVISED GAS MASK

You can make an improvised version of a gas mask by putting a piece of cloth into a gallon of water and adding one tablespoon of baking soda to the mix. Strap this moistened rag over your mouth and nose.

Shelter In

Getting off the X might mean you are forced to move indoors and "shelter in." Most toxic agents are heavier than air and tend to settle and stay close to the ground. You want to make your indoor evacuation by heading upward to a safe haven.

1. Get to an interior room on a higher floor.
2. Shut down all air-conditioning or heating systems.
    • If in a car, shut off air or heating, close air-intake vents on the dashboard, and roll up windows. If you detect or believe toxic fumes or a gas has entered your car, then keep the windows open fully while driving away from the exposure site. Once the car is sufficiently aerated, then close windows.
3. Ensure all windows are closed and sealed tightly. Use duct tape to cover seams.

As if CQC (close-quarters combat) isn't challenging enough, one of the contingencies we would train for was unexpectedly encountering a biochemical agent. We would be working our way through the house when the instructor cadre started yelling, *"Gas, gas, gas!"* So after saying the usual *"F this,"* half the team would don their gas masks, while the other half held security . . . and their breath. Then we would switch it up, with the gas-masked guys holding security while the other half masked up before continuing on with the mission. Let's just say that a 100-degree temperature and 100-percent humidity with a fogged-up gas mask makes it feel like you are breathing through a straw. Just another beautiful day in the teams!

What to Do If You've Been Exposed

You must begin decontamination procedures as soon as you have cleared the area of the attack.

1. Remove all of your clothes immediately. Do so by pulling them *down and away*. Don't pull them over your head because the eyes, nose, and mouth are then more susceptible to exposure. If you are wearing a pullover-type garment that cannot be stepped out of and has no buttons, zipper, or snaps, then cut it with scissors or a knife, or tear the garment, though always in a downward direction. This should get rid of 90 percent of any agents to which you have been exposed. Have a plastic bag at hand and put the clothes into it while undressing. Seal the bag immediately.

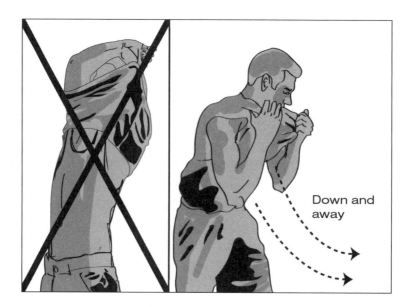

Down and away

2. Wash. You want to find any source of water, be it an outdoor fountain, hose spigot, or body of water. If indoors, use soap and cold water and wash yourself down thoroughly yet gently—you do not want to scrub abrasively, as this will open skin pores and increase toxin exposure. It's best if you can make a mix of water, soap, and a touch of bleach or chlorine. This will help disinfect your skin and neutralize toxin concentrations. Remember to flush nostrils,

clean ears, and wash all cracks and crevices of your body. If in a tub, make sure this water is flushed away and the area afterward cleaned. Wash. Rinse. Repeat.

3. If you do not have water available, talcum powder can be used, or even flour will act as a dry wash and absorb toxins. When using a dry cleanser, cover your body in it and let it stand for about thirty seconds. Brush it off with whatever you have, be it cloth or gauze, and repeat this. Make sure to seal these cleaning rags in plastic bags. If outdoors, mud can be used as a form of nonabrasive cleaner, as long as it's retrieved at least twelve inches below the surface. Let some of the mud harden. In doing so it will absorb toxins from the outer layer of the skin. But remember, flake off or gently brush away whatever substance you use to clean exposed areas. Don't rub your skin too roughly, as abrasion will cause more toxins to enter.

   - Remember: Any item that has been on the ground during the toxic assault should be considered contaminated and not good for decontamination purposes. For example, using a newspaper you found on the street could potentially only introduce more of the toxin into your system versus removing it.

4. Seek medical assistance as soon as possible.

BOMB

A bomb is any of a number of explosive devices both civilian and military that rely on an explosive material to provide an extremely sudden and violent release of energy. They can be low-explosive, high-explosive, or nuclear. They can be positioned in advance for follow-on detonation, dropped from the air, or even precision guided. For the purposes of this section, we will focus on the types of bombs that are most commonly used by terrorists to inflict injury and death.

Car Bomb

In early maritime warfare, ships packed with gunpowder were set on fire and cast adrift toward enemy fleets. These bomb ships or fire ships were a hit-or-miss tactic. Most times the fire was extinguished before it ignited the combustibles aboard. The Dutch sent dozens of these bomb ships, called Hellburners, packed with seven thousand pounds of gunpowder, to ultimately break the Spanish blockade at the Siege of Antwerp in the 1500s. In the 1920s, Communist anarchists parked a horse-drawn cart filled with explosives in the financial district of New York City, killing thirty-eight. Car bombs were used by the Vietcong in Vietnam, and also by terrorists in both Palestine and Israel.

It got to the point where it was common to hear these going off all day long throughout Baghdad. A boom in the distance and I'd take a second to pray nobody but the assholes who made it got killed—then back to work. Freaking Wild West over there.

Car bombs have been used to kill people for more than a hundred years, but not to the extent and unfortunate effectiveness that we have seen in Afghanistan and Iraq against our troops. Today, the car bomb is known as a VBIED, or vehicle-borne improvised explosive device, and has been responsible for the death or injury of tens of thousands of people, including, most regrettably, many of our armed forces. More than 60 percent of all U.S. casualties in Afghanistan and Iraq were caused by car bombs or IEDs (improvised explosive devices).

SITUATIONAL AWARENESS

The most important weapon against car bombs is situational awareness. Again, alertness is one of the most vital and key tools needed to acquire a SEAL mindset. In the case of detecting a possible car bomb, ask yourself questions such as these:

❏ Why did the driver park in a no-parking zone, park awkwardly, or park in haste?

❏ Why did the driver park in front of a certain business or building, but head in the opposite direction from it?

❏ Why does the vehicle appear to be heavy (low-sitting suspension)?

Since the car bomb is such a cheap and effective way to do harm and cause chaos, incidents of this nature can only increase. Economical handheld technological inventions are being tested that will offer a way to detect whether or not a car contains explosives. Perhaps there will be a day when these detectors will be as common as smoke alarms in the house. Until then, situational awareness is our best weapon.

The main problem with situational awareness being the best defense is that detection of a car bomb will require an *exceptional* degree of alertness in everyday life. Any vehicle can become a car bomb once it is loaded with explosives. The metal of the car itself turns into shrapnel. More than the explosive, the shredded car parts cause the most widespread and indiscriminate damage, killing anyone near it. Explosives used in car bombs could be ammunition, pyrotechnics, or dynamite. These don't require ingenious concealment and are simply placed under the seat, put in the trunk, or magnetically attached underneath the car. The charges can be detonated by numerous means: timers, ignitions, the opening of doors, the pressing of brakes or accelerators, switches (tilt, pressure), or remote devices (such as cell phones).

Seeing people talking on cell phones is a normal, common thing here in the States. You don't give it a second thought. But when you're rolling around in Iraq and you see this, you are always waiting for the BOOM. It's strange how during wartime such an everyday thing can be a threat. But since we knew IEDs could be detonated by cell phone, we were always on the lookout for the random guy standing by himself with phone in hand. Really got the hair standing up.

Because military compounds and important buildings tend to have a lot of security in place against bombings and the like, prospective car bombers oftentimes target low-security locations—soft targets—such as markets or busy street corners.

Another brutal tactic that has been employed is the use of sequential car bombs. One is detonated to lure first responders and those trying to help, after which a second one is detonated, killing even more.

INDIVIDUAL PRECAUTIONS FOR COMMUNITY SAFETY

The absolute randomness of a car bomb makes it such a difficult thing to defeat. However, there are several things you can do to avoid your vehicle's unknowingly being recruited as a car bomb or rigged with explosives. A potential car bomber will not want to use a car that can be traced to them, so they will often use a rental car obtained fraudulently—or your car. In Israel, it is not uncommon for random cars to be chosen and rigged with explosives, unbeknownst to the owner. Personal safety thus depends somewhat on everybody in the community taking basic precautions.

1. Park your car in a secure location whenever possible. If a secure lot or parking space isn't available, then always try to park it in a very public place. It would be difficult for someone to remain unnoticed if they attempted to attach an explosive under your car or wire it to go off when you opened the door, for example.
2. Lock your doors and trunk to avoid undesired access to your vehicle.
3. Take a look under your vehicle frequently. Look for anything that shouldn't be there, such as a wire that seems out of place or is hanging down. You may see an object that is relatively clean in comparison to the normal grease and dirt under your vehicle. Mirrors attached to a long handle are ideal for this task.
4. If you even remotely suspect something is wrong, back away immediately and contact the police.

The NYPD has established a saying that applies to every city in the United States—"If you see something, say something."

In 2010, when a car bomb attack was planned for the theater district in New York City, it was two street vendors who noticed smoke coming from the car and alerted mounted police.

STRUCTURAL SAFETY

In 1995, Timothy McVeigh packed a rented moving truck with five thousand pounds of ammonium nitrate, a type of fertilizer, which he doused with highly combustible racing fuel. He parked the truck in front of the Alfred P. Murrah Federal Building in Oklahoma City at nine A.M. and lit a two-minute fuse. At 9:02 the truck exploded and killed 168 people. Two minutes! In this case, McVeigh had been recorded on security cameras making practice runs and driving near the building in the same truck a few days before. On the day of the explosion, he parked the vehicle in a pickup zone for a day-care center, which was housed in the building, and abandoned the vehicle. He fled on foot, moving away from the parked and abandoned truck, and jogged far from the building toward his getaway vehicle. What we can learn from this in retrospect is how important situational awareness is in detecting a car bomb. Unusual behavior, such as a driver running rapidly from a parked car or truck, is not part of the normal baseline, as discussed earlier.

One deterrent put in place after the Oklahoma City bombing was the installation of concrete barriers at all federal buildings, and eventually at the entrances to all buildings with high occupancy, such as malls and many schools. The following techniques for fortifying your house, estate, or compound are essential. These will also serve to protect you in the event that a catastrophe, civil unrest, or rioting occurs in your area.

Standard methods of fortification

- Gates and barriers at a distance far from the entrance.

- An approach to the entrance that requires vehicles to slow or stop completely. You don't want a car to have the ability to race through rapidly. Use barricades or an obstacle, forcing an approaching vehicle to make a series of S-turns before arriving at the gate.

- Limited exits and entrances, so there is less traffic flow to control.

- Permanent bunkers at a structure's other susceptible areas. Note how this technique is used at main pedestrian entryways at malls and public buildings.

- Inspection of all undercarriages, hoods, and trunks of cars.

- Visual sweeps of a vehicle's occupants.

IED and Booby Trap

The use of explosive devices to kill or injure is not limited to vehicles. The true leading cause of casualties during both the Afghanistan and Iraq wars was the use of IEDs and booby traps. An IED is simply any homemade device packed with explosives. Intensive situational awareness is the best defense against IEDs. As always, be alert to things that seem out of the ordinary, such as an unexpected delivery, or a package wrapped or boxed, for example, in an unusual manner.

IED delivery methods

- Disguised as a package.

- Thrown from a hideout along the road—in this situation it is usually two males doing the throwing. That's how it was in Afghanistan and Iraq, though the throwing was not always done by adults.

- Placed in potholes and covered with a thin layer of dirt, to act as land mines. They can be on major roadways or on trails used only by the military.

- Placed near a pile of cinder blocks or rubble. Now and again after a battle, the IEDs are planted where they will kill rescue workers.

- Placed in dead animals.

Yes, the insurgents use dead animals on the side of the road to conceal IEDs. Animals using animals. I'm a master of the obvious when I say that you need situational awareness, cranked up to the red line, while operating in an environment like Afghanistan or Iraq. Every time we drove past something that "didn't look right," we would sort of wince or hold our breath for a second. It just became second nature.

Suicide Bomber

What's called a "person-borne" bomb, the person being a suicide bomber, is a very lethal weapon and difficult to spot. These volunteers, or "recruits," are fitted with a special vest or belt, or modified clothing, which is packed with high explosives. To achieve as much collateral damage as they can, these modified carrying devices also contain fragmentary objects, such as ball bearings, bolts, nuts, or any kind of metal scraps. Most often, this type of bomb will use a "command detonation firing system," which is some sort of switch or button the person activates by hand. The downside of this method of delivery is that sometimes these bombers lose their nerve and fire off the bomb when not yet in place. Their clothing is bulkier than normal, and many times they seem nervous, sweaty, and preoccupied.

CONFRONTING A SUICIDE BOMBER

The opinions are mixed on how to disable a suicide bomber, if, in fact, you have the opportunity to know for certain that a person is vested with explosives. Given that many suicide bombers need their hands to detonate a device, many police departments train officers to shoot the suspect in the head—literally between the eyes—so as to immediately halt all motor skills.

For the civilian without a weapon, the best method might be to get behind the bomber and grab him or her by the shins and lift them off the ground. They will fall face-first and instinctively use their hands to stop the fall. If you are standing face-to-face with the bomber, use violence of action and strike forcefully at his face, then grab his hands. Call out to bystanders to stay clear, to take cover, and to call police for assistance.

If detonation is imminent, one idea is to sacrifice yourself and embrace the bomber to prevent those around you from receiving the full force of the blast. In most circumstances, this would be an extremely hard choice, but if it came down to you dying or your children who were standing next to you, the appropriate action is clear— pull the trigger! Remember, action makes a hero, and as we say in the SEALs, "the greater good for the greater number."

SEAL Michael Monsoor was acting for the greater good of his teammates on September 29, 2006, while part of a sniper overwatch security position in Iraq with three other SEALs and eight Iraqi Army soldiers. On that day, an insurgent threw a fragmentation grenade at their position. It struck Monsoor in the chest before falling to the ground. Although he was right next to an exit, Monsoor shouted to others to take cover, and then, without hesitation, he spread his body over the explosive, saving his fellow SEALs. He passed away approximately thirty minutes later from his injuries. Michael Monsoor was posthumously awarded the Medal of Honor.

If a Bomb Detonates

If you are in the vicinity when a bomb goes off, it happens so fast and unexpectedly that there are limited survival tools that will help. The best response is to hit the ground and lie flat, covering your head with your fingers laced. Keep your legs crossed and your mouth opened. If your mouth is closed, the concussion or shock waves from the explosion can burst your lungs and your eardrums. The scenarios depicted in movies with the character leaping away, spread-eagle, will only increase your chance of sustaining more injuries.

I can't tell you how happy it made me every time I heard that a suicide bomber attack had occurred and the result was only one dead: the bomber. I knew things were getting desperate in Iraq when they started sending women and kids with explosive vests to do their dirty work. Not only did they run out of virgins, they ran out of anyone with a sense of courage. Shit bags!

BRIDGE COLLAPSE

In the last fifty years, more than a hundred bridges gave way unexpectedly and collapsed. Whether from wind, flood, overload, or an engineering flaw, any of the nearly six hundred thousand bridges in the U.S. that have spans of more than twenty feet could fail without warning. In 2007, for example, the I-35W bridge that spanned the Mississippi River in Minneapolis, Minnesota, collapsed during the height of evening rush hour. It was built in 1967 and carried 140,000 cars across its 1,900-foot span daily. Despite inspections, the bridge failed, ultimately causing 13 deaths and injuring nearly 150. As America's infrastructure continues to decay, it is wise to be alert when driving across any elevated roadway.

When a bridge collapses, there will usually be no warning. When the Tacoma Narrows Bridge collapsed in 1940, its span wobbled and twisted well before it finally gave way, which allowed vehicles to clear off, causing no casualties. Typically, a bridge will simply collapse, similar to how destruction is caused during an earthquake. If you are in your car and see the vehicles ahead of you disappearing below, and realize that your turn is inevitably next, keep your seat belt on and brace for impact. A one-hundred-foot plunge from a bridge into the water would be similar to a collision at 60 mph. If the car drops more than twenty feet, the front end, where the engine is located, which is the heaviest part, will usually cause the vehicle to nose-dive. Air bags will be deployed upon your impact with the water. (Refer back to "Auto Accident," page 77.)

Several years ago, I had an opportunity to go through the Naval Aviation Survival Training Program. The highlight (or worst part of the training, depending on whom you ask) included a ride in "the Dunker." It's a device you strap into that is meant to simulate a plane or helicopter crashing into the ocean. It strikes the pool water and flips upside down. Once the movement stops, all you have to do is get out of your safety harness and swim to the surface. If you ever watched *An Officer and a Gentleman,* you'll know what I'm talking about. (In the movie, David Caruso freaked out in it, before he became ultracool in *CSI: Miami.*) I enjoyed the hell out of my try in the Dunker. But the thought of impacting the ocean at night, at four times the speed, and crammed in with twenty other guys wearing a ton of gear and with only a couple of escape routes, is something else. That would not be fun. Yep, I still hate helicopters.

Bracing for Impact

If you are about to plunge into the water:

1. Place your hands on the steering wheel at four o'clock and eight o'clock to allow the air bag to deploy without striking your arms or hands.
2. Scrunch your shoulders up so your neck is between them. Even though air bags will still be deployed, the danger will be in getting thrown against the roof of the car and breaking your neck. (Of course, you *are* wearing your seat belt, no?)
3. Fully extend your legs so that your feet are flat on the floor, off the pedals. The more spread the better.
4. Keep your head all the way back against the headrest.
5. Keep your lungs full of air.

How to Escape a Submerged Vehicle

Finding yourself in a car submerged in water is far more likely to occur due to human error than to roadway or bridge failure. In the U.S., more than ten thousand vehicles annually end up in an accident classified as an "auto immersion incident." Numerous roads border canals, rivers, and lakes, and it is usually some sort of driver distraction that results in a car ending up in the drink. Whatever caused you to wind up there, once the car is in water, the next phase of survival must be implemented immediately.

Once a vehicle enters the water, you have less than two minutes before the vehicle completely sinks below the surface. If you panic, you lose valuable seconds. Remember, the brain is the strongest muscle in the body. Now is the time to remain calm and yet act with purpose. You will be mentally prepared. After rehearsing the following steps, in addition to making a mental movie of the proper response, you will survive.

GET OFF THE X

Once you hit the water, you need to get free of all restraints so you can exit the vehicle. Your only goal is to get out of the vehicle. If the air bag deployed, the unit will automatically begin to deflate, designed as air bags are to prevent the risk of suffocation during any accident. If this does not occur, or the process is keeping you compressed against the seat for too long, then lift out of your seat and away from the air bag.

Do not waste time trying to open the car doors. Once a car is in water, the outside pressure will make it impossible to swing the door open. Only when the car has sunk completely and the interior of the car is entirely filled with water will the forces of pressure equalize and allow the door to open. That's not a good situation to be in.

The best way to exit the vehicle is through the windows. If your car has manually operated windows, you will put all effort into opening the window fully. You do not want to get snagged up on anything during your escape. If you act quickly, even power windows will retain enough charge to operate. A vehicle's electronic system should continue to operate for about one to two minutes, even if the battery is wet. While you're taking off your seat belt, use your other hand to press the window-open button. Do this upon impact. If you are very prepared, even try to have the windows down while you are in mid-flight, powering them open during the fall.

MUSCLE MEMORY

Remember, it takes many repetitions for any action to become "memorized" by the muscles. Here's an exercise you can practice in your driveway: Time yourself as you try to get your seat belt off while pressing the window button or cranking your window open, until it becomes a sort of reflex reaction.

BREAK THE WINDOW

Many people who drown in such instances do so because they believe incorrectly that if all the windows are closed, their car will stay water-tight, like a mini-submarine. Water will enter through the undercarriage and through the firewall of the engine and dashboard very quickly. You must break the glass if the windows did not open or opened only halfway. Your best escape route is the side windows, as the windshield is much thicker, made of "unbreakable" safety glass, and secured more firmly.

- Use the heaviest object you have at hand as a battering ram to break a side window. Good choices include a camera, a laptop, or a hammer that you keep under the front seat. Even better, if you have one of the glass-breaking devices I list in the "Gear" section (page 295), use it now with maximum force. You can even use your keys, if you are strong enough. No matter what you use, *strike at the very center of the window*.

- Foot method: Even if you are not in top shape, your legs are far stronger than your arms. Position yourself sideways in the seat and jam your feet at the center of the side window. Keep doing this until the glass breaks.

WHEN YOU HAVE TO USE THE DOOR

If you are unable to break open the window, you must remain very calm and regather your strength. Take even breaths and be sure you are free of obstacles. Remain calm and continue breathing the air closest to the roof of your car. You will still have an opportunity to escape when the interior of the vehicle has almost completely filled with water. It will understandably be an unnerving experience to wait in the car as it floods, but use combat breathing techniques to remain patient yet ready to act. When there are only a few inches of air remaining, take a deep breath, and then open the door. *Ensure it is unlocked first!*

With the pressure equalized, it should be fairly easy to open. Then exit the vehicle and proceed with your escape.

Escape

Again, remain calm and climb through the window or door. Push off the car and swim to the surface. Your greatest danger is getting caught up or tangled on something while attempting escape, so make sure to take a moment to check that no part of your clothing can create a snag. You may become disoriented, or your vehicle may be upside down. Look for light and head toward it, or follow the bubbles—they always go to the surface. If there is a child in the car, attempt to give them something buoyant to hold on to and send them out the window first.

On the Surface

Swim away from the vehicle. Do so in a direction opposite from where you entered the water, especially if this accident was a result of a collapsed bridge. Now that you've made it out and survived, you don't want to get struck by another vehicle or falling debris.

Immediately gather and do a head count to find out if anyone is missing. If there's another person still down there, then, of course, make the attempt to reach them if you see that no other rescuers are in sight. But this should be performed only by the strongest swimmer, and only if there is a reasonable chance that you won't also become a victim.

SEALs say: "Slow is smooth—smooth is fast."

Life before property: Don't even think of trying to swim back down to the car to retrieve something.

BURGLARY AND ROBBERY

People have been taking things that don't belong to them since the beginning of time. It used to be called outright stealing, but now there are distinctions in types of thefts, especially when it involves unlawful breaking and entering into a house or apartment, convenience store, or bank. For the purposes of survival, it is important to note the differences in the various scenarios so that you know how to respond accordingly. Burglary, by definition, involves breaking in with the intent to steal, without the use of force, while robbery is when goods are stolen with force or the threat of it. A third category, called home invasion, is robbery with the intent to assault; we'll address that in a later section (see "Home Invasion," page 186).

Remember: The motivation or rationale for theft, no matter how it is classified, is to take something of value in the easiest and most expedient way possible—so keep this in mind as I list the ways to deal with these situations. By following a preparedness checklist, you can defend yourself against all types of theft, from the opportunist, petty theft to highly planned robberies. Here are the steps you need to take to prevent being victimized, and the best way to respond if your castle is ever breached.

Prevention

You can prevent burglary and the likelihood of professional criminals choosing your house as a target by making your dwelling appear as one that seems too risky. First, install alarms, or at least use security signs and decals that are prominently displayed on all windows and doors. Security bars on windows, strong locks and doors, big dogs, and alert neighbors are also keys items that will frequently deter burglars and even the more violent home invaders. Remember, burglars want to get in and out easily, and more importantly, criminals don't want to be seen.

POINT OF ENTRY

While in the field, there were many times our ops required days or even weeks to complete, so we had to set up defensive positions. The first rule of defense is to limit vulnerabilities. If we were holed up in a cave or had our backs against a mountain, we chose locations that would force any would-be attackers to come at us from a limited number of directions. This applies when securing your home, so that the opportunity to violate it is limited. Remote garage doors are easily activated with a master opener, and thieves can drive up and down a block to see which doors open with their device. Side or back doors often have fewer locks than the front door, and many sliding glass doors can be simply lifted off their tracks.

Of course, while we were in the field, we always had at least one of us on security watch, focusing on the place from which the threat was most likely to come. For the home, lighting and motion detectors can be used as sentries. Exterior defense, such as outdoor lighting that makes a clearly lit perimeter of one hundred feet, forces the home invaders to attempt only the front door. A security door or grate that remains closed while the main front door is open is the best way not to be tricked by the fake-deliveryman scheme. In lieu of that, there are now several inexpensive camera kits that allow you to view a live feed from a camera on your laptop anywhere with an Internet connection. These sentries are easy to install, come in stylish options, and let you know who is knocking on your door even if you are away on vacation. Even a dummy camera, not actually wired, makes home invaders think twice.

BE A GOOD NEIGHBOR

Once you establish that a neighbor can be a trusted ally, they can be one of the very best deterrents to potential crime at your residence.

How to form a neighborhood watch:

- Get to know all your adjacent neighbors: Make friends, or at least form a common bond for the good of neighborhood protection, with the occupants of the house on each side of your home and the three directly across the street.

- Invite them into your home and establish trust.

- Agree to watch out for one another's homes.

- Allow a neighbor to have a key. (This solves the problem of hiding a key outside the door, where most experienced criminals will find it.)

- Do small tasks for one another to improve territoriality.

- Offer to pick up newspapers and mail while they are on vacation.

- If they are away, occasionally park your car in their driveway to make it seem that someone is home.

- Return favors and communicate often.

EXTERIOR LIGHTING

The proper outdoor lighting is definitely a deterrent to criminals, since they know it makes them more easily noticed and identifiable.

- Attempt to light the entire perimeter of your home or apartment.

- Make it bright enough for you to see within a hundred-foot radius. Illuminate the area strongly enough to identify colors.

- Use good lighting along the pathway and at your door.

- Use light timers or photo cells to turn lights on or off automatically.

- Use infrared motion-sensor lights on the rear of a single-family home.

- *Do not* leave the garage or porch light turned on all day;
  that is a dead giveaway that you are out of town.

DOORS AND LOCKS

As mentioned, most forced entries are made via the front, back, or garage door. Experienced burglars know that the garage door is usually the weakest point of entry, followed by the back door.

- Use a solid-core or metal door for all entrance points.

- Use a quality, heavy-duty deadbolt lock with a one-inch throw bolt.

- Use high-quality Grade 1 or Grade 2 locks on exterior doors to resist twisting, prying, and lock-picking attempts.

- Use a quality, heavy-duty knob-in-lock set with a dead-latch mechanism.

- Use a heavy-duty, four-screw strike plate with three-inch screws to penetrate into a wooden door frame. Lightweight moldings are often tacked on to the door frame and can be torn away with a firm kick.

- Use a wide-angle 160-degree peephole mounted no higher than fifty-eight inches.

SLIDING GLASS PATIO DOORS

These are very vulnerable to being forced open from the outside because of inherently defective latch mechanisms.

- Use a secondary blocking device on all sliding glass doors, like a wood dowel, a sturdy pole, a two-by-four, etc., laid in the bottom of the track, or a pin that goes through the door and frame. These pins and secondary latch devices are sold in all hardware stores and are easy to install.

- Keep the latch mechanism in good condition and properly adjusted.

- Keep sliding-door rollers in good condition and functioning.

- Use antilift devices such as through-the-door pins or upper-track screws.

- Use highly visible alarm decals, BEWARE OF DOG signs, or block-watch placards.

WINDOWS

An open window, visible from the street or alley, may be the sole reason your home gets chosen for a burglary.

- Secure all accessible windows with secondary blocking devices.

- When you do wish to open windows for ventilation, open them no more than six inches and use a blocking device to prevent them from getting pried open further.

- Make sure someone cannot reach through an open window and undo the blocking device or unlock a door.

- Use antilift devices to prevent windows from being lifted out. The least expensive and easiest method is to install screws halfway into the upper track of the movable glass panel to prevent it from being lifted out in the closed position.

- Use crime-prevention or alarm decals on ground-accessible windows.

INTERIOR LIGHTING

To create the illusion of signs of life and activity inside a residence at night, interior lighting is necessary. A darkened home night after night sends the message to burglars that you are away on a trip.

- Use light timers on a daily basis, not just when you are away.

- Light timers are best used near front and back windows with the curtains closed to simulate actual occupancy.

- Light timers can also be used to turn on radios or television sets to further enhance the illusion of occupancy.

ALARM SYSTEMS

Alarm systems definitely have a place in a home security plan and are effective if used properly.

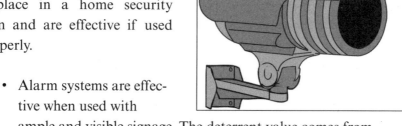

- Alarm systems are effective when used with ample and visible signage. The deterrent value comes from the alarm company lawn sign and from the alarm decals on the windows, generally causing criminals to bypass that property and go to another property without such signage.

- Alarm systems need to have an audible horn or bell to be effective.

- Alarm systems must be properly installed, programmed, maintained, and tested with your alarm company on a monthly basis.

- Consider adding a front-door camera to your system.

- If you don't add an active camera system, use of a dummy camera can also be very effective. For purposes of safety, deterrence is better than after-the-fact evidence gathering anyhow.

- Make sure your alarm response call list is up to date.

- Inform your neighbor how to respond to an alarm bell.

DOGS

Dogs can be one of the most useful deterrents to someone thinking about breaking into your home. A barking dog, even a smaller one, is about as inviting to an intruder as a shotgun being pointed at his face.

Burglary

Of course, the goal of a burglar is to steal something of value without getting caught and to do so with the least resistance. Sometimes, simple burglary turns confrontational when a homeowner or occupant happens to be present when the thief had mistakenly believed the premises vacant. Burglaries occur mostly during the day, when people are generally at work or doing errands. Most burglars work alone and tend to prowl a neighborhood looking for the right residence and the right opportunity. Many of these operations are not highly planned, so a house is often targeted if it looks like it would be easy to get in and out without detection.

In general, these petty burglars want to avoid getting recognized or having to deal with physical conflict and will usually flee when approached. Remember, most burglaries do not result in violence unless the criminal is cornered and then resorts to force in order to escape.

If you encounter a burglar in your home, you should perform a **threat assessment.** Although you will understandably be surprised to encounter a stranger in your home, remain calm in order to immediately determine the level of threat the intruder presents.

SITUATIONAL AWARENESS CHECKLIST for encountering a burglar:

❑ What is in their hands? Do they have a weapon?

❑ What do they want, or what item does it seem they are in your house trying to steal?

❑ What is their physical condition and general appearance?

❑ Do they seem drunk or on drugs? If so, then they will be completely unpredictable and utterly irrational—*very dangerous.*

TARGET RECOGNITION

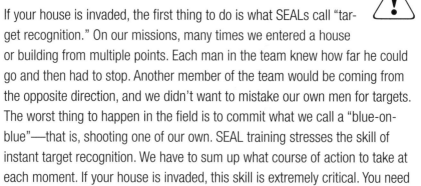

If your house is invaded, the first thing to do is what SEALs call "target recognition." On our missions, many times we entered a house or building from multiple points. Each man in the team knew how far he could go and then had to stop. Another member of the team would be coming from the opposite direction, and we didn't want to mistake our own men for targets. The worst thing to happen in the field is to commit what we call a "blue-on-blue"—that is, shooting one of our own. SEAL training stresses the skill of instant target recognition. We have to sum up what course of action to take at each moment. If your house is invaded, this skill is extremely critical. You need to assess the attacker's manpower or firepower quickly.

Again, the typical petty burglar is there to steal whatever appears valuable and what is readily lying about in the open, such as electronics or a visible jewelry box. A majority of these types of burglaries are committed by addicts or by perpetrators under the influence of drugs or alcohol. This makes them very unpredictable; in addition, they will be dealing with their own "fight or flight" response. I don't condone giving criminals a pass, but think about these factors:

• Do you have kids, a wife, a husband, a girlfriend, or a boyfriend in the house who could be in danger if this escalates?

- Even if you could beat the hell out of this guy, is it worth potentially getting injured or infected during a violent scuffle?
- Is your own or your family's safety worth a few dollars?

Threat assessment

DO NOT TURN THE BURGLAR INTO A CORNERED ANIMAL

You must attempt to **de-escalate the situation.** The best decision, in most cases, is to stand away from the most obvious exit pathway the burglar has, use your body language to indicate that you will offer them no resistance if they rightly choose to get out while they can, and then let them go. Once they exit, call the police but do not pursue the criminal on your own. For what happens when de-escalation is not possible, see "Robbery" (below), "Home Invasion" (page 186), and "Fighting" (page 146).

Robbery

In contrast, robberies are generally carried out by career criminals who have made stealing their profession, so to say. Robberies often occur at night and on weekends, when homes are more likely to be occupied. These invaders will have scouted out the target, assessing a house's exits, types of windows, or other physical vulnerabilities. They will also target a house based on the resident who occupies the dwelling. Their selection process may include targeting a woman living alone, a wealthy senior citizen, or an owner of a local store, for example. It is not unheard-of for a robber to follow you home based on the value of the car you are driving or the jewelry you are wearing. Some of these robbers could have been in your home before as a delivery person, installer, or repair technician. This class of criminal rarely works alone and relies on a measure of planning before they choose a target. They are also armed and willing to use their weapons to complete their crime.

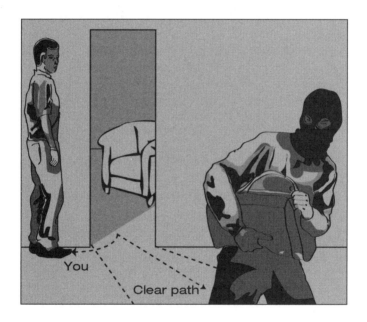

YOUR RESPONSE: 911

If you hear an unfamiliar sound around your house, especially at your windows or doors, assume it is someone attempting a forced entry. Immediately call 911 and report, "Someone is breaking into my house. Send help." If possible, call from a landline, because your address will instantly appear on the dispatcher's display. Maintain the connection with the dispatcher until help arrives, even if you have to put the phone down.

Remember, 911 will always *work*, even if you don't have landline phone service (like many people who rely entirely on cell phones). Additionally, you may wish to have a cheaper, spare cell phone plugged in and charged somewhere in your house as you may be unable to get to the phone you normally use.

If you are certain a break-in is in progress, you might not have time to wait for the police, or even have the chance to call for help. In any regard, now is the time to initiate the threat assessment:

- Am I alone, or do I have a wife, a husband, kids, a girl-friend, or a boyfriend in the home?
- Fight or flight: Should I simply leave the premises now through an exit in the opposition direction, or do I investigate?
- Do I have the ability to fight off one or more intruders? If there is one intruder, the answer might be yes. If there is a group of heavily armed men, for example, the answer will be no, or rather, not just yet.

If you are going to investigate, get something you can use as a weapon. (See "Improvised Weapons," page 301.) When investigating your house, move from room to room, making as much noise as possible. Shout out that the police have been called and that authorities will arrive shortly. You should also warn the intruder that you are armed, instructing them to get out of the house now.

FIREARMS

I have often been asked what I recommend for home defense, specifically with regard to firearms. My answer is always the same: If you are going to get a firearm for home defense, you need to be proficient with it. Just buying a gun and not knowing how to use it could do more harm than good to you and your family during a stressful situation, such as when a robbery is in progress. In addition, you need to be willing to use it and take a life if it comes down to that. Also, if others live with you, especially children, it is very important to understand firearm safety and how to properly store a weapon. (See "Gear," page 295.)

ENCOUNTERING THE INVADER

Regardless of whether the robbers entered through the front door by a ruse or gained access through a softer entry, such as a rear door, window, or garage, you must quickly make a threat assessment of the multiple variables present. Once you are face-to-face with your intruder, and you have determined that they will attempt to cause you harm rather than accepting the exit pathway you have provided for them, make sure your first blow is fast, without hesitation, and directed at the throat of the intruder. (For more on this, see "Fighting," page 146.) However, if you see three, four, or five assailants entering, it could be better to hold back because striking out will get you killed. Being dead, obviously, makes you of no use to the rest of your family. But if the opportunity arises, remember violence of action. Hold nothing back. Time to *pull the trigger!*

If during a home invasion you are overwhelmed and outnumbered, there are other techniques that will help you survive. If you are bound or corralled by weapons into submission, then in effect—even if you are in your own home—you have been kidnapped. I discuss survival methods for this situation in "Home Invasion" (page 186) and "Tiger Kidnapping" (page 187).

In Special Operations we use close-quarters combat to clear a house. It is methodically done at a very fast pace. Dynamically and aggressively, we enter each room and immediately sweep from the far left corner all the way over to the far right corner. In the case of the bin Laden raid, the team had landed, entered, cleared a three-story structure, and killed the world's most wanted man within fifteen minutes. That was a great day—a result of great training and preparation!

CONVENIENCE STORE OR BANK ROBBERY

Although each situation is different, individuals who decide to hold up a convenience store, for example, will usually be armed, desperate, and unpredictable—which is a *very* dangerous combination. Keep in mind, this person is committing a serious felony and can become extremely dangerous if you present yourself as a disruption to their intent. You have very important decisions to make in a very short time, which is why the threat assessment is again so important.

1. If you have access to a quick escape before the robbers control the scene, take it!
2. Failing that, your best response is to stay low, and find cover if possible.
3. Comply with any instructions the robbers have, up to the point at which you foresee harm coming to yourself from doing so.
4. Remember, "Life before property." If you think the assailant will simply leave the premises after taking what they want, then let them. Let them finish their bank robbery without drawing attention to yourself or intervening.
5. Keep an eye on their movements without direct eye contact. Don't be curious and stare at them to see what's happening, since this will actually increase your chances of being considered a witness that the assailant might be inclined to eliminate.
6. However, as I stated earlier, "If I die, let it be on my feet." I'd rather take the risk of fighting than risk being gunned down by a drugged-up criminal while lying on the ground. These assailants are usually so dangerous that they could start shooting everyone present, even if unprovoked. If this is your threat assessment, and you are in the immediate proximity of the assailant, fighting is the only option. Pull the trigger and disable the thief with your maximum effort.

7. When it's over and police arrive, don't move, and make sure to show your hands, so as not to be mistaken as a threat. (See the instructions for encountering law enforcement in the "Active Shooter" section, page 37.)

CARJACKING

Since the day the horse was left in the barn and the automobile became the standard means of transportation, cars have been getting stolen. Until relatively recent times, the average car thief knew how to hot-wire a car and take it when the owner was unaware. Carjacking, defined as forcibly stealing a car while it is occupied, increased in popularity proportionately as more and more antitheft devices became included in autos.

For the criminal, it's easier to steal a car that is running or one that has keys in it than it is to steal a vehicle with a screeching alarm system that may alert authorities. That you happen to be in the car, or are about to get in it, is an asset to the thief, since the car is ready to steal and drive away quickly. However, you are also the carjacker's greatest liability, and one that needs to be overcome swiftly with an element of surprise. Unlike in other crimes that require planning, such as home invasions, the carjacker usually makes a rapid choice of which car to target. Still, they do have criteria and are generally looking for several things when picking their targets:

- Someone who seems preoccupied and distracted (such as on a cell phone).
- Individuals who seem weaker than the carjacker or look like they will not fight.
- Vehicles with only a single occupant.

Situational Awareness

Carjacking happens when the car is stopped. Nearly 95 percent of all carjacking takes place in urban and suburban areas, usually no more than five miles from the victim's home. These crimes occur more often in broad daylight than at night, and usually at intersections or in large commercial parking lots when the victim is either entering or exiting their car. According to the FBI, a weapon, predominantly a gun or a knife, is used in 75 percent of all carjacking incidents. Since most law enforcement agencies do not track carjacking separately from general theft and/or assault, it is difficult to precisely profile the type of person most often victimized. However, the National Crime Victim Survey suggests that men driving alone are more frequently targeted at night, while lone women are the primary victims during the day. In either case, situational awareness is the first defense against carjackers.

No carjacker is going to jump into a moving vehicle, so be particularly alert at:

- ATMs—they get money and a car
- Gas stations—the carjacker gets a full tank of gas and a vehicle
- High-crime areas
- Freeway exit and entry ramps
- Less-traveled roads (in rural areas)
- Intersections where you must stop
- Isolated areas in parking lots
- Residential driveways and gates

The level of awareness required while driving in the towns and villages of Afghanistan was off the charts. We slowly crept through streets filled with people with nothing but hatred in their eyes, and we were constantly scanning for the individual or group that was ready to attach an explosive device to the vehicle or hose us down with automatic gunfire. We continuously had to identify avenues for escape should we be engaged. It made driving through the most dangerous crime areas of any American city seem like a visit to Disneyland.

Typical Strategies

Learning about the strategies thieves use will help you determine precautions you should take to avoid them. Be aware that in these first three methods there is some type of **"story"** associated with the carjacking. Pay attention to the tale that is being told to help you avoid danger.

THE BUMP AND JUMP

One technique carjackers use, particularly in quiet areas of suburbs or on country roads, is to hit your car from behind. The normal procedure following such an incident is to stop the vehicle and exchange license and insurance information. However, check out if the scenario seems a bit too manufactured, and scrutinize who is in the car that just hit you, especially if you see that it is occupied by two people who seem particularly focused on your reaction. I'm not saying that an elderly lady with a poodle on her lap accompanied by another senior couldn't be a carjacker. However, this scheme is usually pulled off by two or more younger males. Once you stop, they've got you. If your gut tells you this seems wrong, keep moving slowly, and wave for them to follow you, until you can stop the car in a more public place. Also, get on your cell phone and notify police of what just happened, who you are, and why you are moving from the scene. Give them information on where you plan to stop.

GOOD SAMARITAN

In this situation, a car may seem disabled on the roadside. One of the jackers will try to flag you down while another person, near the car, feigns injury. Once you stop to offer assistance, they pounce.

Again, I'm not advocating that you avoid helping those in need, but remember to be aware of the situation. Think before stopping to assist in an accident. Immediately call 911 and report the situation, location, number of cars involved, and any injuries. You may choose to wait until the police arrive instead of intervening directly.

If you need a closer look, with your windows rolled up and doors locked, slowly approach the scene but keep at least ten to fifteen feet of distance. This will allow you plenty of time and distance to flee the scene should things go wrong.

THE RUSE METHOD

This is when a car drives alongside you or flashes its lights, apparently wanting to tell you that something is wrong with your car. They may say there is an object dragging from your rear bumper, or even that it seems that there is fire near your muffler. It will always be something that seems to demand immediate attention for the purpose of getting you to pull off the road and stop your car. Generally, the bigger the story, the less accurate it will be, so be aware and listen to your instincts and keep your BS detector on high alert.

THE TRAP TECHNIQUE

They follow you home and wait until you pull into your driveway or a gated community. They ambush you when you park or while you are waiting for the gate to open. In this scenario, the attacker drives up from behind and blocks the victim's car.

SURPRISE ATTACK

Some carjackers don't bother with a narrative and merely open your door and yank you out. This is not usually the case at an intersection, since the car will most likely be in drive. This could happen while in a parking lot, when carjackers see that your car is running but you are distracted by texting or whatever.

Prevention

Always remember: Carjackers count on the element of surprise. So the first point of prevention is to not be distracted in high-risk areas. This means no cell phone conversations or seat-dancing to your music. Additionally:

- Keep your doors locked and windows up. Most new vehicles will automatically lock the doors when you put the car in gear.

- When stopped, use your rear- and side-view mirrors to stay aware of your surroundings. This increases your safety and makes it more difficult for an attacker to surprise you.

- Keep some distance between you and the vehicle in front so you can maneuver easily, if necessary. Always remain about one half of your vehicle's length from the car in front of you when stopped at an intersection.

- It also may help prevent your car from getting carjacked at intersections if you install the maximum allowed legal tint on the front windows. This hinders carjackers from knowing how many people are in your car or if you are alerted to their planned attack. Don't be distracted with texting, for example, while approaching your parked car on foot. Enter the car while remaining attentive and wait to send your messages or place your phone calls at another, well-lighted location.

- If you are bumped from behind, or if someone tries to alert you to a problem with your vehicle, pull over only when you reach a safe public place.

- Think before stopping to assist in an accident. It may be safer to call 911 and report the location, number of cars involved, and any injuries you observed.

- If you are parked at a mall or at an office building, and the lot seems abandoned when you wish to return to your car, ask the building's security for an escort.

- If you are driving into a gated community that doesn't have security personnel and uses only an intercom, call ahead to have the gate opened. Then wait on the street until the gate is open before turning in and possibly getting trapped.

- In all cases, keep your cell phone or radio with you and immediately alert someone regarding your situation.

During a Carjacking

In most carjacking situations, the attackers are interested only in the vehicle. In many instances, you can get off the X by simply surrendering your keys and stepping aside. If this is not an option, try to stay calm, and if given the time, perform an immediate threat assessment. From this threat assessment information, you must decide the best course of action: compliance, flight, or fight.

- Type of attack: nonviolent or violent?
- Environment: isolated or public?
- Mental state of attacker: reasonable or nervous?
- Number of attackers.
- Weapons.
- Whether or not children are present in your vehicle.

Never risk your life for property.

COMPLIANCE—GIVING UP YOUR CAR

In most cases, giving up your car is absolutely the right thing to do. When doing so, make sure you:

1. Listen carefully to all directions.
2. Make no quick or sudden movements that the attacker could construe as a counterattack.
3. Get your seat belt off. If this becomes violent, you don't want to be pinned in your seat.
4. Always keep your hands in plain view. Tell the attacker every move in advance.
5. Inform the carjacker that the car is installed with a locator device that cannot be deactivated.
6. Make the attacker aware if children are present. The attacker may be focused only on the driver and not know children are in the car.

FLEEING

Most of the time, the carjacker wants your keys and you out of the car. However, if you have a child in the car or feel that complying will mean certain death, *pull the trigger!* If you are already outside of the car, "accidentally" dropping the keys or tossing them a short distance might give you the moment you need to flee on foot. If still inside, finding a way to distract the carjacker momentarily might enable you to use the power of your vehicle and drive away.

WHEN A CARJACKING BECOMES AN ABDUCTION

If you are driving

In a number of cases, the carjacker will want you to drive the car, perhaps to participate in an even larger crime, or even to rape or murder you. If you find yourself in this situation, the carjacker might be in the passenger seat or in the seat behind you, and will most likely have a weapon pointed at you. If you are driving, you must remain calm, while feigning that you are overly panicky to the attacker. By acting as if you are uncontrollably nervous, you can drive erratically, with the goal of getting spotted by the police.

- Draw attention by gradually drifting across the centerline.

- Tap your brakes to set the brake lights off repeatedly. If tapped lightly, this will only cause the brake lights to go on, not slow down the car—a good signal to the outside world that the carjacker likely won't be able to notice.

- Leave a turn signal on.

- If it's night, attempt to turn the headlights off.

- Run a stop sign or travel far below or above the speed limit.

- If pulled over, act as if you are under the influence. Use slow, slurred speech, or hand the officer the wrong ID, such as a credit card instead of your license. Do whatever you can to get yourself out of the vehicle. Your goal is to communicate to the officer that you are in a dire situation. If you are acting intoxicated, the officer will usually ask you to leave the car, at which time you can divulge the true seriousness of your situation. Get off the X any way you can!

Carjacked as a passenger

If you are a passenger in the abducted vehicle and the carjacker is driving, look for an opportunity to escape. Ideas include:

- If you know how to disengage the door lock from your seat, look for an opportunity when the car slows and is away from oncoming traffic to leap from the car.

- Get sick, act as if convulsing, and, if possible, vomit; the idea is to make yourself a hindrance to a quick escape. If your abductor thinks you are about to die right there in the car, it may help you. Some criminals don't want to get charged with manslaughter in addition to grand theft auto.

- Pull the emergency brake.

- Reach over and throw the car into reverse, which will stall the vehicle and distract your assailant.

If confined to the trunk of the vehicle

- Disconnect the rear brake-light wiring (in an attempt to have the car pulled over).

- Use the trunk escape or release key, which is on the interior of the trunk in many new cars and glows in the dark.

- Attempt to open the trunk using tire jack hardware by inserting it between the trunk and body of the car and using a prying motion. You may also be able to use the jack on the trunk the same way you would to lift a car and pop the trunk open.

- Try to sneak into the backseat by forcing the seat back to fold down (forward). If the backseat has a fold-down arm-rest, there is generally only a thin layer of fabric separating the seat from the trunk.

In 1995, a woman by the name of Janette Fennell was locked in her trunk by robbers. After surviving the ordeal, she led a campaign to have emergency releases installed inside car trunks. All cars built after 2001 are required to have them. *Know where it is on your car and how to use it.*

PREPAREDNESS DRILL

Open up the trunk of your car. Look at the lock mechanism carefully until you are familiar with its particular design. If you were abducted, it would likely be your own vehicle in which you would be trapped. Is there a gap at the lock device? Is it screwed in or welded? Also, know where your jack is located so that if you had to find it in total darkness you could. Take time to note how the wall of the backseat or trunk barrier, the part that separates this area from the interior of your car, is constructed and figure out how you would dismantle it from the inside.

EARTHQUAKE

On the list of natural disasters, earthquakes instill the greatest fear. There's something inherently unnerving about the idea that the very ground we are standing on could instantly tremble and split open. In addition, despite the advances in technology that can forecast tornadoes, hurricanes, and even tsunamis, the ability to predict earthquakes with any accuracy, and with adequate time to provide a way to prepare for this disaster, remains elusive.

Earthquakes are caused by shifting tectonic plates and by subterranean pressure and heat that has been trapped in the earth since the planet was formed. Scientists tell us that all the continents were once joined in a huge landmass as one supercontinent, called Pangaea. Earthquakes are among the natural forces that shifted all the continents to where they are today. The power of these things carved out rivers, pushed up mountain ranges, and created basins to form the sea. In other words, the earth is *supposed* to move, and we should *expect* it to happen. This is why you need to know what to do and rehearse the actions that you need to take in order to survive this natural disaster.

Thirty-nine U.S. states have ongoing earthquake activity. The U.S. Geological Survey (USGS) detects an average of 20,000 earthquakes each year—about 50 per day. Worldwide, there are more than 150 earthquakes measuring over 6.0 on the Richter scale, which can cause damage within a 100-mile radius, each year.

Preparedness: Secure the Compound

Study the map on page 130, provided by the U.S. Geological Survey. If your house is located in the most risk-prone areas, preparedness is required.

Falling debris is the greatest cause of death and injury during the initial earthquake tremor. Go from room to room and make sure things like bookcases are bracketed to the wall. Remove the bigger objects from high shelves and place on the floor. Install a permanent block or wood strip in front of appliances to prevent them from rolling forward. If you have gas appliances, make sure there is enough flex in the hose; it's broken gas lines that provide the most potentially serious fire hazards in the aftermath of an earthquake. Strap down your water heater, and bracket or remove mirrors or pictures hanging near beds.

Earthquakes can strike day or night. Periodically check supplies in your designated safe room and practice drills in how to respond with the entire family. Familiarity and rehearsal equals quicker response time and proportionately increases chances for survival. Unlike basement safe rooms, which are ideal in tornado-prone regions, in earthquake zones a mid-level floor might be a better place to create your safe room. This can prevent injury from falling debris. A room that has a window that can allow for escape when the trembling ceases is another consideration.

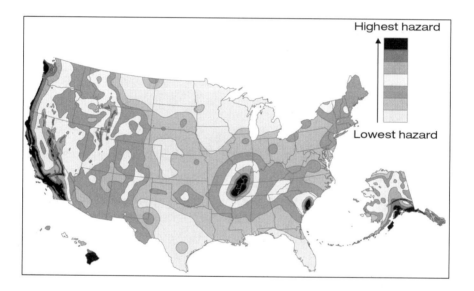

In addition, if you live in a single-family house, be observant of structural flaws, such as foundation cracks or sagging roof areas. Weakened structures will buckle even during smaller tremors. Pay particular attention to chimneys, and make sure the mortar is in place.

If you live in a multiunit building, choosing a safe room is dependent on the size of the structure. Mid-level is more or less ideal, though the strategy is a balancing act between seeking shelter that's too high, and which will increase your chances of tumbling downward among falling debris, or being too low in the building and getting trapped or injured by that same debris.

For earthquake emergencies, elevators are absolutely eliminated as evacuation exits. Take the stairs!

In 2002, a 5.2 earthquake hit the Ohio-Pennsylvania border. Only one man died during this event, killed by debris when a chimney collapsed.

What to Do in an Earthquake

There are myths and misinformation on what to do first if an earthquake hits. Most think you should run outside, get in a doorframe, or get against a wall.

All wrong!

IF YOU ARE OUTDOORS

Get to a clearing and away from buildings, poles, and overhead power lines; the risk of injury or death from falling debris is greater than that from getting swallowed up in a fissure. Remember, the safest distance away from a building is at least three times the height of the building. Ideally, if you can get to a large parking lot or to an open park area, you should be safe. Pay close attention to nearby trees, rocks, and boulders, situating yourself far enough away in the event that they should fall or tumble. In addition to falling debris, beware of the chance of a sinkhole forming. If you are near a hill or natural incline, make your way to the summit, as tremors could cause soil movement and landslides at lower elevations.

IF YOU ARE IN A VEHICLE

Stop your car as soon as possible. Try to make sure you are far enough away from buildings, highway on-off ramps, and utility poles. How far is enough? Rule of thumb is three times the height of any item that has the potential to fall on you—if a nearby building is thirty feet tall, try to get at least ninety away. Attempt to drive off elevated roadways or bridges before stopping. Stay in the vehicle. Hunker down, and get as far as you can from the interior roof, in the event something crashes onto the car. However, if you are in a garage or multilevel parking facility, get out of the vehicle immediately and crouch next to it. The roof of the vehicle won't be able to withstand the weight of collapsing concrete.

IF YOU ARE INSIDE

Stay inside. It is counterintuitive to remain in a building that may collapse on top of you during an earthquake, but again, the risk of injury or death from falling glass and debris is much greater if you try to exit once the tremor has begun. There are two methods of coping when inside a structure during an earthquake.

Drop, cover, and hold on

Find a sturdy table or piece of furniture and get under it. Cover your head with your arms and hold on. This is recommended for more-developed countries because of improved construction and safety requirements for structures. In Third World countries, depending on the nearness of exits or windows that you observed during your situational awareness exercises, making a dive to get out of the building might be prudent. Remember: If it is man-made, Mother Nature can destroy it in a heartbeat.

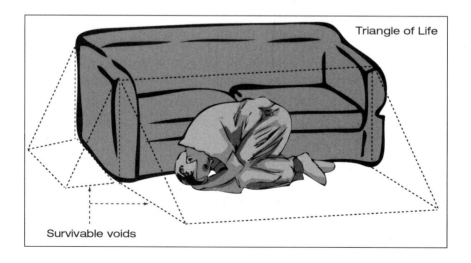

Triangle of Life

Survivable voids

Triangle of Life

In this alternate method, position yourself next to a sturdy piece of furniture so that if a wall collapses, it will create a crawl space or void space in which you can survive.

Stay put until the shaking has stopped. It will rarely last longer than a minute, although it may feel like an eternity.

When I was in college in San Diego, I experienced my first of several earthquakes. And I have to admit I did what any earthquake rookie would do—I ran outside. So I talked to my neighbor for a couple of minutes, reflecting on the experience, before I realized I was buck naked. Let's just say that my situational awareness ran a little thin in the college years. She didn't seem to mind, though.

Aftermath

If you were at home or in your apartment when the earthquake hit, and you escaped physical injury, then get up and go outside immediately. Aftershocks can occur from minutes to days after the first major shake. The next one could bring the structure down.

If you live in a single-family house, make sure all gas lines are closed at the main, and turn off the electrical breaker; there may be loose and bare wires that can cause fires. You should be able to do both of these from outside your home. You should never attempt to reenter a building after an earthquake unless a structural engineer approves it as safe to do so.

Don't think that the danger is over because the earthquake has stopped. Aftershocks continue for days following the initial earthquake and frequently do more damage to structures already compromised. Some aftershocks are just as strong as the first tremor.

If you are on the move, be alert and remember that what was once normal landscape is now a very different environment. Postquake dangers are numerous.

- Avoid entering structures without approval, unless for rescue purposes. (See "Search and Rescue," page 273.)

- Sleep outdoors, make a shelter, or go to a designated shelter center. If in a city, try to set up a base in a park or wide-open area.

- If living in a coastal region, get to high ground as quickly as possible because of the possibility of a tidal wave (See "Flash Flood, Flooding, and Tsunami," page 167.)

- Avoid bridges, overpasses, and elevated walkways.

- Watch out for downed power lines.

WHAT TO DO IF YOU'RE BURIED IN RUBBLE

1. Try to cover your nose and mouth with a cloth or part of your shirt. There will be a ton of dust and particles and you want to protect your airway. Concrete dust—and there will be plenty of it—can actually reharden in your lungs and throat and choke you to death.
2. Call out to let someone know you are there, but don't waste too much time or energy doing this, especially during the first hours of the aftermath.
3. If you can move, look for light and *slowly* crawl toward it. You don't want to start moving too many obstacles, as these could be keeping more deadly debris from tumbling down on you. As you are crawling, make sure you move only items in front of you that are non-weight-bearing or easily movable. Don't start yanking or tugging at debris. If you attempt to move even a small item like a piece of two-by-four wall stud, in this scenario, the thin wood might be serving as a weight-bearing beam, and moving it could cause the small area you are in to collapse.

4. If you can't move, again, don't waste too much of your energy yelling. The best thing to do is find something that you can tap or bang on. The vibrations from this will travel much farther than your voice. Make sure your tapping is inconsistent or rhythmic so it sounds out of place and will be more easily noticed. When in doubt, you can always tap "SOS": three short taps, three long taps, three short taps. Continue doing so until help arrives.

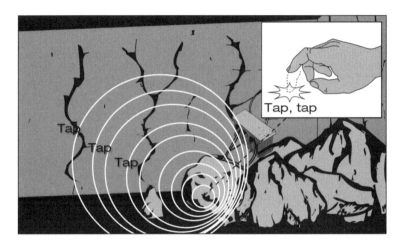

SEALs say: "If trapped, tap."

ELEVATOR EMERGENCY

There are more than 200 billion trips made annually in elevators. Considering that elevators account for only approximately 150 deaths and 18,000 injuries each year, they are a safe means of transportation, at least statistically. However, many of those fatalities could have been avoided. By following SEAL survival techniques, even during the most mundane daily activity, such as riding an elevator, you are retraining your mindset. This is how you should handle an elevator emergency.

Situational Awareness

Normally, you push the button, the door opens, and you get in. How the elevator works, what the flooring and cables are made of, or when the elevator was last inspected are of no concern. Understanding the basic operation of many of the common technological advancements you use frequently, such as elevators and escalators, is part of being aware and prepared, and will give you an advantage in the event of an emergency. In the military, for example, we know the mechanics of a parachute, the design of tanks, and certainly the detailed components of weapons before we use them.

Many serious injuries and deaths caused by elevators are due to door malfunctions. The door opens and there is no car there; those who died falling down the shaft did so because they simply stepped forward when the door opened, totally unaware of their situation or surroundings. Other times, the door signal malfunctions and a car begins to move before everyone has entered or exited. Do not place blind faith in technology, especially in something that can malfunction and kill you. Be alert. It's important to know not only how to properly ride elevators but also what to do if the elevator becomes stalled.

In 2008, a man was stranded in a Manhattan elevator for forty-one hours and survived.

Elevator Entrapment

On average, rescue from a stalled elevator takes three hours, so it's best to wait. Even though most elevators have hatches concealed by paneling, which provide a way to get to the top of the car, this is an option to consider only under the direst of circumstances. Depending on whether the elevator is powered by hydraulics or counterweights, there are many hazards in the shaft that can kill you instantly; only those with prior knowledge of the elevator's design should attempt this escape. It is better to stand by for trained personnel.

Those who experience entrapment often suffer extreme panic, and in instances this can bring about a heart attack. In this situation, when you can do nothing physically to aid in your survival, you can keep yourself and those around you calm by using your mind.

Know your destination

1 2 3 4 5 6 7 8 9 10

Elevator certificate

Use handrails

Wait for doors to open all the way

If the elevator should ever stop between floors, do not panic. There is plenty of air in the elevator. Even if the air temperature feels warm, there is plenty of air circulating in the elevator and the shaft.

1. Push the Door Open button. If the car is, in fact, at the landing, the door will open. Be certain you sense no movement in the car before departing rapidly.

2. If the door does not open, you are still safe. Never climb out of a stalled elevator, especially if the door opens between floors.

3. *Never* try to exit a stalled elevator car. This is the second-greatest cause of fatalities, which result from limb severing, crushing, and decapitation when the elevator unexpectedly begins to move again while a passenger is only halfway out of the car.

4. Use the Alarm or Help button, the telephone, or the intercom to call for assistance. Do not be concerned if you cannot be heard on the phone or if it seems not to work. Some phones are designed to only receive calls. Use the Alarm or Help button in this case. *Always* wait for trained emergency personnel.

5. If service response time exceeds thirty minutes, 911 or the fire department should be called to report the entrapment first; if you can reach a friend on the outside, assign them the task of helping to locate or call the relevant facility operations manager of the building.

6. Your best course of action is to relax, get comfortable, and wait for professional assistance. Emergency lighting will come on in the event of a power failure, so most likely you won't be in complete darkness. You may be inconvenienced, but you are safe.

At SERE (during POW training), I spent a week in a three-by-three-foot concrete box. To combat the feelings of entrapment and isolation, I started building things in my mind. I found that the more detailed and specific I was in my imagined design, the better. I broke it down to every nut and bolt of what I wanted to assemble. I even pondered paint options. When the week was over, I envisioned having a fully restored 1966 Shelby GT-350 classic car sitting in my garage at home. This is another example of utilizing the mental movie, an essential tool in many aspects of survival. The brain is our strongest muscle. To endure confinement or entrapment, use it, and let it take you on a mental vacation.

Free Fall

Fifty-seven percent of elevator fatalities are due to **fall deaths.** Some are caused when the door opens but no car is there. Other incidents are due to the collapse of the floor of the elevator car. Many older elevators have plywood floors that rot or have support brackets weakened by excessive overload. When the floor gives way, just the slightest load can send it tumbling below. That was the case in 2001, when an eighty-five-year-old Richmond, Ohio, woman entered an elevator alone. At the sixth floor, the flooring apparently had carried one load too many; the woman fell down the shaft when the floor of the elevator suddenly gave way.

- When you are waiting for an elevator and the door opens, be alert and pause. This may sound so incredibly obvious, but practice the most minimal form of situational awareness—look to make sure there is an elevator car to step into.

- In the event of a fire or other situation that could lead to a disruption in electrical services, take the stairs.

- When available, hold on to the interior handrail while riding in an elevator.

- Report unusual metal sounds, grinding cables, car jerkiness—even adverse floor conditions, like if it feels spongy or uneven—to building management.

- Again, *use the stairs until you have proof that the situation has been rectified.*

LONGEST FREE FALL

In the summer of 1945, a B-25 Army bomber got lost in the fog while attempting to land at LaGuardia Airport. It crashed into the seventy-ninth floor of the Empire State Building, killing fourteen people. When the plane hit, the engine ripped from the fuselage and torpedoed through the building. The engine cut loose all six cables of elevator car number 6, then on the seventy-eighth floor. The only occupant was elevator operator Betty O., who then experienced the longest free fall of an elevator car before or since, plunging a thousand feet toward the subbasement, which ended in a thunderous crash. The woman miraculously survived by holding on to the handrail and thus becoming weightless during the fall.

FALLING THROUGH ICE

With water covering more than 70 percent of the Earth's surface, it's inevitable that many people will find themselves submerged whether they want to be or not. A particularly dangerous scenario frequently occurs in the early winter or during the spring thaw, when ice-covered lakes, rivers, and ponds aren't as safe as they may appear. Ice is deceiving, and it's difficult to know by looking at it if it's thick enough to hold the weight of a person. Environmental factors can cause sudden changes to ice, and it's never certain whether or not you are literally walking on thin ice.

Every two minutes a person drowns. Worldwide, more than a million people drown every year, the greatest percentage being children. Drowning by falling through ice is not classified in a separate category, but there are unique techniques for surviving a fall through ice, even if you are otherwise a fairly good swimmer.

Going In

Remember how I suggested ways to expand your comfort zone in Part One, "SEAL Mindset and Survival Psychology," and recommended ending a warm shower with a thirty-second blast of cold water? Well, no matter if you are bundled up for the winter chill, falling through ice is that same sensation multiplied by a factor of ten. The work you did expanding your comfort zone will definitely pay off in this scenario. However, instantaneous submersion in near-freezing water will physiologically cause your body to experience a phenomenon known as cold shock response. When the blood temperature changes so dramatically, in some cases, it can lead to cardiac arrest and sudden death. The sheer surprise of being submerged will cause the onset of shock, and you could find yourself breathing rapidly—or hyperventilating—which causes a loss of coordination of the limbs.

Swimming Out

Fortunately, cold shock response lasts only a minute or two before the body can get its circulatory system realigned to cope. If you know this is happening to your body involuntarily, you must remain calm and attempt to keep your head above the waterline, or merely keep your mouth closed, holding your breath. It is fear of drowning and a panicked mind that are the base causes of most drowning deaths, since floundering and breathing uncontrollably hinders our natural buoyancy. If you fall through ice, know that the cold shock response condition will subside. When it does, it's time to get out of the water.

1. Do everything you can to keep your head above the water. Your only goal for the first minute is to not drown.
2. Swim back to the place where you initially fell through the ice. This will be your escape route. Don't panic—you should have anywhere from three to eight minutes in which you will have enough strength to get out.

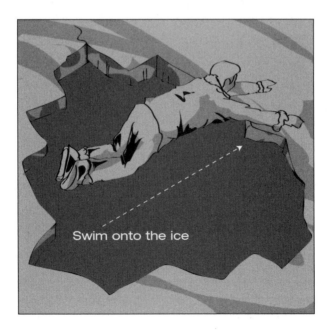

Swim onto the ice

3. In general, it's most likely that the ice surrounding the area where you fell in is also weakened. You will not be able to simply grab at the edge of this hole and hoist yourself out. You will have to lengthen your body as you would in a normal, horizontal swimming position. As you approach the edge of the ice opening, continue the swimming motion until your head and arms are out of the water. Once you have your elbows up on the ice, keep kicking as if swimming. Then proceed by inching forward, using your arms and fingers to pull yourself along the ice.

4. Your propulsion will be provided by your kicking feet, still underwater. If you stop kicking too soon and you put too much of your upper-body weight on the ice before you are fully out of the water, more ice could break, and you will become submerged again.

Rolling Out

Sometimes it's possible to get out of the water by rolling yourself out of the hole, especially if the opening in the ice is large. You need to get on your back and float to be in the correct position near the opening to make this maneuver successful. When your body is aligned and floating as close to the surface as possible, reach an arm out of the water and sling it onto the ice. Then lift the leg that is on the same side as your arm out of the water and onto the ice. Once you are half out, thrust the rest of your body upward while at once starting to roll away. Staying horizontal on the ice will create less pressure and give you a chance to roll to a place where the ice is firm.

Whichever method you use, *do not* stand up immediately. Assume the ice is still too thin to support your weight and roll toward the nearest shore. Once you feel that you are on more solid ice, get to your knees and crawl until eventually you are on your feet and off the ice.

Stop and Save It

If after five to eight minutes of attempting to climb out you are still unable to free yourself, then you need to shift gears. You need to think about improving your chances of survival by conserving your energy and helping your body to maintain heat. Water can take the heat from your body twenty-five times faster than air of the same temperature.

If you can get only halfway or partially out of the water, do so. Usually, you will be able to keep your upper body or chest out of the water by holding on to the edge of the ice. Stretch your arms on the ice and keep them there. Your goal is to stay alive and conscious as long as possible, in the hopes of being discovered. If your arms freeze to the surface of ice, in this scenario, it might be a good thing. It will help to keep your head out of the water without your exerting energy.

How to Help If You Are a Bystander

If you witness someone fall through ice, identify possible hazards and decide whether it is safe to enter the ice or attempt rescue from shore. If you react inappropriately, such as racing onto the ice yourself, you will probably be joining the victim underwater.

1. Take the time to send someone for help or make a call on your cell phone before trying to help the victim.
2. Attempt to talk to the victim by giving clear, concise instructions. Call out in a firm yet reassuring manner, relating the steps and methods described above.
3. Find something you can throw to them. Ideally, a rope that you tie a loop onto one end of and toss toward the person in the water is the best option. If you know how to tie a bowline in the rope, this is when to use it. The person may not be able to maintain a grip on a rope that doesn't have some kind of loop or knot on the end.

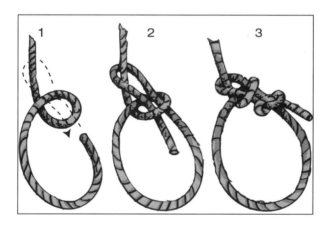

4. Sometimes, public parks or places where people skate have ladders for rescue purposes located at various points along the shore.
5. If nothing is available to throw and there is no rescue ladder at the scene, attempt to find a tree branch or pole. Or if in a residential area, send someone to fetch a ladder.
6. If you use a ladder, place it flat on the ice and push toward the opening. Again, depending on your scene size-up, you may need to tie a rope to the end of the ladder to retrieve it. Then push the ladder with a branch or pole to the per-

son, so you don't get too close and put yourself in danger. Give instructions clearly, telling the victim that the ladder is above them and to grab the end.

During BUD/S, on any particular day, we spent hours in what we called "surf torture" sessions in the Pacific. I always used to laugh when the instructors would repeatedly say, "You may be cold now, but in the unlikely event you make it to the teams, *you will be colder.*" To which my response was: "Bullshit." I changed that opinion during Winter Warfare Training in Alaska. There, I found myself once again neck-deep in the Pacific, for "polar bear appreciation." In this training, the new guys, or "meats," were stripped and submerged in the ice water. It was the longest ten minutes of my life. Let's just say it took longer for some of my anatomy to start working again than other parts. I feel your pain, George Costanza.

FIGHTING

In any number of survival scenarios, there could be a time when the only option to save your life, or the lives of others, is to fight. Even if it never comes down to getting into a physical confrontation, knowing how to fight—correctly—brings **confidence.** An important aspect of incorporating the SEAL mindset into your daily life is having the tools to defend yourself if the situation arises. This is important in order to live free and unafraid. You may not have the self-defense skills that SEALs or martial arts experts possess, but if you practice the following basic and effective fighting techniques, this knowledge will keep you alive, and in many instances, incapacitate your assailant. When the situation calls for an immediate physical response, it undoubtedly would be to your great advantage to have trained and practiced the following techniques. I have talked about muscle memory, and when it comes to hand-to-hand combat, only by doing certain moves again and again will you develop the skills needed to fight efficiently without forethought. This gives you an incredible edge—not to mention the element of surprise—when the time comes to use them. I must also add that I encourage you take some form of self-defense training as well. It not only will help should you find yourself in a life-threatening situation, but it will give you many benefits, such as self-confidence, physical fitness, and discipline. Learning self-defense will make you both physically and mentally tougher.

In SEAL teams we spend a lot of time training in hand-to-hand combat because it's a blast—in training, anyway. In the real world of modern-day combat, if you find yourself engaged in hand-to-hand, then you can pretty much assume that everything is totally screwed. Why? Where is your air support, your team, your rifle, pistol, and knife?

Prefight

Fighting is a violent, physical battle. Yet, before the first strike lands or any contact is made, fighting to win begins in the mind. Even if hand-to-hand combat is physical, the prefight aspect is 100 percent mental. Once your mindset is geared to fight, it creates a powerful force, not only by telling your muscles what must be done but by giving you the proper command of presence to do it. Oftentimes, once a person gets into this fight-zone mode, it can project that you are a seriously dangerous opponent. If nothing else, your mindset and apparent willingness to fight with reckless abandon—or, as SEALs say, "unleash the beast"—is enough to make your assailant think twice and could end the threat before anything begins.

Commanding Presence

Confidence and posture are two things that could mean the difference between your walking away undeterred and getting subjected to a life-threatening beating, or worse. Attackers tend to prey on the weak; don't represent yourself as such a target. The look of someone approaching with their chest out, shoulders back, and a confident and determined facial expression will be much less alluring to an attacker than someone hunched over staring at the ground and cowering in fear.

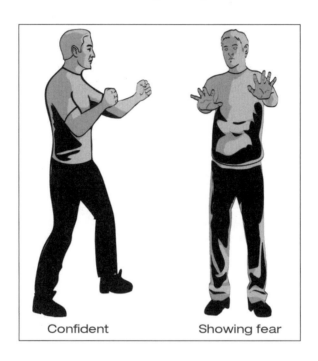

Confident   Showing fear

When I was living in a certain part of Santa Monica, I found that for some reason I couldn't walk half a block before an aggressive panhandling desperado asked me for money. I fully understand that there are many people out there dealing with a variety of hardships. That said, the folks in my old neighborhood had a less-than-sympathetic approach. So I began to do a little experiment. Any time I saw one coming, I would make eye contact immediately and maintain an agitated stare until I passed the individual. I rarely, if ever, was asked for money. This was done to prove the point that even the most aggressive and utterly rude people who might want to stop you as you go about your business won't bother if you present confidence and display a no-nonsense posture.

Situational awareness is your best friend in prefight situations, and even more so to prevent a fight. Stay away from danger areas like alleys, dark parking lots or garages, high-crime sections of the city, and groups of people loitering.

> **SITUATIONAL AWARENESS CHECKLIST** when confronted:
> ❏ Know how many opponents there are and how they are positioning themselves.
> ❏ Assess what their condition is: sick, under the influence, crazed?
> ❏ Do they have a weapon? Always look at the hands.

Distance is a key factor when it comes to avoiding a fight: distance from dangerous areas; distance from potential attackers. Distance will also give you options and the ability to see things unfold. You can create distance through your movement, or create distance with an object like a pole, a broom, a large stick, or even an extended arm (use caution not to get grabbed).

The Fight

Violence of action means the unrestricted use of speed, strength, surprise, and aggression to achieve total dominance against your enemy. I'm repeating this to drive home the concept that any fighting technique is useless unless you first totally commit to violence of action. Don't be afraid to hit first, and when you do, hit hard. Remember, you are fighting because this is the best and only option. Pull the trigger—because you are in a battle for your life!

Your instincts, assessment, and situational awareness have told you that you are in mortal danger. You don't know the other person's intentions fully, and you never can. What you can do is survive—*it is your right to not be killed or harmed by another person.*

As with most things survival-related, fighting has its own set of priorities that need to be addressed at lightning speed.

1. Protect your face.
2. Stay on your feet and keep moving.

3. Hit hard.

4. Haul ass (a.k.a. get off the X).

One of the training techniques we use in the SEAL teams is called the hooded box drill. Basically, you are placed in the middle of a darkened, noise-filled room with all of your gear on. You have your primary (rifle) and secondary (pistol) weapons. Then, a two-by-two-foot hood drops from the ceiling to cover your face. The idea of this drill is to train for making an immediate assessment and response. Once the hood is raised, you have less than a second to evaluate your situation and take action. In military operations and in real life, that's how quickly situations can change. It's an amazing training tool. Especially when the hood flies up and there are four guys a foot away who start to beat the hell out of you.

Please repeat: *Violence of action!*

---

1. PROTECT YOUR FACE

On the human body, the greatest number of vulnerable points are located upward from the clavicles, or collarbones. This will be discussed more thoroughly, but it is important to remember that you must protect these vulnerabilities on your own body before you attack.

- Make fists by curling the fingers tight to the palm with thumbs outside of the index fingers, gripping in.

- Bring arms up so that elbows are against your chest and fists are close to your face, with thumbs a few inches forward from the outer eye sockets.

- This is the ideal position to protect much of your upper torso while creating a barrier around your neck, face, and head. This will also allow you to strike and immediately return to this defensive and protective position.

2. STAY ON YOUR FEET AND KEEP MOVING

Unless you are very good at wrestling or jujitsu, the best place to be in a fight is upright and on your feet. This is especially important if you are fighting more than one attacker, because it will give you the ability to move around during the attack. A moving target is much harder to hit than a static one, so stay mobile. Circle often and keep your attacker(s) in front of you. Don't allow them to surround you.

- Keep your feet shoulder-width apart.
- Lower your center of gravity by crouching slightly.
- Shuffle your feet; never cross them.

If you should fall to the ground, curl up on your side and cover your head while delivering kicks to your attacker's legs and knees. As soon as possible, get back to your feet.

3. HIT HARD

Again, back to violence of action: Make every blow count, and you could walk away; otherwise you may be carried away. Punch, kick, elbow, gouge, bite, stab, rip, crush—you name it, you should do it, because this person is trying to take your life. The only rule in fighting is to live.

Vulnerable points exist all over the body, but remember that the greatest number of them exist from the collarbones up. Within this relatively small area of the neck, you have:

- Two carotid arteries that feed blood to the brain.
- The windpipe, which is the airway for breathing.
- The spinal cord, which controls all motor skills for the body.

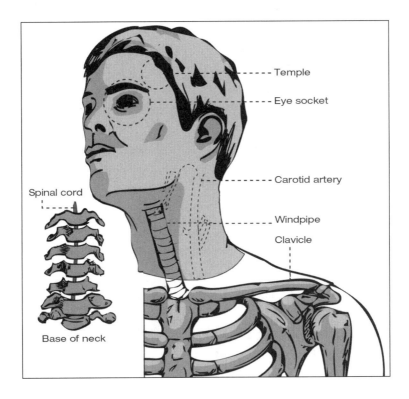

Your attacker may be three times your size, but if you take away even one of these functions, the fight is *over*. Even a 250-pound man made of solid muscle will stop fighting if he can't breathe, which is why you must concentrate the full force of your attack on the face and neck area.

Punches

Make a fist as described and deliver a punch so you are ideally striking with the knuckles of the index and middle fingers and punching *through* your target, as if you were trying to reach a place a few inches behind where you're aiming. Then immediately return the hand to the defensive position by your face. You will increase the power of a punch by twisting your midsection in conjunction with the blow.

- **Jab:** This is a punch thrown straight out, using your fist on your lead-leg side; it's not the most powerful, but is great for maintaining distance.

- **Cross:** A punch straight in from opposite the lead leg—very powerful.

- **Hook:** An outward-arcing punch delivered by either fist—great for targeting the ear or jaw.

- **Uppercut:** An upward-arcing punch delivered by either fist—great for targeting the chin, and the best for lights-out!

Palm strike

In addition to the above punches, your hands can also be very effective when clawing or jabbing with fingers, and an open-palm strike can be devastating. The palm of the hand contains one of the densest bones in the body.

1. Open your palm; cock your arm back, just as you would for a jab punch.
2. Strike directly at the front of the nose and aim upward.

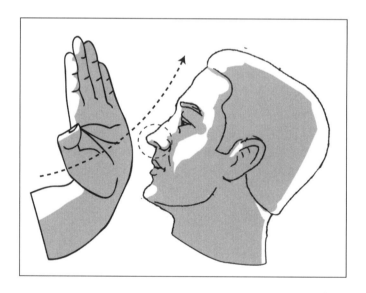

A nose broken this way is much more painful than one that's been hit from the side, and will take the fight out of nearly anyone.

Feet

Feet can be used in a variety of ways during a fight. There are numerous kicking techniques that can stop a fight before it even starts, but for the purposes of teaching you fighting survival methods, I would strongly recommend that you use your feet to stay upright and move. If on the ground, kick to keep the assailant way until you are back on your feet. In general, save the spinning-back roundhouse kick to the temple for the professionals.

Elbows

Elbows are very effective and can be used when tight against your attacker. If you perform this properly, not only will you strike when slashing in, but you can deliver a second and equally devastating blow by back slashing (returning the elbow to original position).

Knees

As with the elbows, knees are hard body parts that can inflict great damage while you're tight against an attacker. The best way to employ knee strikes is to grab the back of your attacker's neck with both hands, drawing them toward you each time you are delivering a knee strike. Be aware that using this technique may cause you to sacrifice some stability because you will have only one foot planted on the ground during each strike.

Chokeholds

The **rear chokehold** method (a.k.a. the sleeper) is a compression grip applied to the throat to disrupt circulation (carotid arteries) and breathing (windpipe), which ultimately causes the person to lose consciousness.

1. It is best applied from behind the attacker by wrapping your left arm around the person's throat, with his windpipe in the crook of your arm and your bicep and forearm on each side of his neck. The positioning of your arm is the key to this technique, so remember, the deeper you can get his throat between your bicep and forearm, the better.

2. Keep your right arm behind his neck and grab your left shoulder.

3. Then with your left arm, reach to grab your right arm's bicep, squeezing tightly, making a full lock, or chokehold.

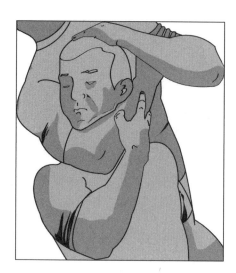

An alternate method is called the **front chokehold,** which works when you are facing your attacker.

1. With your right hand, reach across and literally grab the opposite corner of his shirt collar—not the person. You will have greater control over your adversary this way.

2. With your left hand, reach and grip the attacker's collar on the opposite side. This will make your crossed arms an X in front of his throat.

3. Grip as tight as you can while rotating your hands forcefully inward to achieve the chokehold. You are twisting the opposite shirt collars as if you were squeezing and wringing out a rag.

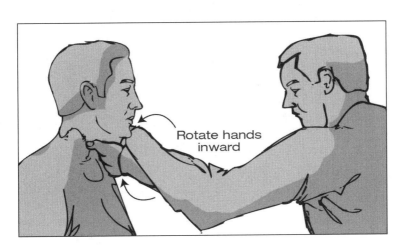

Rotate hands inward

Thumb drop

This move will bring a person to his knees within moments.

1. From a standard handshake grip, rotate your hand upward as you grip the attacker's hand, so that your thumb is above his thumb knuckle.

2. Lock that knuckle down with your thumb.

3. Bend his thumb, turning it and pushing his entire hand directly up toward his forearm. Keep doing so until you have full control and can force him down to his knees. (See illustration on page 158.)

Fighting an Assailant Who Has a Gun or Knife

If your assailant has a weapon, then your choices in defense will change. Disarming a person with a gun is incredibly risky. It takes a second to pull the trigger, so the best option might be to comply and wait for an opportunity to attack. However, if you are close enough and the situation necessitates you attack, your goal would be to use maximum effort and **attack the weapon** with the full intention to deflect his aim. Trying to wrestle the weapon from his grip is less likely to work than pushing his hand away, be it up, to the side, or downward. At this point, you may get the opportunity to strike at vulnerable areas and disable the attacker enough to get off the X. If the person has a knife, again, keeping your distance is the goal. Use your shirt, coat, or whatever you can find to deflect his thrusting arm, which then could provide an opportunity to use defensive tactics.

4. HAUL ASS

Although this is the last step in this section, avoiding fights altogether needs to be your first priority. Get off the X and save your fighting techniques for the gym. But you might need to strike first and hard to have the chance to get away. Don't stay engaged if you can escape. The moment you have an opening, take it and leave the scene, because fights can change instantly and drastically.

Final Note

As I have aged (matured), I have learned many valuable lessons. One of these is that when big kids (adults) get into fights, three things can happen:

- Someone goes to the hospital.
- Someone goes to jail.
- Someone goes to the morgue.

MUSCLE MEMORY

If someone were to unexpectedly punch you in the face right now, even if the blow was weak, the shock of being hit would likely immobilize you. I can think of no other activity that requires practice and repetition more than some form of martial arts or physical defense training. The above methods of defense would be nearly useless if you merely read how to do them and didn't train to perfect them. In addition, being physically ready to defend yourself or your loved ones brings confidence and freedom. Remember: Repetition, repetition, and more repetition help your muscles respond quickly and with effectiveness. You will therefore become victorious during the most strenuous or violent encounters you might have to deal with, even if, hopefully, you'll never have to use them.

I would *never* tell someone not to defend themselves. I do however subscribe to the following policies:

1. Don't start a fight; finish a fight.
2. If you see a guy with ears that look like chewed-up bubble-gum, keep walking!

FIRE: FORESTS, BUILDINGS, HOMES

Each year, an average of more than five million acres of U.S. forests burn. The fires cost $1 billion to extinguish, destroy $500 billion worth of property, and cause the deaths of at least three thousand people. Fires are started from natural factors, such as lightning, which is blamed for more than thirty thousand fires annually; or from human carelessness, such as from campfires or cigarettes; or by arson. And with the vast amount of tree death due to beetle kill leaving behind abundant dry timber in some states, an absolutely devastating forest fire is a mere lightning strike away. Nevertheless, once a forest is ablaze, its force and destructive powers create a formidable survival challenge.

Situational Awareness: Know Your Risk

A number of government agencies monitor national areas that are susceptible to fire, including the National Weather Service and U.S. Forest Service, which have updated maps posted online. If you live near or plan to be in fire-prone regions, stay alert to environmental factors such as droughts or seasonal periods of low rainfall.

Outdoor Fire Threats

If your house is located in the vicinity of a fire, be prepared to evacuate well in advance. Do not ignore official alerts. As a preemptive attempt to save your property, you should be watchful of hot, flying embers that can travel miles from active forest fires. Wetting down roofs and activating lawn sprinkler systems, if available, will help, but evacuation should be the primary plan of action.

If venturing into forests or brush areas during these periods, be aware of the location of natural firebreaks, such as rivers, lakes, ravines, and paths purposely cleared of trees. Try to stay in close proximity to these, as fires can start rapidly, and depending on levels of moisture and wind, flames can burn vast swaths of land, raging at speeds of more than 80 mph. That's slightly faster than you can run. The most furious of these fires have even overtaken vehicles trying to flee.

If you are in a forest or brush area, the smell of smoke should be an immediate call to move to a safe area. The problem is that the smoke alone will not indicate from which direction the fire is approaching. You can assume that fires will travel more intensely in the same direction as the wind is blowing. However, as mentioned, embers that emanated from the fire may jump ahead of the main wall of flames and could easily surround you. Before you plan an evacuation route, take time to observe the direction of the wind and consider the type of terrain in which you will move. Fire burns more rapidly in an upward direction, so with fire, *do not* head to high ground. The best choice is to evacuate toward low-lying areas, waterways, or roads. Sometimes, you might need to cross a section of burning grass to get behind a fire, where the already-scorched earth might be the safest place to be. Do not panic. Use the Rule of Three—then make the decision and go.

SURVIVAL CHECKLIST
❏ Be familiar with fire-hazard conditions.
❏ Avoid or evacuate well in advance of a fire. If you live in a high-fire-hazard area you should already have valuables packed and ready to go—don't delay your evacuation to do this! (See "Gear," page 295.)
❏ If within range of smoke, wear a respirator, or use a moistened cloth over your nose and mouth.
❏ In a wildfire or forest fire, head to low ground. Get to firebreaks, rivers, lakes, gullies, ditches, or ravines.
❏ If overtaken while in your vehicle, do not leave the car. It should sustain you for at least two to three minutes and might allow the intense flames to pass. Staying in a car longer than that will mean death, and you may have a better chance of fleeing in the direction from which the fire approached.

❏ If you must cross a fire, douse all clothing with as much water as is available. Remove any clothing that is made of synthetic fiber (material that will melt) and remove jewelry. Cover your head and all extremities with moistened blankets or with whatever is at hand. An outer layer will prevent your clothes from igniting and give you an opportunity to get to an area already scorched.

❏ If your clothes catch fire, do not stand, as the smoke will enter your lungs. Roll on the ground to extinguish clothing—**stop, drop, and roll!**

Building and House Fires

There are more than 350,000 home fires in the United States every year, which account for approximately 3,500 deaths and 15,000 serious injuries. Nearly 85 percent of all U.S. house and building fires are primarily caused by unattended cooking, space heaters, cigarettes, or candles. (Candles are responsible for approximately 6,800 fires annually.) Most fire-related deaths result from toxic fumes and smoke inhalation.

PREPARATION CHECKLIST

Although the discovery of fire has been a major factor in humankind's dominance and survival since prehistoric times, once fire goes unchecked and is burning rampantly, it is a fearsome enemy. Like an especially combative opponent, it is ruthless, indiscriminate in its destruction, and will not stop until extinguished. In addition, its attacks are unannounced and can happen at any time. Considering these characteristics of fire, the first course of action is prevention and preparation.

- If you live in an apartment building or work in an office building, know the location of the nearest fire exits. You should know no less than two evacuation options for each floor of your residence. Never use the elevator, as these are virtual wind tunnels for fire to move between floors. If bedrooms are located on the second floor, for example, rope ladders can be used and stored in easily accessible areas.

- As for physical toughness, you should be at least in minimally acceptable physical condition to use the fire escape or designated stairways.

- Practice evacuation during nonemergency conditions so that in the event of a fire you are familiar with it. You should know this escape route thoroughly, counting the number of doors from your office, for example, to the fire exit door. Rehearse this route several times, and when rehearsing at home, include your family. Be able to find your way to the exit with your eyes closed. The evacuation path then becomes a mental file you can draw on in the event of an emergency. There could be no visibility during an actual fire, in addition to your being impeded by other panicking occupants.

- Install and check smoke alarm batteries regularly. It's a good practice to make this test at a designated time, such as when the clocks have to be changed in the spring and fall. This is especially important if you are renting a place and are unaware of the age or reliability of the smoke alarms installed.

- Install fire extinguishers and check expiration dates. Secure fire extinguishers in areas that are close to likely fire hazards, such as stoves, but not in cabinetry.

- Practice varying evacuation routes, and have alternate paths, depending on the origin of the fire.

- Have means to escape from upper floors. Ensure *all* fire escapes open and operate correctly, especially in older and multistory buildings.

- Establish a designated meet-up point, so that all escaping family members can be accounted for immediately.

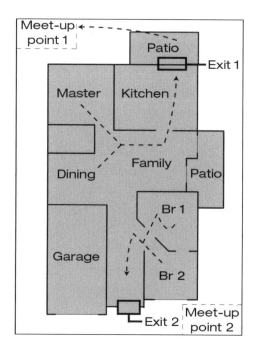

FOR RENTERS

If you rent, you must rely on others to correct hazards you observe. You should know the building you live in thoroughly in order to respond effectively to any number of life-threatening situations. If you find any flaws that could impede your survival, such as padlocked exit doors, do not hesitate to contact the landlord or management company (by phone and in written format) to have these unsafe items corrected. It is better to be a politely persistent person and demand to live in a safe environment now than to have a tag on your toe as a temporary tenant of the morgue later.

WHAT TO DO IN A FIRE

If a fire breaks out in your house, attempt to extinguish it primarily with the proper fire extinguisher. If you have a garden hose near the front or back door, make sure it is long enough to reach kitchen areas. You could attempt to extinguish the fire with water if it remains locally contained, but *do not use water if the source of fire is electrical.* As a final attempt to extinguish the fire, use a nonflammable blanket or coat and attempt to smother it, but do not create a gust of more air by beating at it. As mentioned, most fire fatalities are due to smoke inhalation. If the fire is beyond any reasonable attempt at control, immediately evacuate. The smoke will kill you before the fire does.

FIRE EVACUATION CHECKLIST

❏ Use a previously established code word (as discussed in other emergency scenarios) to alert all family members to the hazard and the call to action.

❏ Close doors when leaving rooms. This will slow down the spread of fire.

❏ Just as fires do in forests, flames move upward in a house or building. Heat and smoke rise; move rapidly, but stay low and as close to the floor as possible.

❏ Cover your mouth and nose with a moistened cloth.

❏ If trapped by flames in a room with a window and the window does not open fully, smash glass in the center with an object and cover jagged ends around the frame with a towel or blanket before exiting.

❏ If evacuation is blocked by flames while on an upper floor, tie bedsheets together and fasten to a firm object, such as a bed leg. If the distance to the ground is more than twenty feet, attempt to use something to decrease the distance.

❏ If you must jump, use the parachute landing fall, or PLF, method. Lower yourself as far as possible while holding on to the window frame or the makeshift rope from bedsheets, and then push off from the wall. Keep your legs slightly bent, with your knees and feet together. If holding onto a rope or ledge, your arms will be raised at first; after you let go, bring both of yours hands in front of your body with your fists close to your face. Roll sideways as you land. This spreads the landing impact throughout the body.

Trust me when I say PLF works. On my fifth jump at Airborne Jump School, I exited the aircraft and looked up to see a nice hole in my canopy. Now, the rule was anything larger than your helmet and you need to ditch the parachute and go for your reserve. Okay—the unwritten rule is the reserves don't work very well, so I decided to ride it in "as is." Well, I hit the ground like a bag of shit and even cracked my hip but was able to limp away, thanks to the old PLF.

BTW—round chutes suck, unless you are landing in water.

❑ Get away from the burning structure and head toward the preestablished regrouping area.

FLASH FLOOD, FLOODING, AND TSUNAMI

An unexpected surge of flowing water—that's the simplest way to describe a flash flood. In the U.S., flooding is the number one cause of weather-related deaths. Sudden and heavy rainfall (especially during tropical storms or hurricanes), melting snow, or dam breaches and water pipe breaks are common causes of flash flooding. The source of the flash flood could be miles away, but water does what it always does and seeks lower-lying ground.

For example, Colorado's Big Thompson Canyon flash flood of 1976 was due to a severe thunderstorm higher up in the canyon. Twelve inches of rain fell in less than four hours. The victims, including 143 dead, had seen little or no rain when the flood rushed down the canyon in a wall of water twenty feet high. Water is a powerful element, weighing 8.3 pounds per gallon, and when moving at flood speed, it sweeps away cars and trucks, demolishes houses and other buildings, ruins roadways, and collapses bridges. Against such a force, evasion is the first course of defense.

In the spring of 2010, an Atlanta woman was driving home during a light rain. Even though the soil surrounding Atlanta's normally hilly roadways was saturated, no flood warnings had been issued. While crossing a small bridge over a creek, the woman's car was suddenly hit by the headwaters of a flash flood. Her car was instantly carried away and tumbled along for miles, without allowing her an opportunity to escape.

During a Flood

Certain areas are prone to floods, such as communities surrounding rivers and lakes, and those at low elevations. The Federal Emergency Management Agency (FEMA) and the U.S. Geological Survey (USGS) have maps showing likely flood areas. These should be consulted as part of preparing your dwelling for all possible hazards. In a flood event, the following actions are necessary:

- If at home, turn off electrical power at the circuit breaker. Close windows and doors and get to the highest level. If you have an attic, bring a ladder to the upper levels and a tool that could help you escape through the roof in the event floodwaters rise to exceptional heights.

- If in a vehicle, do not attempt to drive through water. The rule is, turn around and find another route for evacuation. If water rises suddenly around your car, get out immediately. The threat of drowning from being trapped is very real. Note, however, that you will *not* be electrocuted if your car battery becomes wet.

- Except when unavoidable, do not try to walk or swim across floodwaters deeper than one foot. The water during a flash flood is filled with fast-moving debris of all types, as well as irregular currents that can change swiftly. In addition, the waters are likely carrying many other unseen hazardous objects, such as timbers or even cars, which, if they hit you, can render you unconscious, or worse.

- If outdoors, always head to high ground, and if you must walk, test waters with a stick as you go to avoid hidden deep spots, and be observant of downed power lines.

- If you find shelter on a roof or on an upper branch of a tree, for example, tie yourself to it, using a belt or whatever is at hand, in the event of a passing flood surge.

Even for SEALs, for whom the water is a second home, river crossings were always a challenge. If we wanted to make a rendezvous point, we would trek at least a quarter mile upriver to account for strong currents and the weight of our gear knocking us off-course. This way we could reach the other side, more or less, at where we planned to be. That's how unpredictable rushing waters can be even to expert swimmers.

Aftermath

If the floodwater was due to a flash flood, the volume will usually recede quickly. You must be mentally tough and physically prepared to ride out the initial surge, which usually lasts no more than thirty minutes. If it is a prolonged flood, such as those caused by breached dams or continued rains, assess the place where you are sheltered and determine if it is structurally sound enough to wait there for rescue. If not, try to get to the nearest roof or tree by latching on to and riding anything that floats. You want to avoid getting into the floodwaters, as they will be highly contaminated with everything from fuel to sewage. Additionally, public drinking water will be contaminated. Drink only bottled water until advised otherwise. If you have prepared and stocked up on water and nonperishable foods, your shelter, if reasonably secured, is the best place to be until a safe means of evacuation arrives.

Tsunami

"Tsunami" is the Japanese word for "harbor wave." It is a giant wave caused by earthquakes or underwater volcanic eruptions. These colossal tides cause massive destruction to coastal regions and often give short notice of their approach. These rogue waves can reach heights of more than two hundred feet. It wasn't until recently that some areas prone to this occurrence began to install tsunameters, monitoring devices anchored to the ocean floor that send signals to buoys and satellites, attempting to offer some warning of a tsunami's approach.

SITUATIONAL AWARENESS

If you live in or are visiting a coastal area, be alert to any known earthquake activity that happens anywhere in the world. One recorded tsunami stemmed from an earthquake in Alaska's Aleutian Islands and sent giant waves a distance of 2,300 miles toward Hawaii. The only warning people had before it hit the small village of Hilo Bay was an unusual receding of the ocean's level before it struck. The bay water suddenly receded two hundred feet from the normal tide line. This lasted for more than thirty minutes, causing schools of fish to flop about without water. People rushed out with baskets to harvest the bounty, believing it was their lucky day to reap such an abundant catch without effort. However, shortly afterward, a 115-foot-high wave surged, moving at 150 mph, and eventually drowned 159 people. This was nothing compared to the 2004 Indian Ocean tsunami, to which more than 250,000 deaths were attributed. Against such odds, evacuation to the highest ground is the best chance of survival. Be alert to anomalies of nature, because its power is unpredictable and lethal.

- As part of your vacation and sightseeing excursions, get maps of coastal areas you are visiting and find possible evacuation routes. Know which roads lead to high ground.

- If you see water leaving or draining from a coastal area, don't watch it in amazement—haul ass to high ground.

ANIMAL BEHAVIOR AND SITUATIONAL AWARENESS

Natural environments have baselines of normal activity just as urban or suburban regions do. Animals, in particular, have historically predicted natural disasters up to two weeks in advance. In 1975, Chinese officials observed hibernating snakes unexpectedly emerging from their burrows, so they immediately ordered the evacuation of the city of Haicheng. Several hours later an earthquake of 7.3 magnitude struck. In Indonesia, local fishermen discovered an unusual pattern of fish migration two weeks prior to the tsunami. They tried to warn officials but were ignored. In addition, flocks of shore birds were seen abandoning their seaside nests days before the incident. Hours before the tsunami struck, elephants were seen actually sprinting up into the hills. In general, many animals' sensory perceptions can pick up on environmental disturbances even ahead of modern technology. Dogs, cats, and livestock often seem unduly agitated before a disaster strikes. Be alert to changes in animal behavior as part of your situational awareness when in rural or more natural environments.

FOOT PURSUIT AND BEING CHASED

There will be situations when escape is the best option for survival. In any number of life-threatening scenarios, moving off the X will require you to flee. After you have performed your threat assessment and your body's fight-flight-freeze response is screaming *flight,* then you must do so without hesitation. In many cases, the attacker or predator will follow you.

If you find yourself in a situation where you are being chased on foot and the outcome of getting caught is potentially lethal, there are methods to follow that will increase your chances of success. Here is a time when the physical toughness you have been working on to improve yourself will play a significant role, and could in fact be the deciding factor in whether you live or die. This is trigger time—because getting caught is simply *not* an option. When fleeing an attacker:

1. Adjust your mindset to change your goal priority. By this, I mean tell yourself that you are *running to safety*. This has a positive impact and allows you to be far less crippled by fear than merely telling yourself you are running from danger.

My team was in a foreign country watching an area where we were not supposed to be. Unfortunately, we were discovered by a group of kids. There is always the dilemma of what to do when a recon goes bad because of someone that you can't necessarily "neutralize." The one cold, hard fact is that when you are "rolled up" (discovered), the op is over, period. So within minutes, the three of us were on foot, putting as much distance between us and the hide site as we could. Even more regrettably, the best and fastest way out meant booking through an area that was known to have land mines. I told my boys to stay in single file behind me and keep up. Won the lottery that day.

---

2. Keep looking forward and be aware of your surroundings. Your instincts may tell you to look behind to see how far away or close your pursuer is. This is not a track-and-field event, with a ribbon as a prize. Looking back not only will slow you down but will increase your chances of falling over an upcoming obstacle or getting run over by a car. Keep your eyes ahead and your mind focused on what's directly before you, not what's behind.
3. Yell loudly and shout for help as you are running. Just make sure you are not doing it so much that it slows your pace. Your lungs and legs need this oxygen to keep you moving. If your pursuer is an attacker, you might be able to alert the police or get people to see your plight and intervene.
4. Make last-minute changes in direction (easier if you know the area you are in). For example, if you know of an open-

ended alley ahead, make it seem as if you are running straight, then dodge suddenly, without indicating that you will make an abrupt turn.

5. Keep alert to the environment, and be particularly observant of objects or items in your path, such as trash cans, which you could use as obstacles to slow your pursuer. If you do not know the area, be alert not to turn onto streets or alleys that could be dead ends.

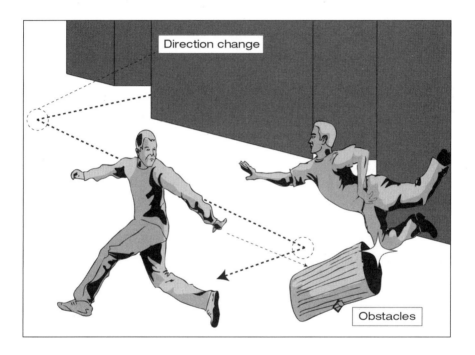

Direction change

Obstacles

6. Run toward large crowds or public places where there will likely be people, such as malls or bus stations. You want to attract witnesses, since most attackers don't want to be seen.

7. If you are in a wooded area, look for concealment, since your pursuer could be in as good or better physical condition than you, and you can only outrun him for so long.

8. If your pursuer doesn't care about being rolled up, when you make it to a public place, try to quickly blend in. You want to get lost in the crowd by taking off your jacket, for example, or "borrowing" a pair of sunglasses from a passerby.

In *The Fugitive,* Harrison Ford presented a dozen ways to lose pursuers, with multiple changes in his evasion tactics. At one point he borrowed a stranger's coat, threw on a green hat, and joined a crowd of proud Irishmen as part of Chicago's St. Patrick's Day parade, becoming invisible in a sea of green.

GANG VIOLENCE

Law enforcement monitors the activities of the nearly 25,000 gangs in the United States, which currently have an approximate membership of more than 950,000 in active status. Nearly all gangs are territorial and, in many instances, much more ruthless than other groups of organized crime. In general, U.S. gangs' primary business is illegal drugs. Most gang violence is directed toward other gangs, but there is little regard for non–gang members caught in the crossfire. Due to gang activity, homicide is the leading cause of death among people aged fifteen to twenty-four in U.S. urban areas. For example, in 2009, eight children and teens were killed in gang-related drive-by shootings in Chicago during one twenty-four-hour period.

In Washington, D.C., in April 2002, a woman and her boyfriend were driving to dinner and communicating in sign language when another car, carrying gang members, stopped at the same traffic light. The gang thought the woman was flashing a rival gang's signs and shot her in the face. Neither the woman nor her boyfriend, both of whom were deaf, was a gang member.

Wrong Place, Wrong Time

In general, it's being in the wrong place at the wrong time that increases your odds of having a confrontation with gangs. Most homicides do not occur due to the random violence of a single angry stranger. In fact, most murders are committed by someone the victim knows. When random acts of violence do occur, however, they are often committed by groups or gangs. So if you find yourself in an area where gang activity is noted, your best course of action is to *avoid* and *evacuate*. If you plan to drive in a city you are unfamiliar with, it should be part of your pre-mission planning to know where the areas with the highest crime rates are located and avoid them.

In 2010, a couple visiting Los Angeles unknowingly drove into a part of town controlled by gangs. They had forgotten to turn the rental car's headlights on, and gang members, fearing an attack by rivals, ran up to the car and fired ten rounds through the windshield.

Keep Your Distance and De-escalate

If you find yourself in a situation where interaction is inevitable, be agreeable and de-escalate. "Kiss my ass" is not de-escalation and will be taken as a threat, or **disrespect,** and considered a challenge. The very foundation of gang mentality is respect and intimidation. In this situation, you really want to be what we commonly call "the gray man" (see also "Torture and Being Held Hostage," page 280, and "Trouble in a Foreign Country," page 286). You must present yourself as someone merely passing through, not knowing or caring who these people are or what they are doing. Don't try to buddy up, pretending you know gang signs or gang language, either. Likewise, you do not want to show fear or weakness, for any of the above reactions will cause immediate confrontation.

If members of the gang attempt to start a conversation, for the purposes of sizing you up, repeat a phrase such as "I have to go." You will also want to be alert to avenues of escape and be ready to bypass a gang hanging around a street corner, for example, by moving out of range. Depending on the number of gang members you are confronted by, flight could be the best choice, which will rapidly de-escalate the situation. Chances are they are merely looking for an easy victim and will not pursue. But at all costs, do not let yourself get surrounded or cornered, or get close enough for one of them to grab you. Gangs operate with a pack mentality, which often enables individual cowards to become emboldened when backed by the power of their numbers. You may be a hell of a fighter, but it is extremely difficult to defeat a group of simultaneous attackers. Let them have their space, or whatever they perceive as their territory, even if you have to cross the street or take a longer route to where you were headed.

Punch and Run: Fight and Flight

When physical contact is a foregone conclusion, you need to do everything you can to limit personal injury. Make no mistake: A ten-on-one fight scenario is not only purely defensive, it is one of mere survival. Don't wait until you are jumped. That is way too late to act. Bolt from the group. You have to do everything in your power to *remain on your feet* and continue moving. Your chances of minimizing injury are far better if you are engaging individuals while on your feet than trying to square off against an entire group, especially if you end up on the ground. Violence of action is a must. However, this is no time to initiate a plan of cleaning up the streets and ridding neighborhoods of the plague of gang violence. Not without community support, at least. In this situation, your violence of action and physical response are used to gain time to get free and escape. Oftentimes, the courage displayed by a group will rapidly dissipate as their numbers thin out. If you drop the right guy, or outrun some of them, the others could give up or quit.

During a down weekend while with SEAL Team One, several of us decided to go drinking at a beach bar in San Diego. Things started to get rowdy, as they often do, and eventually the shit-talking began with one of the locals. Well, we didn't realize the obnoxious local was there with forty of his closest friends. The hornet's nest erupted onto the street outside the front of the bar, with the five of us circled up back-to-back, dealing with the swarm. SEALs are tough . . . but not forty-against-five tough. Pretty funny how the whole thing shut down once we took out the big guy of the group. Almost instantly, this de-energized the rest of them. We were lucky to get out of that with just a few scrapes—and ahead of the cops.

HIJACKING

Unlike wresting control of a vessel from a ship's captain, which has been going on throughout naval history and still is, taking over an aircraft while in flight is more or less a new form of crime. Between 1940 and 1970 there were only a dozen incidents. From 1970 to 2000, there were nearly sixty such "skyjackings" or "sky-controlling" incidents, or what are now commonly known as hijackings. The motive for ship seizures is usually robbery, but the majority of aircraft hijackings are for political reasons, or to hold passengers hostage as collateral, or to use the plane as a weapon, as was the case in the 9/11 attacks. In most scenarios, the pilot is forcibly made to fly the plane to where the hijackers demand; in only some incidents do hijackers actually take over flying.

Previous to 9/11, airlines trained pilots primarily to cooperate and attempt to de-escalate the situation. The plan was to stall and gain as much as time as possible, and see what delays could be used while seemingly complying with the demands of the hijackers. Most hijackings ended, in general, with few casualties. In addition, there were very few preventive security measures in place. The cockpit door was rarely locked; flight personnel entered and left the cockpit with no more than a knock.

After 9/11, airlines took a dramatic turn and adopted entirely new tactics to thwart unlawful seizure of an aircraft. Time was your friend in the old days of hijacking, and the chances of getting out alive were very good. Not anymore.

With vastly tightened security measures and an overhaul in intelligence efforts, only the most sophisticated operations will have a chance to take over control of an airplane. So understand that if you find yourself involved in a hijacking, you are likely dealing with a highly trained individual or group.

Before You Even Board

The Israeli airline El Al has one of the best safety records in the industry, primarily because they were the first to realize that security starts before passengers even get to the airport. The use of an ever-growing database of names, which includes genders, birth dates, and people's flying history, is now in place. "No-fly" and watch lists, including lists of those with suspected ties to terrorist groups, lists of the names of known criminals, and other intelligence reports, are now used as the first net of security. The next phase of prevention is surveillance, both audio and visual, which consists of actively monitoring passengers as they arrive at the airport. When arriving at a terminal, crank up your situational awareness to very high. You are surrounded by people from all over the world with vastly different backgrounds and beliefs.

Focus on the basics:

- Does something or someone ready to board your flight seem out of place?
- Body language is a great indicator—does anyone seem unusually nervous or stressed?

If you notice *anything* during the situational awareness drill while boarding an airplane that causes an instinctual reaction, *do not ignore it*. Do not hesitate to voice your concerns to airport security (TSA) or someone connected with the airline.

Settling In

As you board the plane, start assessing the situation, as described in "Airplane Crash" (page 58). Look at all the passengers you pass and make mental notes of the ones who, again, seem out of place in some way; remember their location in relation to your seat. Also make a metal note of passengers who might seem capable of assisting in the event of trouble.

- Always try to get an aisle seat, because it will enable you to get to your feet immediately and be more ready to deal with any situation.

- Stow all of your belongings in the overhead bin. Make sure there is nothing below your feet that could in any way impede your movement.

- Also remove or tuck in any loose clothing; keep your shoes on and ensure they are tied. This isn't the time to get comfortable for your flight—not yet.

- Once seated, continue your visual sweep of the plane. Take note of passengers who could be a potential problem or threat.

- Identify passengers in your immediate vicinity who you feel would be either an asset or a liability if a conflict were to arise.

- Rehearse in your mind what you would do if someone in front of, behind, or next to you starts trouble.

Threat Assessment

If air marshals are onboard, it will become immediately apparent in the event of an incident. Air marshals are trained for handgun accuracy, investigative work, and operating independently, and know tactics for subduing assailants quickly. Don't get in their way, but help if asked or if you can. However, you can't assume they're on your flight, so don't wait for them, and perform your own threat assessment.

- Who is attempting the hijacking? Is this a terrorist mission or an individual who seems deranged or psychotic? How quickly can they execute their intention?

- How many hijackers are there? Multiple hijackers are clearly going to require a greater number of responders. It also indicates that this is a very sophisticated operation.

- What types of weapons are being used? Given the heightened security measures at all airports, it is unlikely these terrorists were able to smuggle anything advanced like a firearm onto the plane. That said, remember what terrorists with box cutters were able to accomplish in 2001.

SEALs say: "Greater good for the greater number."

Charge!

When you see that someone clearly has the intent to harm or kill you and everyone else on board, you must make a decision. You may take a few seconds to several minutes to contemplate and assess all variables, but it will surely come down to a physical confrontation. If you are in such a situation, it's time to *pull the trigger!* If at such a crossroads, the use of violence of action could never be more appropriate.

In this situation, if I can prevent the plane from crashing, even if it means that I might get swiped with a knife, then let's roll. Gather the troops from the passengers you previously marked, and formulate a plan.

I urge you to *lead the charge.* For most people, fighting is a very unnatural thing, and many want to avoid it. But in life-threatening situations, it takes only one person to initiate an action, and others will follow. Step up and be that person. I always say that if I'm going to die, let it be on my feet, fighting for my life and giving it 1,000 percent effort.

The More, the Better

Quickly coordinate your efforts with as many passengers as possible to overwhelm the hijackers. Flood them with bodies, attacking them from all directions. Try to have at least a 3:1 ratio—that is, three passengers for every hijacker—when initiating your assault. Again, more is better.

Improvised Weapons

(See also "Gear," page 295, and "Fighting," page 146.) You can increase the odds of making your attack successful by utilizing some of the things in your immediate area as weapons. Most anything can be used to help in the fight. But let me reiterate, no matter what you choose as a weapon, it must be employed with violence of action. Half an effort will not work. Possible weapons include:

- Car keys between your fingers
- A belt
- A tightly rolled-up magazine
- A high-heeled shoe
- A laptop computer or cell phone
- A seat-bottom cushion, to use as a shield
- A coat, wrapped around your lead arm to cushion a blow
- A ballpoint pen

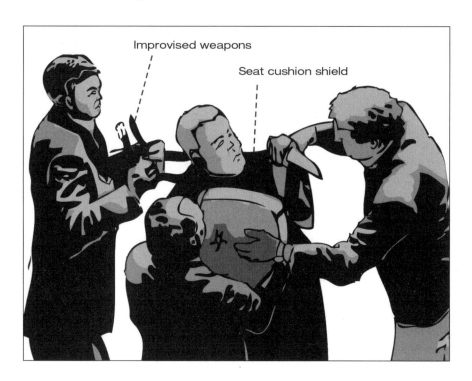

Improvised weapons

Seat cushion shield

Possible Explosives

If you think the hijackers may be carrying some type of explosive device, then you must act immediately. Attempt to get them to the floor, preferably away from the wings, where the fuel is stored. Try to spread their arms and legs apart, and keep their hands over their head. A manual explosive device will probably require their hand to detonate it. Remove their ability to do so. If, however, you don't feel in *immediate* danger, you could have a brief amount of time to formulate a different response.

Search, Handle, Restrain

If all goes well, you will have physically subdued the hijacker(s), but you're not done yet.

1. Have several people position the hijacker facedown, with arms overhead and spread and palms facing down. Also spread his legs wide. Keep a knee in the middle of his back. Have one of your passenger team control the back of the assailant's neck, forcing the head tight against and into the floor. Have others straddle each leg.

2. It is very important to perform a quick search of the hijacker. If you find an explosive device, the danger is far from over. Whether to attempt to remove the device or not will be a difficult decision. Generally, it is best to leave the device alone. If, however, you believe the device may have a timer or there is a chance the terrorist will still have the ability to detonate it, you should consider removing it. If you are able to remove the device, it should be jettisoned from the aircraft. This must be coordinated with the pilot or flight crew.

   • In recent times, many airlines have installed doors that allow for a **controlled detonation,** since there may be insufficient time to jettison the explosive. Airlines have retrofitted and fortified particular exit doors that are sturdy enough to sustain a small to medium explosion without damaging any of the plane's operating systems. Usually this is the aft starboard door, the farthest rear door on the right side when facing the front of the plane. The key to this is to place the explosive against the door and build a makeshift bunker around it. Use carry-on bags, blankets . . . anything that will help to contain the explosion, such that the majority of the explosion's force is against the door.

3. If no explosive is discovered during the search, the next thing to do is move the hijacker to the galley at the rear of the plane. This should be done using what we call **prisoner-handling techniques.**

   - Again, maintain control with a 3:1 ratio.
   - Place both the hijacker's arms behind their back, and create an arm bar by placing your arm under theirs and cranking their arms up high behind their back.
   - Have someone control both their neck and their waist.
   - Slowly pull the hijacker up from the ground while maintaining positive and aggressive force on them.
   - Keep the hijacker lower than you. They can make the trip to the rear of the plane on their knees. If they get feisty, slam their face right back down to the deck of the aircraft. Remember, this person will still try to kill you and everyone else if given the chance.

4. Once you have the hijacker in the rear galley, you are going to want to restrain them for the rest of the flight. Utilize anything you can find—belts, ties, shoelaces, carry-on-bag straps—to bind their arms behind their back and tightly secure their feet and knees together.

5. When you are certain the hijacker is thoroughly restrained, remove their ability to see, hear, and speak. Blindfold and gag this person thoroughly.

6. At least two people must maintain a constant watch on the hijacker. If the hijacker moves or tries to get free, be ready to pounce.

I enjoyed using these techniques to subdue a prisoner when my platoon had the opportunity to take a very bad man responsible for over twenty thousand deaths to the war crimes tribunal in the Hague. Old poopy-pants did not enjoy that night one bit. Wish we could have sent him free-falling without a parachute. Dare to dream.

The Outside World's Response

While you are dealing with this life-threatening situation inside the plane, there will be a whole series of events put into motion in the world outside. If the pilots are still in control of the plane, they will "squawk," or transmit a code that lets everyone know they have been hijacked. NORAD (the North American Aerospace Defense Command) will then scramble fighter jets to intercept, and the FAA will work to clear the area of other aircraft while establishing the best location to land.

Understand that since 9/11, one of the mission options of the fighter jet interceptor is to shoot down a hijacked airliner. This would clearly be a worst-case scenario, which is why it is so crucial to establish or reestablish communications with the outside world once the hijacker is subdued. If NORAD doesn't know what is going on inside the plane, they could destroy it.

If the pilots are still in control of the plane, the flight crew will notify them (using specific protocol) of the situation in the cabin. The pilots will then convey that information to NORAD and the FAA.

If, however, the pilots are for some reason incapacitated, it will be up to the flight crew or perhaps even some of the passengers to take control of the plane and reestablish communication. To do so, go to the communication portion of the cockpit and dial in the following frequency: 121.5. This is a common frequency used for emergency situations. In a very clear and controlled tone provide the following information:

- Who you are.
- Flight number.
- Current situation ("We've regained control of the plane!").
- Status of plane and pilots.

Remember, the clock is ticking, and you have a couple of fighter jets with authorization to shoot you down. Follow all instructions you are given once you have established communication on the emergency frequency. You probably didn't plan on flying a jumbo jet when you woke up this morning, but that may be exactly what you're going to have to do.

HOME INVASION

In the United States, one in forty homes was targeted for a home invasion in 2012. Home invasions now account for one in four robberies, since the traditional targets like gas stations and convenience stores have initiated plans that make less cash available and make targeting them not worth the trouble for professional criminals. Law enforcement now makes a distinction between burglary or robbery, in which assailants unlawfully force their way into a home, apartment, or hotel room to commit a crime, and home invasion, a predetermined, more sophisticated, better-planned, and often much more violent crime that occurs within a person's residence.

Tactics used by home invaders have become increasingly brutal, with a third of all home invasions turning physically violent, often leading to rape, torture, and even murder. Home invasions are just as frightening as any apocalyptic event, since these are life-threatening situations that jeopardize our person, our family, and our right to live in a secure environment. Having your property stolen is an enraging and frustrating experience. Add intimidation, assault, and other heinous acts committed in the sanctuary of your home to the list, and home invasion becomes an intolerable crime. Learning the skills necessary to fight back and survive a home invasion are essential now and would be of paramount importance if the stakes for survival were even higher, especially in the aftermath of a catastrophic event.

Home invasion is motivated generally by the intention to steal property, and less frequently to commit kidnapping. Targeting a home is less risky for criminals than robbing commercial establishments. Unlike with robbing a retail store, a home invasion is far less likely to be interrupted by police on the beat or by random pedestrians entering the scene. Once the offenders take control of a residence, they force occupants to open safes, locate hidden valuables, supply keys to the family car, and provide PIN numbers to their ATM cards. Home invaders will try to increase their escape time by disabling the phones and sometimes will leave their victims bound or incapacitated. It is not unheard-of for robbers to load up the victim's car with valuables and drive away without anyone in the neighborhood taking notice.

There is no single correct response to a life-threatening home invasion scenario. There are tools to help you, but ultimately the choice is personal, based on your own assessment of your physical and mental capabilities and your evaluation of the level of imminent danger. But if you continue to remember that the goal is to *survive*, you will endure.

Tiger Kidnapping

Police refer to a more sophisticated and dangerous type of home invasion as a tiger kidnapping. It gets its name from the fact that highly trained professionals stalk their victim's every move for weeks or months like a predator prior to striking. In a tiger kidnapping, a person of importance to the victim is held hostage and is used as collateral until the victim has met the criminal's demands. For example, the president of a bank is told his family will be killed if he does not empty the safe at his branch.

Tiger kidnapping is the most sophisticated and ultimately the most dangerous of all home invasions. It involves two separate crimes committed in tandem. The first crime usually involves the abduction of a person to be held hostage, but sometimes blackmail is employed instead—sensitive information, or the threat of revealing damaging information, can be used as a means to coerce collaboration from the abducted. Instead of simply robbing the victim, the captors demand that a second crime, which could be anything from robbery or murder to planting a bomb, be committed on their behalf by someone close to the hostage in exchange for the hostage's safe return. Although a similar situation could be enacted via blackmail and without kidnapping, home invaders know this method expedites results. Hostages are held by captors as collateral until their demands are met. Unlike with blackmail, perpetrators don't have to wait for response to their demands via phone calls or notes, or take the chance of getting police involved. Instead, in these scenarios, the goal of the captors is to have their dirty work performed by another person, who is referred to as the "human key." In addition, in many instances, the victims of these tiger kidnappings are less likely to report the offense to authorities since they too, technically, were involved in committing a crime. As in the example of a bank employee who helps in a robbery, even if he does so under threat that his family would be harmed, he has in effect also committed a crime, and often remains secretive. Fearing repercussions in regards to the level of their involvement, or concerned about the criminal's return, many victims are reluctant to report their ordeal to authorities. In any case, tiger kidnappings are well-planned operations, in which the victims have been under surveillance and stalked for a considerable amount of time.

It's a very strange thing to know that another human being is stalking you. With the work I did in Iraq, I knew that every time we left our secure compound, we were under surveillance by the "bad guys." You wondered in the back of your mind: "Is this the time they're going to pounce?" This is what keeps you at a maximum state of alert. And each time we returned to the safety of our compound, I said: "Not today."

STAGES OF TIGER KIDNAPPINGS

After the target is stalked and their daily routine is well recorded, then the attack begins. In contrast to burglaries and robberies, which are often crimes of opportunity, home invaders are usually very familiar with the layout of the home or apartment. Nevertheless, the most effective way to gain entry is through the front door or garage. Occasionally, well-armed home invaders forcibly enter the home by kicking open the door and then deal with whomever they find inside. More commonly, home invaders prefer not to make such a scene on the street, especially if the front door is visible to neighbors or public roads. Various ruses are used to get you to open the door, such as pretending to deliver flowers or packages. Some may pretend to solicit some service or say that they are working on a neighbor's house and wish to give a free estimate of some sort, or that they were in an accident and need to use your phone. The list of ways to get you to open the door by simply ringing the bell is long. It's surprising how many people do just that and swing open the door upon the first knock.

In Special Operations, when our mission involved the entry, or "breaching," of a house or structure, there were two ways we got in. The most dramatic, and the type portrayed in movies, is called "dynamic entry." This is when we blow away the fortified entry with explosives or use a "hooligan tool," a crowbar-type device, to give us instant access. However, given the enemy's knowledge of our tactics and use of fortification, the "soft entry" has become the preferred method. Using this technique, we exploit the house's weaknesses and enter without making undue noise. This gives us the upper hand via stealth and surprise. Home invaders aren't going to use dynamite, and nearly always try the soft entry. The best way to make your house a difficult target for home invaders is to identify all the soft entry points and install basic hardware and safety devices. (See "Burglary and Robbery," page 106.)

Prevention and Rehearsal

As with most survival techniques, it is better to contemplate the unthinkable beforehand. Look at your home and create and play your mental movie of what plan of action would be best in the dire event of a home invasion. In Special Ops we always focused on rehearsal prior to a mission. You can do the following to rehearse for a home invasion with your family:

- Establish a code word that everyone knows means trouble. This will initiate an escape plan and a proper course of action. The seriousness of this word must be made clear; it should never to be used unless in a do-or-die situation.

- Draw a sketch of the interior of your home and mark alternate points of exit that could be accessed while avoiding the area the attackers have breached. Also, have more than one escape route, including alternate escape plans for the front, rear, and second floor.

- Set up a safe room in your home. Use a signal or your special code word to notify family members when to get to it without question or hesitation.

- Do not make rehearsals a scary situation for children. As in a school fire drill, children can be great assets if taught to remain calm when under stress.

- Teach children how and when to dial 911, activate an alarm panic button if you have an alarm system, or escape to the neighbor's house to summon the police.

MAKING A SAFE ROOM

If space allows, choose a certain room as a designated safe room. This is a good plan not only for home invasions but for other emergencies or in the event of natural disasters. This particular room should be a safe retreat to accommodate any number of emergencies. Primarily, the door should be fortified enough to delay an intruder during a home invasion or other terrorist threat. It should be equipped with an alarm panel, or a landline phone, or an inexpensive cell phone left there on permanent charge. A step further would be to have a police-band radio or any other means of communication to summon help. A safe room can be created and furnished with relatively little effort and expense.

- Select an interior room or large closet with no windows or skylight.
- Install a solid-core wood or steel door, and hang it so it opens or swings outward.
- Replace the wooden doorjamb with a steel one, or reinforce the door trim with steel angle iron to prevent the door from being kicked open.
- Install a keyless Grade 1 deadbolt (if your deadbolt can be opened with a key, you risk having the keys fall into the wrong hands).

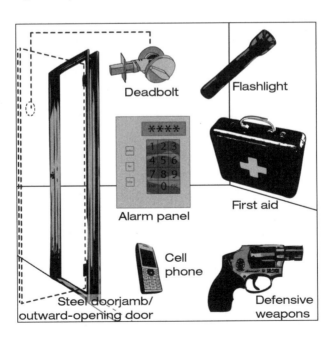

Deadbolt

Flashlight

Alarm panel

First aid

Cell phone

Steel doorjamb/ outward-opening door

Defensive weapons

- Stock the safe room with necessary emergency items and a way to summon aid or defend yourself. This includes a cell phone, a flashlight, a first-aid kit, food, water, and defensive weapons.
- Install an alarm panel, a direct-dial phone or a cell phone, and an electrical outlet for cell phone charging.
- If possible, install a secret escape hatch with a way to get to the attic, the basement, or an alternative escape route.

You are home, it is the evening, and suddenly you hear a very loud crash in the other part of your residence. You should:
1. Call 911.
2. Initiate security plan.
3. Yell code word.
4. Exit residence or move to safe room.
5. Wait for the police to arrive.

If unable to call 911:
1. Initiate security plan.
2. Yell code word.
3. Exit residence or move to safe room.
4. If inside safe room, attempt to call 911 again. *Do not leave.*

If outside, move to prearranged location for help, such as a neighbor's house, while calling 911.

If unable to exit residence or move to safe room:
1. Make an immediate threat assessment.
    - Why is this person here?
    - Are they going to harm my family or me?
    - Can I overpower this person to subdue them or allow for my escape?
2. Allow them to leave if possible. Never risk life for property.
3. Fight or comply, based on your threat assessment.
4. Keep a cool head. Sometimes fighting and screaming works, especially if there are neighbors who will intervene or call police. But it makes no sense to risk fighting if you

are physically incapable of doing so effectively, especially if the invaders are armed and you are not.

5. If you do decide to strike a blow, do it fast, suddenly, and forcefully to the nose, eyes, or throat without concern for the damage you will inflict. (See also "Fighting," page 146.) While the assailant is momentarily stunned, make your escape. Don't stand there waiting to throw more punches or gather family members.

6. Alternatively, total compliance sometimes works. At first there may be no chance for escape, but after a while you may see an opening. The invaders could just leave without harming you. However, compliance may increase the duration of the invasion and therefore increase the potential for molestation. Continue reevaluating the situation as it evolves.

When Violence Comes

The modus operandi of home invaders is to gain control of you and your family, regardless of your family members' ages, instantaneously. Once they get into your home, they will become extremely aggressive and threatening. The greatest violence of a home invasion occurs within the first minutes; success depends upon instilling shock and fear in the victims. Frequently, in addition to weapons, home invaders bring handcuffs, ropes, duct tape, or plastic bands to bind the home's occupants. It is not unusual for the home invaders to pick one family member to physically assault, for the purpose of rendering all witnesses absolutely submissive. If this happens, and the surprise has made it impossible to fight back, the victim should curl up into a ball and try to protect their head and face with their arms. Feign that you are more injured than you really are, and perhaps even consider appearing unconscious.

At this point, do not look directly at the attackers, or talk or argue with them. It's important to defuse their initial rage and adrenaline rush by acting in a nonthreatening manner. They will likely divide family members and place them in separate areas of the house, as another means to gain psychological manipulation. These professionals know they must show dominance and control, so at this phase, let the intruders believe they have executed this part of the assault successfully. This will not only limit physical violence but will give you more time and allow for an opportunity to escape.

While it will be difficult to be assaulted, or watch a loved one be assaulted, this is the time to remain alert and gather intelligence that can be used against your attackers. This information will be valuable as you form your plan for survival and ultimately for your escape.

- Identify the leader of the group and who's who in their chain of command.

- Consider why you were targeted: Is it access to money or valuable information?

- Who is valuable among your family members, and whom would the attackers consider expendable? Are they here to make one of your group a "human key"?

SERE: Survive, Evade, Resist, Escape

The first course of action in a home invasion is to have at least one family member escape so they can summon police. Everything you do is geared toward achieving this goal.

Now that you have survived the initial violation of your home and person, you must use your intelligence to outwit the attackers. When you're bound or captured, the idea is to gain time. An opportunity will arise to get away, as long as you keep your cool and stay alert. There are ways to establish a bond with your captors. The more personable and calm you are, the greater the possibility of establishing communication with your assailants. It is ideal to attempt to humanize the attackers, such as by calling them by name. Again, this is for the purposes of buying time and making it through the ordeal.

BEING A POW

One of the many grueling aspects of SEAL training is the two weeks we prepare for what I would consider to be the worst-case scenario in war: getting captured. We must pass two horrendous weeks of being a POW. The skills learned from this can help if you find yourself bound and subdued during a home invasion. When I went through it, I lost twenty-two pounds and came out looking like a different person, though hardened and more experienced. POW training stresses what we call SERE, which stands for "survive, evade, resist, escape." Remember this acronym as your plan of action. All of these techniques could save your life in a home invasion. Our training included being placed in a three-by-three-foot concrete box for one of the weeks without food and nothing more than a coffee can to urinate into. We were taken out and interrogated, beaten, and worse. Our simulated captors tried to make us tell them the secret we were told, and in so doing we learned how to survive, giving up only pieces of information at a time. This makes captors think we are useful and keeps us alive another day, which is actually giving us another opportunity to escape. Time is your friend.

HOW TO ESCAPE RESTRAINTS

Rope, Tape

- **Cutting method:** Search for any object with an edge, such as a piece of broken glass or a vase shard that smashed during the initial assault. Secretly attempt to get this into your bound hands.

- **Friction method:** If left out of view of your attackers, you might have time to escape bondage using friction. For example, you can make a friction saw with shoelaces by looping each end, running the length over your restraints, and placing a foot in each loop. Bicycle your feet, causing the laces to cut through the rope or tape from the friction they create.

- **Burning method:** Use matches or a lighter to actually melt through the restraint.

- **Wiggle method:** With the exception of metal handcuffs, many restraints have a certain degree of elasticity. It will greatly improve your ability to use this technique if you take a deep breath and expand your chest and upper body while you are being bound. Once you exhale, you will already have a little slack, making it easier to get free. Attempt to use constant movement to establish enough slack to get out.

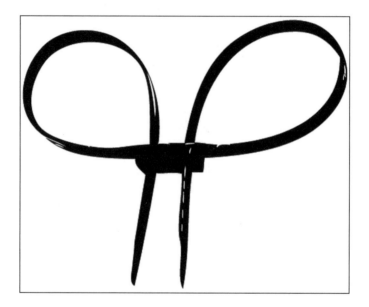

Flex Cuffs

Flex cuffs are increasingly popular with both law enforcement and hostage takers due to their strength and low cost. These plastic ties are usually more durable than rope or duct tape, but you could escape using:

- **The shim method:** Find an object to wedge into the latch. Flex cuffs have small plastic teeth that can be worn or broken. If you can get a shim into the tie slot, it could be possible to prevent the one-way catch from activating and allow you to pull one end free.

- **Break:** Flex cuffs can also snap if jammed against something hard enough. If there is nothing to strike against, escape flex cuffs by using your own chest as a ramming board. This will hurt but is often effective: Try to stretch your arms out directly in front of you, then, in a powerful motion, drive your arms back toward your chest. Keep doing this until the band lock latch is breached.

Handcuffs

Handcuffs work using a very basic one-way locking mechanism. The arm of the cuffs has a series of teeth on it known as a ratchet. As the ratchet travels through the pawl, or the locking pin, it allows the arm to tighten, but the pawl will not allow the arm to loosen due to the one-way nature of the teeth.

The best way to defeat handcuffs is by using a handcuff key you have stashed on your body. I always carry a plastic one taped to the underside of my watch. If, however, you don't have a spare key, there are two other methods for removing handcuffs.

- **The bobby-pin method:** Remove the plastic from the tip of a standard bobby pin, place the pin an eighth of an inch deep into the handcuff keyhole, and make a 90-degree bend at the end of the bobby pin. Then take the bobby pin and place it directly into the keyhole about an eighth of an inch deep. Rotate the bobby pin so the bent end pushes the spring-loaded pawl down far enough so that the teeth on the ratchet clear the pawl, allowing the arm to swing open.

- **The shim method:** Take a bobby pin with plastic tip removed or another, thinner piece of metal, and place this in the slot just below the ratchet arm. Shim the space between the teeth of the ratchet and the catch of the pawl so the one-way lock is defeated, allowing the arm to swing open.

ONCE YOU'RE FREE OF RESTRAINTS

Now that you are free, don't squander this small opportunity. If you escape your restraints, keep a cool head and act as if you are still in your restraints. You have the advantage of not being in the condition in which the invaders think you are. Fighting may not be wise; however, the attackers may let their guards down once you appear to be restrained.

If you can keep your wits, you can increase your options for survival by waiting for the right moment to act. You must seize this chance because there might not be another. Now that you are free and have gathered intelligence about the group, you can assess if this is a robbery or if the attackers intend to turn this into a tiger kidnapping. In either case, time is running out, and you must take the one opportunity you have to escape.

Remember, the base goal at this point is not to attempt to free everyone but to **get at least one of you out of the house.** If someone in the household can escape and call for help, the home invaders will have lost their advantage. If you have the chance, it may be difficult to leave your loved ones behind. But remember, if you can get to a phone, this entire ordeal will be over in a few minutes. Nevertheless, seek an opportunity to create a diversion to allow the member who is freed of binding to make an escape. Set off a car alarm triggered from your keyless remote, or feign illness, or call out to the captors. If you are fleeing, you will have only a moment to go undiscovered; create barricades between you and the intruders as you go. Jumping or dropping from a height may be your only option for escape.

You won't want to leave anyone behind, but doing so could save everyone. To some, running away from your family in crisis is distasteful, especially to men or women with children. However, the alternative could be far worse. And don't ever follow an intruder once they leave your home. Leave that to the police.

HURRICANE AND TORNADO

Put your hat out the window of a car doing 75 mph and it gets flung backward. At 110 to 150 mph, it would be nearly impossible to hold on to it. Wind, rain, and the flooding caused by hurricanes make for a life-threatening natural disaster that must be taken seriously. When a storm system has sustained winds at speeds of 74 miles per hour or greater, it's classified as a hurricane. As natural occurrences, hurricanes form from storm clouds that gather en masse over large, warm bodies of water, and depending on various other environmental factors, begin to circulate. Wind speed will determine the storm's potential hazard, which is measured in categories: Category 1 has winds from 74 to 95 mph; a "Cat 5" has maximum sustained wind speeds of at least 157 mph.

A hurricane's concentrated pressure and barometric fluctuations are what cause the most serious structural damage. Even if you are sheltered in an adequate dwelling, the pressure can literally cause an improperly braced house, for example, to implode. In addition, those who don't take this powerful force of nature seriously greatly increase their chance of being killed by blowing debris. Deadly floods can also be part of the aftermath of a hurricane.

The Galveston, Texas, hurricane of September 8, 1900, claimed the highest death toll of any hurricane in U.S. history, with more than 8,000 fatalities due to flooding. More recently, the nation's third-worst storm occurred on August 29, 2005, when Category 5 hurricane Katrina devastated the gulf coast from Biloxi, Mississippi, to New Orleans, killing more Americans than any other single natural disaster in more than fifty years. The storm surge broke a five-hundred-foot section of levee that kept the below-sea-level areas of New Orleans dry, flooding the historic streets with up to twenty feet of surging water and causing 1,400 deaths.

Preparation, Preparation, Preparation

Hurricane forecasting has improved tremendously since the turn of the last century, when the folks of Galveston had no clue as to what was heading their way on that fateful day. A hurricane is one natural disaster for which we are given plenty of time to prepare and/or evacuate. I can think of no greater example of how easily you can increase your odds of survival than by taking the time to do a serious preparation checklist and being ready for the worst.

The parallels between a nasty hurricane and combat are unlimited. Survival often comes down to knowing when to hold your position and when to move. You must decide when to fight, when to make a planned evacuation, and when to bunker in. Once the winds blow, the chances of dying from flying debris are great. As in combat, surviving a hurricane requires having the right gear and supplies to keep you alive. Preparation and rehearsal are keys to success in surviving this natural disaster.

Home Prep

Sheltering in a dwelling unprepared can be lethal. Use the following checklist to prepare your home.

- ❏ Cover all openings. Use hurricane shutters with clearly marked windstorm ratings, or precut and predrilled plywood, and use permanent fasteners to attach them to the walls.
- ❏ Make sure the straps that attach the roof to the wall plate of your house are properly nailed. If a house has a gable-end roof (looks like there's a triangle at one corner), then use two-by-four cross-bracing to reinforce these parts for the horizontal force the gable ends will bear. The uplift force of hurricanes frequently blows entire roofs off homes.

❏ Tie down or remove exterior lawn furniture, etc.
❏ Survey for overhanging trees and trim. Remove trees that are within falling distance of your roof.
❏ Know how to turn off electricity and gas.
❏ Pets are not allowed in most emergency shelters, so make sure you have a plan for them.

Equipment

Be prepared for a short-term lack of power and water. Make a checklist of essentials, and each year check that emergency supplies are functioning.

ESSENTIAL SUPPLIES

• Medications for yourself and family members for at least a week.

• A good first-aid kit to treat cuts, abrasions, and other general illnesses or injuries.

• Water: Fill bathtubs and stock up on water jugs. The rule is to have at least one gallon of water per person per day. Bathtub water can be used for hygiene, and bottled water for drinking. Water-purification supplies, such as chlorine or bleach, can also make long-standing bathwater or even pool water drinkable.

• A stockpile of nonperishable foods that can be eaten without cooking.

• An emergency National Oceanic and Atmospheric Administration radio, or any radio with plenty of extra batteries.

• Cell phones that are fully charged.

- Valuable documents and emergency contact numbers stored in sealable plastic bags.

- Cash. ATMs could be down and banks may be closed for some time.

- Sleeping bags ready and a well-stocked safe room.

- Ample flashlights and chemlights.

VEHICLE
- ❏ Get the car filled with gas.
- ❏ Make sure windshield wipers are new.
- ❏ Check spare tire and jacking equipment.
- ❏ Have a map showing several evacuation routes.

When to Evacuate

People are naturally reluctant to leave their homes. Hurricane paths and strengths, as mentioned, are followed and forecast well in advance. However, since the predicted path of a hurricane has a two-hundred-mile (plus or minus) margin of error, it is not certain exactly where a hurricane will make landfall, which leads many to merely hope for the best. If you do decide to leave, then make the assessment early—the rule of thumb in such scenarios is always the sooner, the better. Understand that in an evacuation there are going to be thousands of scared people all trying to flee. Traffic jams will be inevitable, and you may see the very worst in people because of the stress of the situation. Stay focused and relaxed. This is an excellent opportunity to utilize combat breathing.

FEMA offers these guidelines to help you decide when to evacuate:

- Listen to weather broadcasts and evacuate if directed by authorities to do so.

- Evacuate if you live on the coast, in a floodplain, near a river, or near an inland waterway.

- Evacuate if you live in a mobile home or temporary structure.

- Evacuate if you live in a high-rise building.

- Evacuate if you feel you are in danger.

When planning your evacuation route during the hurricane-preparation phase, know the routes firsthand. Look for what are called "blue lines" on highway maps, or less-traveled roads, and know how to circumvent likely traffic jams. Use in-car navigation systems that monitor traffic to look for alternate routes. If you live in a hurricane area, drive the route during nonemergency situations. When people flee, panic sets in, and tempers and frustrations rise. The obvious route may not be the best one. Get to the highest ground you can and away from the coast and other waterways.

Make sure you have an out-of-town emergency point of contact that anyone in your family can call in case you are separated.

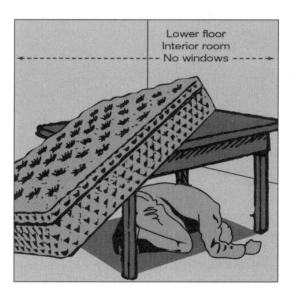

Holding Your Position

If you were unable to evacuate and are going to have to stay put, set up base in an interior room on a lower floor, preferably without windows or external walls. In a two-story house, consider what heavy furniture is located in the room above. You can further bunker in by positioning yourself under a heavy table and using mattresses and blankets to block the open sides.

Caught Outside

If you find yourself threatened by a hurricane when you are outside, you should abandon your vehicle if you're in one, and find shelter immediately. If no structure is available, lie flat on the ground, seek out a ditch, or hunker down behind a rock outcropping. Change to the other side of the rock formation after the eye passes, as the wind will then be blowing in the opposite direction. Look above and stay away from poles or trees that could be uprooted. Your greatest danger is being struck by flying debris, so stay as low to the ground as possible. Use the low or slightly raised crawling technique, making your way from cover to cover until you find suitable shelter. Once there, try to find something you can use to offer additional cover or cushioning from blowing debris.

It's Not Over Yet

If all goes quiet, don't assume the hurricane is gone. You may be in the eye of the storm, which makes for a deceptive and eerie calm. But depending on the size of the storm system, this sudden reprieve may last only a few minutes before the violent winds return, blowing from the opposite direction. In a 2004 Florida hurricane, a woman went out during the false calm to search for her lost cat and was killed by a flying water heater when the winds picked up. When the winds finally do subside, a "scene size-up" is required. The landscape will have changed. One totally avoidable cause of death that occurs after a hurricane is downed power lines, often submerged in puddles. Do not walk through standing water.

Tornado Survival

More deaths occur each year from tornadoes than from hurricanes. Tornadoes form rapidly, and the warning time is considerably shorter. Home preparation is the same as for hurricanes, but often there will be insufficient time to fortify windows.

- A designated safe room is the best option. Choose one in a basement, far from exterior windows and doors. Also, pick a place that does not have heavy furniture on the floor above.

- If living in a tornado-prone area, have a battery-operated National Weather Service radio. The radio will issue warnings when tornadoes are in your area. These extra minutes of warning are often a matter of life and death.

- Practice and rehearse with your family what to do in the event of a tornado, including how to move to your safe room in the event of a power failure.

- If outdoors, seek low areas, such as a ditch or gully, and lie flat.

- If you are in a vehicle, get out of it if you see low areas nearby and take refuge there. If nothing is in sight, stay inside the car and keep your seat belt snug, hunker down in the seat, and brace your hands on the steering wheel.

JAIL

Your chances of being incarcerated at some point in your life are higher than you might realize. And by the nature of how one ends up being arrested, it usually means that you weren't planning or ready for it to happen.

This section is not intended to help the hardened criminal or repeat offender ease their time behind bars. It is for someone who is going to jail for the first time: Maybe you had one drink too many at dinner; you were in the wrong place at the wrong time; someone made an inappropriate remark to your wife or girlfriend, husband or boyfriend; or perhaps you had a simple misunderstanding with the entire staff of a Northern California bar, as in my case. At any rate, you are about to be locked up due to a minor, though regrettable, mistake. Knowing some survival tips could not only lessen your troubles but, in the worst case, may prevent you from injury and death. Whether it's for a day or a month, jail is definitely not a fun-filled environment, and any number of SEAL survival techniques will be useful to you.

What Kind of Jail Is This?

There is a huge difference from one county jail to another. If you were taken to New York City's main jail complex, Rikers Island, you would be among twelve thousand inmates. This jail holds a wide range of offenders, from those jumping a subway turnstile to mass murderers ("Son of Sam" spent time there). You will be among a mixed inmate population, including anyone who couldn't post bail at the local precinct lockup, those serving a sentence of one year or less, and those waiting for a transfer to a larger prison, having been convicted of a serious crime. Given this, you could be exposed to a lot of violence.

On the other hand, if you were fortunate enough to get sent to jail in Palm Springs County, California, their facility is noted for less violent behavior; inmates describe their stay there as being locked up in a very strict boarding school. In any regard, during the first days in jail, inmates are generally not separated by the nature of their crime. If you're there for a warrant issued when you didn't show up to court to pay a motor vehicle fine, for example, you could find yourself sitting in jail next to a gang member or a rapist.

At any given time, at least 10 percent of the U.S. population is either incarcerated or on probation. Of those incarcerated, 85 percent are repeat offenders. On average, more than 160 inmates are killed annually by other inmates and 6,000 are raped, and more than 2,000 corrections personnel are injured seriously enough to require medical attention.

Mental Preparation

Here is the payoff for your mental toughness training, because you are going to harden up now whether you like it or not. Remember, the anticipation of a frightening event is almost always worse than the reality. The media likes to hype up time behind bars, but be thankful and take comfort in the fact that you are going to an American jail and not a hellhole in a foreign country, or, for that matter, a POW camp in Vietnam. Once locked up, you want to shift into a "one day at a time" perspective, or better yet, one hour at a time. Tell yourself this will pass and your life will continue. If you will be there for more than a day, establish a routine and stick to it. If you must remain behind bars longer, remember that it takes about a week to adjust to any different environment. Keep the idea of mental toughness foremost in your mind, and you will endure.

Just Locked Up

Try to make friends with someone who knows what's going on and follow their lead. Every jail is different. There may be little things that set inmates off. Find out as soon as possible what these things are so you can avoid them. Don't spend time explaining why you committed your crime or why it's not as bad as the crimes committed by those around you. This will only agitate other inmates.

THE WHAT-NOT-TO-DO-IN-JAIL CHECKLIST:

❑ Don't discuss your charges or your case. The less other inmates know about your reason for being there or your personal affairs, the better. Not to mention the use of snitches and scams that might have you looking at a much higher chance of conviction. Save it for your lawyer.

❑ Don't draw unwanted attention to yourself.

❑ Don't use inflammatory words, especially toward other inmates.

❑ Don't be a **snitch.** Jails house the worst of our society, so unless whatever goes down involves you directly, you need to look the other way. Never talk to a guard unless you feel you are in immediate danger—other inmates will be watching your every move.

Violence Behind Bars

It is highly probable that you will see violence during your time in a U.S. jail. Even at Rikers Island, which has more than eight thousand correctional staff guarding its twelve thousand inmates, prisoners are mostly supervised from afar. If you follow the rules and advice mentioned above, you can limit your chances of getting involved in a violent situation. In jail society, respect is huge, and your apparent confidence and attitude of mental toughness is the key to earning it. If you start crying or show weakness, be prepared to be taken advantage of. However, if someone threatens you, make sure they know that you are prepared to defend yourself. It's the law of the jungle, where the weakest become prey, and in jail, being fearful and uncourageous will oftentimes attract more violence. Conversely, you don't want to present yourself as a tough guy who needs to be taken down. Your "firepower" is the techniques you learned developing the SEAL mindset and practicing the defensive tactics we use. This is one secret weapon that adds to your confidence, but use it wisely, for the element of surprise will be effective only once.

A good friend and fellow SEAL was down in Mexico for a weekend getaway when he was pulled over and arrested on suspicion of drinking and driving. My friend is a big boy and was unlikely to get into any serious problems while waiting to get bailed out of the local jail. However, the *policía* didn't wait for this to happen and decided to move him to another, larger facility farther south. My buddy didn't realize that he would spend the next four days fighting for his life. He compared the experience to some sort of gladiator games, with the cops betting on how long the big American would last. After a final fight, after which his opponent was no longer moving, my friend was suddenly and without explanation set free. With two broken hands, a broken foot, a screwed-up knee, and a body full of bruises and cuts, he made it back to America. "Don't fuck around in Mexico" is all he would say.

It may be useful to make some friends, because others might not be as likely to start a fight if you have people willing to stick up for you. However, even if you'd like to think it is not so, prejudice and racial division exist more in jails than in the outside world. If you are in a jail and frequently grouped with many inmates in large areas, you need to size up who is who and what gangs or groups are dominating. The reality is that you may need to consider aligning yourself with people of your own background. Understand, however, that by joining this group, you are also putting yourself at higher risk for violence. This is of greater importance if you have a longer sentence. If you are going to be in for only a short time, then by keeping to yourself and using mental toughness as your tool, you should fare well.

Be Good

Your goal in jail is to pass the time as quickly as possible, incident-free, and move on with your life. Almost all jails will reduce your sentence in what is known as "time off for good behavior." Actually, it is difficult to lose this status. Los Angeles county jail inmates generally serve only 10 percent of the time to which they were sentenced. Just ask Paris Hilton. So unless you are fighting guards or get caught with drugs, your time should be reduced.

Once you find yourself in jail, remember:

- Don't do anything illegal—unlike in the movies, all will not be forgiven when the authorities finally figure out you were innocent of the charge that got you arrested to begin with. You will only make things worse.

- Be good.

- Be a ghost.

Released

You made it—now stay out! Be part of the 15 percent who don't return.

LIGHTNING

Lightning is the sniper of natural disasters. It strikes from a distance, it usually kills one at a time, and you never know when you are in its crosshairs. Its kill record is fairly impressive: It causes approximately 2,000 deaths per year. Right now, there are 1,800 thunderstorms happening somewhere on the planet, which produce more than 600,000 lightning strikes per day. One in four of the people who actually get hit by lightning die, but fortunately there are survival techniques to employ that will minimize your chances of becoming a target of these random shots fired from above.

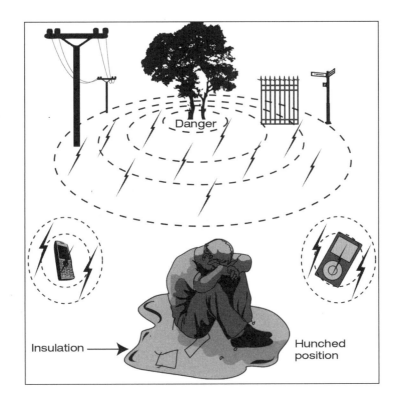

Know the Enemy

As it is when sizing up any adversary, be it human or natural, acquiring "intelligence" on lightning's means and methods is an essential part of planning and preparedness that always gives you an advantage. Scientifically, it is not completely certain how lightning forms in the atmosphere, but what is known is that it is a charged electrical current that is hotter than the surface of the sun. It travels at a speed of 3,700 miles per second, or at "lightning speed"; that's faster than a bullet from an M4 assault rifle, which travels at 3,000 feet per second, or 30 feet per one-hundredth of a second. Lightning can strike as far as ten miles from where it's raining; people have been killed by a bolt of lightning while standing in the sunshine. A lightning strike seeks to balance its either negative or positive electrical charge by seeking out an item below it, which could be a tree or a human. The idea is to make yourself insulated and not an attractive conduit or target.

Targets

Those who have been killed by lightning were usually taking cover under a tree or standing next to a telephone pole. Some were talking on their cell phones while leaning against a metal signpost, or walking on top of a metal sidewalk grate, or touching a metal fence. Lightning generally hits the tallest object within its general striking range, but it also seeks out metal and electrical conduits. People have been hit while inside their homes, washing dishes in a metal sink or talking on a corded, landline phone near a window. Unlike hurricanes or floods, which are prone to devastate particular areas, lightning is less discriminatory. While Rwanda, Africa, is the lightning capital of the world, and Florida is the state with most strikes in the U.S., lightning occurs everywhere.

Lightning is the second-highest cause of death by natural disaster, behind floods. In Florida, for example, hurricanes account for 8 percent of weather-related fatalities; tornadoes account for 13 percent; while lightning-related deaths are at more than 53 percent.

The 30/30 Rule

Victims of lightning can be grouped into two categories: (1) those oblivious to their surroundings, who ignore the dangers of lightning and make no attempt to seek shelter in a storm, and (2) the truly unlucky. However, you can increase your "luck" by following some basic safety tips. There is truth to the well-known phrase "Where there is thunder, there's lightning," since lighting creates the sound of thunder by forming a sonic shock wave. Thunder is the warning shot fired across the bow; if you hear it, then you are close enough for lightning to hit you. When SEALs hear the crack of gunfire somewhere up ahead, we don't ignore it; we pay closer attention. Do the same when hearing thunder.

The National Weather Service (NWS) tries to educate the public about the fact that alertness and quick action can save most from getting struck. The NWS's **30/30 Rule** urges you to measure and count what is called "flash-to-bang time." If you see a flash of lightning, begin counting to thirty. If you don't hear a thunderclap before you reach thirty, then make for shelter immediately. If do hear one before you reach thirty, you need to hit the ground where you are. A good way to estimate how far away lightning is from you is to count out the seconds from the time when you see the flash of lightning to when you hear thunder. For example, if you see lightning, begin to count, "One thousand one, one thousand two . . . ," until you hear the boom. If you hear thunder on "two," you can assume that the lightning struck the ground approximately two miles from where you are.

ACTION CHECKLIST

❑ Seek shelter in a permanent structure and move to the interior. Neither a beach hut nor under a picnic table is safe.

❑ If indoors, stay away from windows. Do not use electrical appliances or computers, or position yourself near plumbing or pipes.

❑ If outdoors and no permanent structures are present, get inside a vehicle, but keep your hands and other body parts from touching any metal parts inside the car. The tires of the car somewhat insulate the vehicle, but the vehicle's metal frame is still a conduit.

❏ Do not stand near trees or tall objects.

❏ Avoid touching fences, signposts, or any metal object.

❏ Power down any cell phones and other portable electronic devices.

❏ If caught outside, sit down and tuck your head between your legs. It is also important to insulate yourself from electrical currents transferring through the ground. Try to sit on a coat, blanket, or anything that limits your body's direct contact with the ground.

❏ If you are in an open field, then avoid this hunched position, as it will still leave you as the highest point. In that case, lie flat on the ground. If possible, try to stay in a slightly raised push-up position. If lightning does strike, it will then pass through your arms and into the ground, thus bypassing your heart and other vital organs.

Just as you watch the lightning flash and listen for thunder, SEAL snipers follow the same principle when using a rifle. As a sniper, you get an appreciation for the speed of sound and the speed of a bullet. You know it's a great shot when the crack of a round explodes as you pull the trigger, then several seconds later you see the impact, or spray. The longer amount of time between sound and visual impact means the further the distance of the shot. A couple seconds in between is always cool.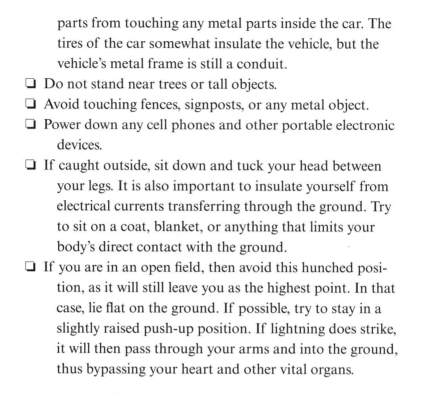

LOST AT SEA

Things have gone from bad to worse, and you've been forced to abandon ship. (See also "Abandon Ship," page 29.) At this point, you have already been through some traumatic experiences, made your threat assessment as to the seaworthiness of your vessel, and gotten off the X. Now you find yourself in the water and away from what was once the security of your ship. You must remember that you got to where you are because it was the best option to save your life. You pulled the trigger and survived a sinking ship, so now is not the time to panic. Even more, you must continue to focus on the varying conditions of your suddenly new situation, remain calm, and do what must be done next. As with most life-threatening scenarios, survival at sea is all about prioritization. And, as obvious as this may sound, your very first goal is to keep from drowning. You surely didn't plan on being neck-deep in the water, but here you are, and now a new mission begins.

Survival Priorities
1. Staying afloat
2. Retaining heat
3. Avoiding sunstroke
4. Water
5. Food
6. Signaling

1. STAY AFLOAT!
You don't have to be a world-class swimmer to survive even rough seas. In fact, you could be a nonswimmer and still keep yourself afloat. If you aren't wearing a life vest, do everything in your power to locate one. If one is not available, find something that is floating and hold on.

Improvised flotation device
This is a great example of a drill that can be rehearsed during non-emergency situations, such as in a pool or while partaking in recreational swimming. This is one of the first drills taught to every new recruit in the Navy. If you have the mindset to endure, there are tools to prevent you from drowning, as long as you remain calm and think.

1. Pull off your pants and tie a knot at the end of each leg.
2. Close the zipper and button the pants at the waistband.

3. In a quick motion, while holding the pants at the waist, throw the pants over your head and dip down into the water. This action will fill the pant legs with air.

4. Keep the waist under the water. This will keep the air from escaping. Then creep up until a pant leg is under each arm. This will lift your head out of the water.

5. You do not want to tie off the waist to keep the air in the pants, as one might think necessary, but rather grasp the waistband while underwater with your hands to create the seal. Pants are not balloons, but they will hold air. You will need to repeat the above procedure as necessary, as the air trapped in the pant legs will diminish.

Survival float

If you aren't able to locate or make a flotation device, *don't panic*. This is where your physical toughness is going to pay off. Remember, you could be out here for a long time, so start conserving your energy now. Use a survival float position to help you do so.

1. Keep your face in the water and your arms and legs dangling; every time you need to take a breath, slowly lift your head out of the water while scissor-kicking once with your legs and pushing your arms together. Pushing your arms and hands together raises your body slightly above the waterline.
2. Then drop your head back facedown and relax your dangling body.
3. The key is to relax your body while getting into this position, which is sometimes referred to as a dead man's float. The longer you are able to relax and conserve energy, the better your chance of enduring.

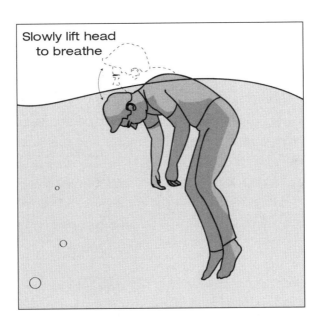

Slowly lift head to breathe

2. DON'T FREEZE

Your next priority is to fight off hypothermia. Even if you are in tropical waters as warm as 84 degrees, for example, your body's core temperature will still drop one degree for every hour you remain submerged. It only takes your core temperature's dropping two degrees for you to begin to feel the effects of hypothermia. Additionally, your body uses a lot of energy to keep warm. And if you have few or no supplies, your problem compounds.

HELP (Heat-Escape-Lessening Posture)

In addition to summoning the power of all the mental toughness you developed, you can use the **HELP** to fight against hypothermia. This is done by positioning your flotation device under you so it will lift as much of your upper body out of the water as possible. The less your body is submerged, the less effect the water will have on your core body temperature. If there are several people, then float together by tying yourselves to one another. This may not be any warmer, but there is strength in numbers.

3. DON'T MELT

You are out of the water but not out of danger. The next thing you need to think about is exposure to the sun and preventing heatstroke. (For information on treating heatstroke, see "Survival Medicine," page 305.) The warm sun may feel good on your wet body and be a welcome sight after a long night, but twelve hours later the sun will become increasingly dangerous. Wet skin will burn, and the burned skin will peel away, leaving exposed blisters and absolute misery. You need to make a canopy to block the sun. Use sheets, towels, even trash bags— the brighter the better, to reflect the sun's rays and for signaling. For example, white will contrast very well against the ocean waters, making your raft more visible to anyone searching for you.

4. GET WATER

The irony of your situation is that you are surrounded by millions of gallons of water, but you can't drink it. You may want to, but don't. Salt water will accelerate the dehydration process. Humans can live about three days without water. *You must ration what you have and gather what you can.* Do not drink any water the first twenty-four hours. You will be relatively fresh during this time, and withholding water from yourself will make your body go into a conservation mode to fight against the effects of dehydration.

Collect drinkable water

Storms are a frequent event in the oceans and seas and may be the reason you are in the situation you are in. There is, however, something good to come from them: rain. Take every opportunity to gather as much as you can, and try to keep it from becoming contaminated with salt water. Another way to produce fresh water is through use of a desalination pump or tablets. This is simply a tool that removes the salt from water, making it drinkable. However, you are unlikely to have access to these items in a dire survival scenario.

Solar still

A final solution for producing or gathering drinking water is the use of a solar still. This is done by causing salt water to evaporate, leaving the salt behind, and then collecting the condensation, which will be fresh water.

1. Get a bucket and pour several inches of salt water into it. You can also use salt-water-soaked towels or clothes.
2. Place a smaller container in the middle of the bottom of the bucket (it must be tall enough to clear the salt water).
3. Cover the top of the bucket with plastic, and make an airtight seal around the outside of the bucket.
4. Place some type of weight in the middle of the plastic wrap.

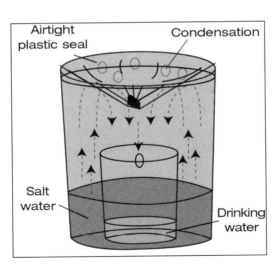

As the seawater in the bucket evaporates, leaving the salt content in the bottom of the bucket, the fresh water will condense on the plastic wrap. This freshwater condensation will drain to the lowest point of the plastic wrap (the area depressed by the weight) and drip into the container below. This is your drinkable water. It won't produce much, but it may be just enough to fight the effects of dehydration and keep you alive.

5. FIND FOOD

As we continue down the list of life-saving priorities, food becomes essential. The ocean offers a vast variety of edible solutions, from kelp to sea turtles to birds. The best and most obvious choice, however, is fish and, to a lesser extent, plankton. Some folks fish for fun, but you will be doing it to survive. You can catch fish in a number of ways.

Spear

This is the best method for catching larger fish, which will provide food for many days. However, proper use of a spear requires the most skill and consumes the most energy. Make sure you feel your chances of successfully spearing a fish are high. Spears can be made from boat hooks, gaffs, PVC pipe, or scraps from metal railings. In addition to a sharp, penetrating point, it will be helpful if your spear has a line attached to it that is fastened to your arm. Retrieving a spear can be an exhausting endeavor.

Net

Provided you have the material, this can be a very efficient way to collect not only fish but other, smaller edible forms of marine life such as plankton. Smaller fish are generally attracted to rafts. They hide under or around rafts or floating objects to naturally protect themselves from larger fish. Nets can be improvised from trash bags, clothing, even a bucket with small holes in the bottom.

Hook and line

If you have fishing line, great. If not, thin twine or even dental floss can be made to serve as fishing line. You can set out lines to wait for the fish to come to you. This is an effective way to get the food you need and expends very little of your energy. Hooks can be made from safety pins, wood, or paper clips, or anything that has a sharpened, pointed end. A small piece of food or blood-soaked cloth will provide great bait. Fishing is all about percentages, so the more hooks you have in the water, the better your chances of catching a fish.

6. SIGNAL FOR HELP

This may be your best and last chance to be rescued, so be prepared to signal at a moment's notice. Understand that based on your height and the curvature of the earth, your visual distance is only ten to fifteen miles. You may see that Coast Guard cutter or helicopter in the distance, but they won't necessarily see you.

Mirror and reflection

Mirrors, or anything that catches and reflects sunlight, can be highly effective during the day and can be seen for miles. Extend your arm toward the object that you to want to signal and make a V with your fingers. The V will act like a gun sight to make certain your reflection hits the target you want. Aim the mirror between your gun-sight fingers and point it directly at the passing ship, for example, or airplane, to ensure that your signal is noticed.

Flare or smoke

A flare at night is one of the very best forms of signaling. Smoke is used for signaling only during the day. If you use a flare, ensure that you are holding it as high as possible and away from your raft. The threat of fire is high with these items. Additionally, a fire extinguisher can be used as an improvised smoke signal.

Dye markers

Dye markers are yet another way to signal. Many of them are water activated and will produce a bright green or orange cloud in the water that can last several hours.

Raft Survival

If you are lucky enough to have a raft, you have greatly increased your chances of survival, but you are by no means out of the woods—or should we say out of the water—yet.

1. If you have just boarded the raft, immediately tie a line to you and to a part of the raft, or to someone else on the raft. If the raft flips over due to wind or waves, you will still be able to climb back into it.

2. Take the next several minutes to locate, and take a quick inventory of, the supplies you now have in the raft and anything in the area that may useful. Pay particularly close attention to brightly colored items that could be used for signaling, and to plastics or other objects that could be used for rainwater collection. This may be your last opportunity to gather these items.

3. Stay in the vicinity of your vessel's last known location. The closer you can stay to that location, the better your chance of being found, since that's where rescue efforts will begin. Therefore, you should deploy a sea anchor. This will minimize the amount your raft travels due to wind and current, and keep you closer to the original abandoned-ship site. If your raft doesn't have a sea anchor, you can make one by using line and a bucket. This will also help to steady the raft in rough seas.

NOT ROOM FOR EVERYONE?

There is a chance that your raft will not be large enough or has been damaged and can't adequately hold the entire group at once. If this is the case, you will have to place some people in the water. This must be done on a rotation. By doing this you are extending the total time for the group's survival *and* building group cohesion through shared sacrifice. Rotation time will be based on water temperature and the strength of the group. Never leave someone in the water long enough that their core temperature is significantly impacted.

Sea-Induced Delusions: "My Mind Is Playing Tricks on Me"

When you are lost at sea, your body and mind will be dealing with an exhausting environment. You will be hot, cold, thirsty, hungry, tired, and stressed. Your mental toughness is going to be pushed to the limit. You will become very aware of the usefulness of your comfort-zone exercises.

Night number four of Hell Week included the epic and unforgettable journey known as "Around the World." Basically, this is an eight-hour night paddle around Coronado Island. As you can imagine, everyone is pretty wrung out at this point, and the lull of San Diego Bay brought out the crazy in everyone. The great thing about it was that the craziness affected one man at a time, so the rest of us got to fully enjoy the show. On our boat, one of my guys thought he was Elvis but sounded more like some kind of goat with laryngitis when he sang. Another of my guys fell asleep and fell into the water. That woke him up screaming bloody murder. (Falling in the water was the last thing you wanted to do, because you would be wet for the next several hours.) As for me, I was *convinced* I saw three 747s floating in the bay ahead of us and began shouting, "*We have to get over there and see if there are any survivors!*" The hallucination lasted only about thirty seconds, and I can remember it to this day. But that night, for those thirty seconds, I was absolutely convinced the hallucination was real. Pretty entertaining.

Additionally, the ocean has other ways of tricking your mind. Because of the constant motion, you may become seasick. Do what you can to limit this, because vomiting will only accelerate dehydration. You can minimize seasickness by focusing your eyes on a fixed space in the distance, which helps you regain a sense of equilibrium. Lying down can also help to relieve symptoms. Another common effect of spending too many days at sea is hallucinations. Try to use tricks to pull the mind back to a state of reality. Perhaps recite the names of all your friends, or make lists of some kind. Given the condition and environment you are in, though, you may just need to accept these mind tricks and even try to be amused by them.

The Long Haul

As soon as you left the vessel, your mindset should have gone into a prioritizing and conserving mode: "I may be out here for a very long time." Remember this checklist:

- ❏ Stay positive.
- ❏ Occupy time with goals to keep you alive another day, such as fishing, water collection, and production.
- ❏ Conserve energy: If you're not actively doing something, then sleep.
- ❏ Inventory supplies, set ration limits, and generally conserve resources.
- ❏ Focus on achieving little victories: View each drop of water collected or each fish caught as a big deal.
- ❏ If with others, prop one another up. Stay strong as a group. Weakness or a breakdown will eventually come to each individual. It is up to the others in the group to boost them back up.

Shark Attack

Another danger you need to deal with while lost at sea is sharks. Although we like to think we are at the top of the food chain, when we are in the ocean that is no longer the case. Sharks are the masters of this environment. Although the fear of sharks, thanks to news media and films, is much greater than the chances of actually getting attacked by one, shark attacks do happen and could create a life-or-death situation. There are more than 360 species of sharks, but only a few are given to attacking humans. Most fatal encounters are caused by great whites, tiger sharks, bull sharks, and white-tip sharks.

In 2011, worldwide shark-related deaths were higher than they've been in nearly two decades. Surfers and others involved in board sports took the brunt, accounting for 60 percent of unprovoked shark attacks; swimmers were attacked 35 percent of the time; and divers accounted for 5 percent of all incidents.

MYTHS

Sharks can't smell one single drop of blood in the water from miles away, as many believe. However, a good amount of blood will surely cause sharks to congregate. Sharks are actually relatively cautious predators and will often circle their prey several times before attacking.

HOW TO PREVENT AN ATTACK

- Pay attention to warnings and be alert to reports of recent shark sightings or attacks in the area.

- Sharks are attracted to light colors that resemble fish. Cover up all skin, including arms and legs, with dark-colored clothing. Even the lighter soles of your bare feet are attractants.

- Remove any jewelry or watches that shine or reflect.

- Excessive splashing or movement will attract a shark's attention.

WHAT TO DO IF YOU'RE IN THE WATER AND YOU SEE A SHARK

1. Remain calm—your goal is obviously to get out of the water, but that is not necessarily the first thing you need to do.
2. Reduce excessive movement or splashing. Start your combat breathing: four-second inhalation, four-second exhalation. It would be a shame to die from drowning in this situation. If you start splashing wildly, you'll look more like a meal. Don't make erratic, sudden movements. This makes you look weak and wounded, which makes you more attractive-looking as prey to a shark.
3. Move away from the shark by doing a slow and steady reverse backstroke, with the bare soles of your feet downward.
4. Until you can get out of the water, keep your eye on the shark at all times. Unlike the case with dogs, this eye contact will not provoke an aggressive response. Be ready to get

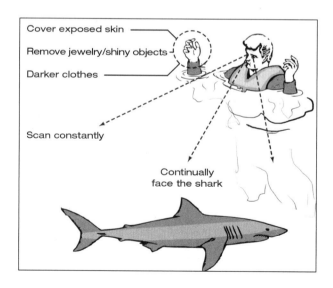

into a defensive position, but always adjust yourself so the front of your body is facing the shark. If you can put your back against a reef or drop-off in the seafloor, do so. If you are with someone else, get back-to-back, so you can see one or more sharks and defend from all directions.

5. Fight or flight: Similar to your chances of outrunning a grizzly bear, your chances of out-swimming a shark are minimal. However, unlike with a grizzly, if you play dead the shark won't care and will continue to tear you up. You have no choice in this situation—*Fight like hell!* Punch, kick, elbow, knee, and stab at anything you can, paying particular attention to the eyes, nose, and gills. If you have a spear or pole or some type of weapon at least a couple of feet long, use it to fend off the shark. The best place to poke at a shark is from the gills forward. And when you strike the shark, let them know it with the maximum amount of force.

6. Once you have made it to shore or to a boat, check yourself for injures. A shark bite is a very violent injury, and if you don't seek medical attention immediately, you could bleed out.

Several years ago while filming a show in the Bahamas, I had the opportunity to dive at Tiger Beach, which has the second-largest population of sharks anywhere in the world. On this day I saw something that has to be one of the top five experiences in my entire life. As I was squared up watching a twelve-foot tiger shark pass from left to right, the shark suddenly changed direction and swam directly toward me. Then I saw the eyelids roll back, which is a protective trait common to these sharks just prior to their attacking. Time stood still. For some reason, I had decided to take a three-foot piece of PVC plumbing pipe in the water with me, and I immediately slammed this into the nose of the approaching tiger shark. It worked. The shark swam away as the water surge from his tail pushed me back a couple of feet. That is a moment of my life forever imprinted upstairs.

LOST IN THE DESERT

If, for whatever reason, you find yourself alone and lost in the desert, know that this unique environment requires you to follow a set of survival priorities. As it is in every life-threatening scenario, the key to enduring is to know what actions to take, and in what order. In the desert your priorities, from highest to lowest, must be *shade, water,* and *shelter*. The distinctive element about surviving in the desert is that it requires you to take immediate action to secure these priorities, yet conserve energy while doing so by implementing a long-haul strategy from the outset.

Of all the environments I've had the privilege of operating in, I can tell you without hesitation that the most challenging is the desert. It is a vast and lifeless place that can reach 130 degrees in the day and drop below freezing at night. The landmark-less terrain can be a combination of sandy dunes and mountainous rock that is not only taxing to navigate but difficult to traverse, with each step a potential ankle-breaker. There is little or no shade to protect you from the abusive intensity of the sun. And if you think the slight breeze that you feel on your face is a welcome relief, just wait . . . it's actually only a warning of a monster, blinding sandstorm to follow. As you inhale and chew on sand particles, your body is screaming for something that is incredibly scarce in this place—water. Oh, and let's not forget we had assholes out there who wanted to kill us.

Survival Priorities

1. Shade
2. Water
3. Shelter

1. FIND SHADE

Getting off the X in this case means finding shade, pure and simple. During the day, you must get out of the sun and into the shade immediately. Don't spend the first hours of the first day in the blazing heat wandering around looking for a way out. Instead, seek temporary shelter.

- Get to the nearest rock outcropping or to the shady side of a dune, or an indenture in the sand, or a gully.

- First and foremost, you must cover all exposed skin, especially your face, neck, and arms. A hat will be worth its weight in gold, and a T-shirt can be pushed under the hat, so that the other end is hanging to cover your neck. If you don't have a hat, make one. Improvise, using whatever scrub brush you can find, and tie it any way you can to cover your head and neck with whatever strip of fabric you have. In the desert, any place the sun strikes is your X; it will literally cook you alive. Getting to shade and covering yourself is the first priority in this environment.

- Conserve your energy until nightfall. Once the sun goes down, that's when it's better to construct a more "permanent" shelter by rearranging rocks, if available, or digging deeper into a gully bank, or by using the shelter-construction techniques below. You need to immediately shift into a conservation or long-haul mode. You should become nocturnal; once the sun goes down, that's when your "day" starts. By doing this, you will minimize perspiration and therefore keep more of the water you have in your body.

2. LOCATE WATER

Now that you are out of the sun in a temporary shelter, the next priority is water. Without water, you won't make it more than a few miles if you attempt to travel in the heat of the day. Even lying dormant, your body will require a gallon of water every twenty-four hours; without water, you will be dead in three days. Do the following, and then use the Rule of Three to decide upon a course of action.

- Carefully examine the widest vista you can see in all directions. Look for signs that may indicate the presence of water, and narrow down your search to these areas.

- Look at the terrain and identify any areas that have vegetation or growth. An area of vegetation in the desert could have a very subtle change of color. It might have only a slightly darker or greener hue than its surroundings. This means water, since vegetation, just like humans, needs moisture to survive.

- Because gravity is a constant and will cause water to flow down, concentrate your search on lower areas like canyons or depressions. Think of areas where rainwater could collect, such as the bottom of rock formations, riverbeds, dry washes, or even a cave, should you be fortunate enough to locate one.

- Some deserts have subterranean water reservoirs lying just below the surface. Plants seemingly growing out of nowhere are tapping into underground water supplies. The roots of most desert plants will point you in the direction to dig, which is usually not very deep below the surface. You can also dig for water at the outside bends of riverbeds, but choose sites for these exploratory searches wisely, as you must conserve your energy.

- If you are in a desert with cacti, find them, because they surely have stored moisture. However, some cacti, like the barrel cactus found in the southwestern region of the United States, require effort to cut into the plant, with only a minimal return of water. Make sure you exert this physical effort to cut into a cactus only in the cool of the evening.

Example of using the Rule of Three for finding water:

1. I see green vegetation but it is at least ten miles away.
2. There are several cacti in my immediate area.
3. There is what appears to be a dry creek down the hill a mile, but the sun is still up and I would have to leave my shelter to reach it.

Solution: Work on the cacti in the immediate area. Once the sun goes down, reevaluate, with the dry creek being a priority.

Building a solar still

Another option for gathering water is the construction of a solar still. If you think you may be in the same area for some time, it is best to build this first, due to the duration of time it takes to produce water.

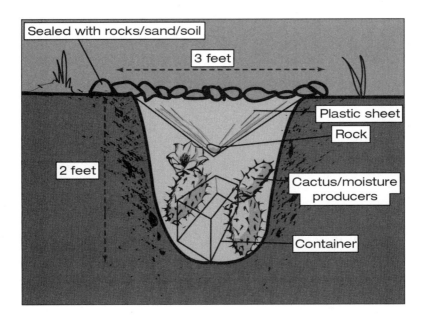

1. Dig a hole about three feet in diameter and approximately two feet deep.
2. In the middle of the hole place a container. Then cover the entire hole with plastic. If you have pieces of cactus, place them around the container.
3. Form an airtight seal around the entire hole by using rocks and sand to hold down the edges of the plastic, and in the middle of the plastic place a small rock to create a slight depression.
4. The temperature in this hole will increase due to the packed soil and the direct rays of the sun, thus causing vapors to rise and condense on the inside of the plastic sheet. Water droplets will form at the depressed part of the plastic tarp and drip into the container positioned directly below.

3. FIND SHELTER

Whether you have decided to stay put and wait for rescue or you need to be on the move, you must have shelter, which will save you from the heat of the day and the cold of the night. A cave or other natural formation is best because it will require none of your energy to utilize it. If you are not so lucky, then you have to make a shelter. Two shelter options follow below.

With both of these shelters, be alert for snakes and scorpions, which are also interested in getting out of the heat of the day. Additionally, if you decide to remove your boots or clothes, or crawl into a sleeping bag, make sure you first shake out the sleeping bag before you get into it, and shake out your boots or clothes before you get back into them. Your situation is difficult enough without adding a sting or bite to the mix.

Open Shelter

1. First, ensure the site you have chosen for your shelter is not near an insect nest or in an area of heavy defecation from desert animals, especially rodents.

2. Dig a trench approximately eighteen inches deep that is long and wide enough to lie in.

3. Cover the trench with some type of material, like a poncho or sheet. Try to raise this covering approximately two feet above the surface of the ground and secure it at each corner. This will offer decreased temperature in the shelter by providing shade while allowing air to circulate through the open sides.

4. If you have enough material, place a second layer approximately twelve inches above the first covering. By having a second layer, you will create airspace between the two layers and further decrease the temperature within your shelter and offer moderate protection from colder night temperatures.

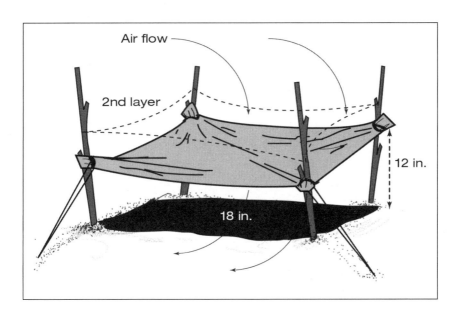

Underground Shelter

1. Again, ensure the site of your shelter is insect- and rodent-free.

2. Dig a trench approximately twenty-four inches deep that is long and wide enough to lie in.

3. Place your covering material across the top of the trench at ground level, and secure it with rocks and sand on three sides so the edges are completely covered. One of the narrower sides should be open; this is where you will get in and out.

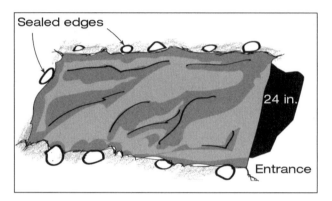

4. If you have enough material, place a second layer approximately twelve inches above the first layer. Build up a pile or make a sand wall to achieve the second level of elevation and cover the same three sides with piled sand. The air trapped in this space will provide additional insulation from the heat and likewise minimize colder temperatures at night.

Walking Out

If you believe help is not on the way, and it's up to you to get out of the desert on your own, then you need to know a few things about movement and navigation in the desert.

- Selecting your route is important. Obviously, your goal is to head toward someone or something that will get you out of this situation. It may be as simple as moving in a direction you know is populated. You could follow a streambed or trail that will ultimately get you out, as most will lead, eventually, to larger bodies of water in addition to giving you sustenance.

- Move at night and attempt to include in your route areas that can offer shelter and possibly provide water along the way.

- A compass would be an excellent tool in this situation, but if you aren't lucky enough to have one, pick a distinctive terrain feature or landmark in the distance and walk toward it. Stars can also be a great way to maintain a bearing at night, so that you don't end up walking in circles.

- Don't overestimate the distance you think you can travel. There is a very fine line that you are straddling between trying to get to safety and overexertion. Remember—*long haul*. You will eventually reach civilization or help if you follow these rules of desert survival.

LOST IN THE FROZEN MOUNTAINS

Unlike the barren desert, which has difficulty sustaining even its own vegetation, mountains readily offer everything you need to survive for months, if necessary—even during the most severe winter storms. You just need knowledge of this type of terrain, SEAL survival tools, and the will to live. As with all perilous scenarios, implementing priorities in sequential order is the key to surviving a cold-weather environment. Here, the cold is the X you must get off. You must retain your core body temperature. In this ice-and-snow-covered landscape, you can at least be thankful that you are surrounded by an abundance of water, an essential for survival, so that's one factor you have in your favor. However, exposure and hypothermia here can kill you faster than will thirst in the desert.

How you got lost and how you'll get out are issues you will deal with later. But if you suddenly get caught in a blizzard or snowstorm, you don't need to take much time doing a threat assessment—because the threat is coming down right before your eyes in the form of a lot of white stuff. Don't panic, but get immediately into action.

In the U.S., there are more than one hundred million acres of designated wilderness areas. It's estimated that nearly 40 percent of all day hikers end up getting lost for at least part of their time in national parks and wilderness areas. More than ten thousand people require search-and-rescue efforts each year.

Survival Priorities

1. Shelter
2. Fire
3. Clothing
4. Water
5. Food
6. Moving and navigation

1. FIND SHELTER

Your first priority is to get out of the cold, especially if your clothing is wet. In this environment, you have several shelter options, which I list below, providing techniques from the most basic and expedient to more advanced shelters, which could accommodate longer-term use if necessary. In each case, the first thing to do in any shelter is to **prepare the floor;** you must create a layer of insulation between you and the snowy ground. This will immediately forestall losing more body heat. Use materials abundant in the terrain, such as pine boughs, to create a padding barrier.

Natural hollows

For immediate cover, seek natural hollows, sometimes referred to as tree wells, which are ready-made shelters found at the base of snow-covered pine trees. These will offer only limited protection from the elements, but it could be just enough for you to warm up while you decide on your next step. Be careful when entering and exiting not to dislodge the snow from the overhanging branches.

Lean-to

This is a fairly simple shelter to construct. Use a series of strong branches that can serve as poles and place them diagonally and as close together as possible, which will create a space below for shelter. Try to use an existing rock formation or several trees as the vertical wall to lean the branches against. Once you have created the diagonal section, you can cover it with additional branches for greater protection below. After this slanted "roof" is fashioned, snow can be used to cover the branches for increased insulation.

Quinze (pronounced "kwinzee")

This shelter is built by piling up snow into a dome shape, then hollowing out the inside.

1. If you have backpacks or other equipment, place these together and start piling snow around and on top of them. This will reduce the amount of snow you need to dig out later. Continue piling on snow until you have a good-sized mound that covers your gear and then some, then pack it down.

2. After waiting thirty minutes for the initial layer to freeze, pile on more snow until the second layer is about three feet thick. Pack down the snow in the form of a dome and wait for it to freeze (about another hour).

3. While the dome is freezing, gather several two-foot-long sticks and push them nearly entirely into the dome at various points, aiming toward its center. These will serve as depth guides, which you'll need later.

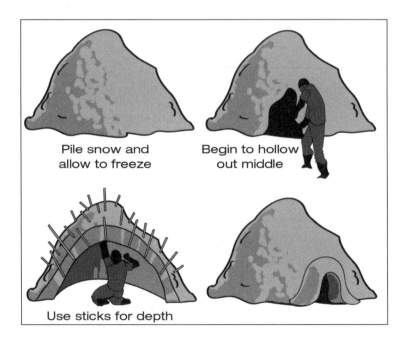

Pile snow and allow to freeze

Begin to hollow out middle

Use sticks for depth

4. At the base of the pile, begin to dig out the snow from one side, working toward the center. Carefully pull your backpacks and equipment out. Keep digging and hollowing out the center of the dome. You'll be able to see the inside and know when to stop excavating when you see the ends of the guide sticks.

5. You have just formed a quickly made igloo-shaped shelter!

Once inside, check the exterior periodically to make sure excessive amounts of heavy snow are not accumulating on the top of your shelter, which could cause it to collapse. This type of snow-mound construction could be enlarged by adding connecting dome "rooms," if you need to be sheltered for longer periods.

In 2001, a fellow SEAL and I decided to attempt a winter summit climb of Mount Rainier as a training climb for Mount McKinley, and then ultimately Everest. Things were going great until we got caught in a whiteout at eleven thousand feet. We spent the next few days in a snow cave. We had sufficient survival gear, and a small candle was enough to keep the cave's temperature at a steady 40 degrees. On top of that, we even toasted the New Year with the airline bottle of Jack Daniel's I had brought along. Talk about being prepared for the worst!

---

2. BUILD A FIRE

You are in a shelter but not out of danger. The chances are great that you are at least mildly hypothermic, especially if your clothes are wet. You need to get your body temperature back up and your clothes dry. Although this snow-and-ice-filled climate makes it more challenging to start a fire, it is still very doable. Just make sure you don't sacrifice the effort and energy you put toward making your shelter by ruining it with a fire that is too close in proximity. Fire and ice don't mix.

1. Find dry wood by breaking dead branches from nearby trees. (Branches found on the ground will be too wet.) Also,

strips of bark will be relatively dry and make a good form of kindling. Gather as many branches and as much kindling as you can on your trip from the shelter to reduce exposure.

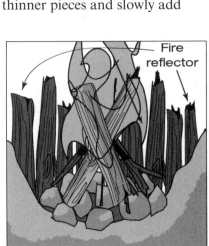

2. Dig a small pit. This will help protect your fire from wind.

3. At the bottom of this pit create a base or platform by laying rocks or logs down side by side. This will keep the fire from melting the snow and extinguishing itself.

4. As with any fire, start with the small stuff (tinder and kindling) and create a teepee-style pile with thin pieces of wood. The key is to ignite the thinner pieces and slowly add larger and thicker branches.

5. Once the fire is going, you can enclose a section of it by building a small wall with stones or ice blocks to provide more protection from wind.

6. To help retain the warmth of the fire, you can build a fire reflector behind you with logs. This will actually bounce the heat back at you from behind.

3. DRY YOUR CLOTHING

In a cold-weather environment, if you're wet, you're dead! If your clothes are wet, they are removing body heat twice as fast as if you weren't wearing any clothes at all. You need to get them off and get them dry. Place your wet clothing items a couple feet above your fire, but make sure they are not close enough to burn. You can use branches or run an improvised clothing line around and above the perimeter of your fire.

There are a number of essential items you to need bring with you when venturing into wilderness areas (see "Gear," page 295), including fire-starting devices, but if you don't have matches or a lighter, you can still start a fire. One item almost everyone takes with them is a camera. The camera lens can be used to magnify the sun. Disassemble the camera and remove the lens. When the snow stops and the sun returns, set up your tinder and teepee of twigs. Hold the lens steady on one spot until the magnified rays begin to make the tinder smolder. Gently blow on the pinpointed area while still holding the lens in place until flames ignite.

---

4. GET WATER

Given your situation, if there is anything to feel lucky about, it's that you will have plenty of water to drink. But don't just start eating snow. Not only will it take more energy from your body to melt the snow inside your mouth, it will also increase your chances of going into hypothermia. The best approach is to find clean snow and melt it before drinking, which can be done in several ways.

- A snow melter can be constructed using a large, flat stone placed at an angle above your fire. Place the snow at the upper end, and with stones, guide the water into a collector at the bottom end.

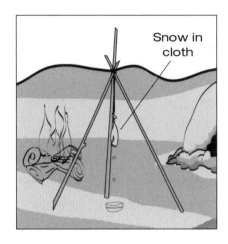

- A water maker is a framework of branches or a teepee-style construction from which a bag or cloth filled with snow is suspended. Place this near, *never directly over,* the fire. Under this bag, place a collector. As the snow melts, the water will collect below. If a shirt or cloth is used as your water maker, it will also help to filter the melted snow.

5. FIND FOOD

Animals are easy to track in a snowy environment. Start with the smaller ones first. Look for exit and entrance holes made by small animals in the snow. Use anything from wire to shoelaces to make a series of snares. This is done by tying a slipknot at one end of your material to form a loop-end slightly smaller than the diameter of the burrow hole.

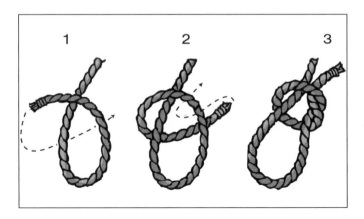

Lay the snare so that the loop encircles the burrow hole. Then anchor the other end of the line. The animal will exit the hole, and the snare will tighten around its neck. Dinner!

LICHEN

The reason that larger animals such as deer, elk, and caribou have stronger antlers in winter than during summer is so that they can dig through the ice and snow to find food, especially a type of plant called *lichen*. These plants are found in most northern zones and even grow in the Arctic tundra. Lichen grows in mats on rocks or close to the ground and comes in colors ranging from dark green to gray. Without getting into a list of various mushrooms and plants that might be edible, or are just as likely to be poisonous and kill you with one bite, lichen is generally safe to eat. But never eat it raw! Gather as much as possible and let it soak in water for at least twenty-four hours. Discard the standing water and add new snow to boil the lichen for about twenty minutes. Eskimos consider roasted lichen a delicacy.

---

6. MOVE TO SAFETY

The decision has been made, and it's time to move. Remember that you are going back out into this very dangerous, potentially deadly environment that may require you to start the list of survival priorities all over again from the beginning. That said, here are some things that will help you on your way.

Improvised snowshoes

Traveling through deep snow can be extremely difficult, with you sinking up to your chest in some cases with each exhausting step. You can make a set of snowshoes that will enable you to walk on top of the snow by gathering several pine boughs and making an

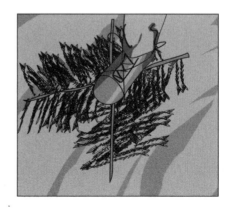

X out of them. Then place your foot over the X and tie them to your feet using rope, shoestrings, etc.

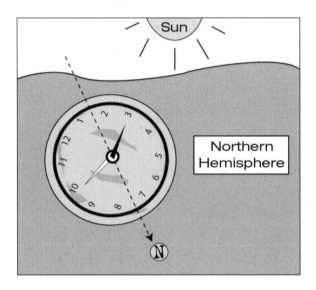

Compass: Watch method

You need direction to know where you are going and not end up walking in circles. You can figure out which way is north by using your watch. Take it off and point the hour hand at the sun. Now imagine a line halfway between the hour hand and the twelve o'clock position. In the northern hemisphere that line is south, and opposite that direction is north.

Compass: Needle and water

If you have a needle, you can make a compass. Magnetize the needle by rubbing it on a piece of silk or other cloth, which will generate a static charge. Get a blade of grass or small piece of wood and float this in a container of water, or in a puddle that is not moving. Place the magnetized needle on the float, and it will orient itself so it points north and south. Also use the sun, since it sets in a westerly direction. The sun can help to mark your bearings and determine which of the needle ends is pointing north and which is pointing south.

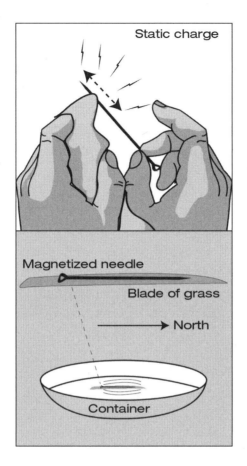

Static charge

Magnetized needle

Blade of grass

North

Container

NUCLEAR ATTACK

The chances of an all-out nuclear war, initiated by any of the world's superpowers, have diminished greatly since the prospect of instantaneous retaliation would mean global suicide. Nine countries, including the United States, China, Russia, the United Kingdom, France, Pakistan, India, Israel, and North Korea, have ballistic missiles with nuclear warheads. Only the United States, China, and Russia have weapons capable of reaching targets anywhere on the globe. Even if a full-scale assault is less likely than it was twenty years ago, however, the possibility of an isolated nuclear attack occurring in the near future is good. A nuclear bomb or even a "dirty bomb" would surely be used if certain countries or terrorist groups had the means to acquire one. If the way Iraqi insurgents killed their own women and children is any indication of the type of enemy that's out there, don't think for a minute that they'd show restraint if given the chance.

Though we use the words "isolated" and "nuclear" together, there can't really be anything isolated about a nuclear attack, since even the smallest nuclear bombs available today are many times more powerful than what was used at Hiroshima and Nagasaki. The bombs used on those cities were equal to 12,000 tons (12 kt) of TNT and killed about 300,000 people. Some modern warheads are 1,000 kt. The deaths and ruinous aftermath caused by an "isolated" nuclear incident would be far-reaching. Any nuclear weapon is absolutely a weapon of mass destruction, but a nuclear attack is a catastrophe that man can survive. Even among the vast devastation of post-blast Hiroshima and Nagasaki there were those who walked among the rubble, those who survived. With the SEAL mindset, survival is possible, even in the face of a nuclear attack—the most vicious kind of destruction we know of.

Preparedness

If you're given warning, the best place to survive a nuclear weapon's shock wave, thermal blast, and radiation is below the surface. The fireball and vacuum effects last for only minutes. But, depending on the terrain and whether the bomb exploded on the ground or in the sky above, it will set off fires miles away and will not only blind you but etch your shadow into concrete.

How It Works and How to React

A nuclear bomb's destructive power can be broken down into three parts. Without getting into the complexity of atomic physics, here is a rundown:

Immediately following the detonation of a nuclear weapon, an incredibly bright and visible ultraviolet light called the **thermal pulse,** or **"flash,"** projects out from ground zero. It may cause flash blindness, so immediately turn away from it and drop to the ground or get behind a wall or other strong cover. Nearly simultaneously, there is a discharge of **thermal heat,** which, at the epicenter, for the first few moments reaches temperatures of tens of millions of degrees. Anything within range and engulfed in this thermal fireball will be vaporized.

Following the thermal pulse will be the **blast wave,** which is the outward burst of air from the explosion. This will collapse structures and immediately burst lungs. The blast wave is strong enough to send a person, car, or even buildings blowing away at a speed of three hundred miles per hour. An **electromagnetic pulse (EMP),** which disables all unshielded electronics within approximately a three-mile radius of ground zero, is created by a nuclear explosion when air around the blast ionizes. Don't expect to use vehicles, phones, computers, or anything non-mechanical after the explosion.

The third destructive component is the **alpha, beta, and gamma radiation** emitted from the bomb, which poses the greatest threat to those not annihilated by the initial blast. The explosion has sent toxic radioactive particles into the air. Eventually these radioactive particles will float back down, resembling snowfall. This toxic snowfall is called **fallout** and comes in three types of particle radiation. Alpha and beta are relatively weak forms that normally require inhalation and skin contact to harm you. Gamma rays are the most dangerous and can pass directly through the body, killing cells, which can become life-threatening after prolonged exposure. There is no way to neutralize the effects of gamma rays once you've been exposed to high doses, and death is forthcoming within about six to seven weeks. Only a dense physical barrier made of solid materials will shield you from lethal radiation.

Now that I have your attention on the devastation such weapons can cause, you may understand better why we go to war or do whatever is necessary to keep these weapons out of the wrong hands. You will need to take prompt action, be at maximum mental toughness, and be physically prepared to survive a nuclear attack.

In terms of prevention, the U.S. government has stockpiled two drugs for radiological emergencies: potassium iodine and a product called Prussian blue. The latter is sold over the counter under the name

Radiogardase. These products can reduce some effects of radiation exposure. Keep Radiogardase and **potassium iodine** in your house. You certainly won't be able to find any *after* a nuclear strike.

MATERIALS THAT REDUCE GAMMA RAYS TO A ONE-IN-ONE-THOUSAND CHANCE OF CONTAMINATION:

Steel that is six inches thick.

A rock barrier that is two to three feet thick.

Concrete that is two feet thick.

An underground trench with a soil roof at least three feet thick.

An ice shelter that is seven feet thick.

A wooden barrier that is eight feet thick.

A tree well (a natural gap created by the branches of trees in snow-laden regions) is a ready-made shelter, given that it can provide roughly twenty feet of snow above you as a barrier.

Surviving the Blast Wave

There are really only a couple of things you can do once you see the thermal pulse, but they are important. If you survive the blast, you will have a decent chance of making it through this alive, but realize this is far from over.

1. Before the blast wave hits you, make sure you are lying on the ground, legs crossed, facing away from the blast.
2. Keep your mouth open so the concussion of the blast doesn't blow your lungs out; a closed mouth allows the pressure to become trapped and will turn your lungs into exploding balloons.

Radiation: Deciding Whether to Run or Shelter In

So you have survived the detonation of a nuclear weapon, which is absolutely amazing. Now you have to decide if you are going to try to outrun the radioactive fallout that will begin to settle back all around, or shelter in. If you are going to try to outrun the fallout, understand that you will probably be *actually* running, since nothing electronic will work.

RUN

Find out which way the wind is blowing. Travel in a direction perpendicular (90 degrees) to that direction, and you will get out of the path of the fallout the fastest. Depending on wind speed, and the magnitude of the weapon, it's estimated that you need to be at least thirty miles from the blast to get clear of the most lethal dosages of radiation, which is measured in **REMs.**

A breakdown of typical exposure:

- 3,000 REMs at thirty miles from the blast;
- 900 REMs at ninety miles (900 REMs causes death in two to fourteen days);
- 300 REMs at 160 miles (300 REMs can harm nerve cells, the digestive tract, and cause temporary hair loss);
- 250 miles from the epicenter reduces damage from radiation exposure to non-permanent levels.

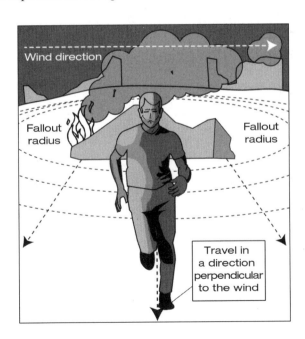

SHELTER IN

The ideal choice for a shelter is a subterranean concrete bunker, equipped with a filtered-air system and stocked with supplies. Russia has about eight thousand functioning public shelters that could house 11 percent of its population, with five thousand additional ones under construction. China is suspected to have more. Switzerland has enough **fallout shelters** to protect its entire population. In the United States, many buildings in urban areas were retrofitted to serve as fallout shelters during the 1960s. Many of the old placards can still be seen on some buildings, but most have not been maintained or regularly stocked with supplies. There are a number of fully functioning locations designed for government officials and military personnel, providing self-sufficient survival in excess of 30 months. The locations are classified.

1. Try to get into a commercial building (brick or concrete) with a basement. If you live in a house with a basement or an apartment building with a basement, get to the lowest level below ground.

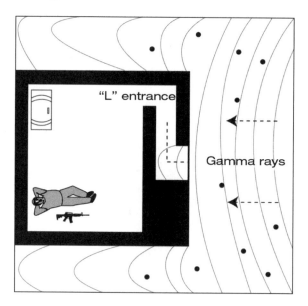

2. If the commercial building doesn't have a basement, move to the highest floor but remain two floors from the roof. For

example, in a twelve-story building move to the tenth floor. This will give you the greatest distance from the fallout on the ground but keep you away from the fallout that settles on the roof. Remember to turn off any ventilation, such as air-conditioning.

3. To protect yourself from the gamma rays, build a structure around you by using filing cabinets, books, desks, and doors. Gamma rays can't turn corners, so make an L-shaped entrance to your structure and stay low.

If outdoors, get to a ravine or ditch, inside a cave—even burying yourself under snow will offer some protection. If you have the time, dig a hole at least six feet deep and as wide, and make a roof of corrugated metal that can be covered with soil. Soil absorbs radiation easily, and this will prevent the initial and most dangerous and lethal radiation from entering your body.

Aftermath of the Blast

Unless you have a Geiger counter, there is no way to measure radiation. It is invisible and has no odor or taste, but it's there. Time to decontaminate.

1. Wash your body thoroughly with salted water, or soap and water.
2. If you have no water, use uncontaminated cloth or even newspaper and gently brush off any fallout, being careful not to rub it into your body. Another option is to use soil to absorb radiation on your skin by sprinkling it on all parts of your body. You must use soil that was well belowground during the blast, or you will only contaminate yourself further.
3. Dispose of the clothing you had on during the blast. Wrap these in plastic and get them out of the area.
4. Stay put. If you are in an adequate shelter, you should not leave it for a minimum of seventy-two hours. After that point, 90 percent of the radiation from the fallout will have

lost its potency. If you are able to shelter in longer, stay put. During this time the irradiated particles of the blast will still be blowing in the atmosphere.

5. Venture out for one hour a day, and slowly increase the time to two to three hours outside at the end of four weeks.

6. Consider all water from lakes, ponds, and reservoirs to be contaminated. All fresh food will also be contaminated if it was merely wrapped in plastic, although canned foods should be safe to eat.

PANDEMIC

A pandemic is a global epidemic or the spread of contagious and infectious disease across huge swaths of the population. Humankind has dealt with these before. The bubonic plague, or "Black Death," of the Middle Ages is believed to have originated in China in around 1330 A.D. By 1347 it had spread via trade routes throughout Europe, and it eventually killed a staggering twenty-five million people, or one-third of the known world's population. The disease originated from rat fleas. The "Spanish flu," at the turn of the twentieth century, killed more than half a million Americans in a few months and is now thought to be similar to SARS, commonly known as "bird flu," which is a viral respiratory illness caused by a coronavirus. Health departments are on high alert for any suspected contagion. Unlike the days when it took years to spread diseases along trade routes, with our modern transportation systems, global infestation can occur within days.

Situational Awareness

It's important to be alert to warnings issued by health officials, but you must also know how diseases spread in order to avoid them. Knowledge and preparation are always vital parts of any arsenal. There are three main methods of transmission.

The Ebola virus is one of the most feared pathogens on earth and has the ability to wipe out the entire population of the planet within ninety days. Its incubation period is two days, with nearly zero signs of symptoms. After exposure you may experience a slight headache and minor queasiness in the stomach. On or about the second day after infection, a person will bleed from every orifice—mouth, nose, ears, sphincter, and even the eyes—accompanied by bursts of projectile vomiting containing parts of their internal organs. One good thing about this virus: It can only be transmitted by direct contact with an infected person's blood or secretions.

FOMITE

This means that contagions can spread via objects, everything from clothing, furniture, doorknobs, and handrails to soap. Depending on the type of virus or other infection and the object that it is on, potency can remain at full strength from twelve to forty-eight hours. People will get ill after touching the infected objects, then transmit the pathogen by rubbing their eyes, ears, or mouth.

DROPLETS

The fastest and most effective way diseases are spread is when the disease is transmitted in bodily fluids by coughing, sneezing, or even talking to someone too closely. The virus is alive and active in droplets of saliva and mucus. A sneeze can exit the nose at an amazing 90 mph and disperse more than sixteen million germs over a radius of twenty-five feet. A five-minute conversation with someone can produce more than three thousand virus-packed droplets.

SPORES

Some diseases are transmitted by spores, which are lighter than air. When the virus is attached to spores, or is itself in spore form, simply breathing in infected air will spread the disease.

Preventing Infection

Limiting contact is the most obvious and commonsense way to avoid disease. Get in the habit of utilizing the following checklist, until it becomes habit:

- ❏ Use a tissue to cover both nose and mouth if you sneeze or cough, and dispose of it properly, preferably in a plastic bag that can be tied and sealed. Don't get others sick.
- ❏ Wash your hands often with soap and water. If soap and water are not available, use an alcohol-based hand rub or disinfectant wipes.
- ❏ Use any type of bleach wipes to clean objects that you frequently put near your face, like a cell phone. Also use them to wipe down shopping-cart handles, for example, or other such objects touched by the general public.
- ❏ If you have a habit of touching your eyes, nose, or mouth with your hands, stop it. These are the most common pathways for infection.
- ❏ During alerts, employ social distancing. Avoid crowds and close contact with sick people.

Pandemic in Effect

The effects of the disruption of a food or supply chain can be as bad as or worse than the actual disease present when it comes to survivability. As mentioned, be aware that if a pandemic strikes and is officially labeled as such by the government, orders will be issued to cancel all public events, and except for medical or law enforcement personnel, citizens will be mandated to remain indoors. Compulsory orders for isolation will be the government's first course of defense. You must be prepared to remain self-sufficient. Unfortunately, the situation can last anywhere from several days to several months. If enough forewarning is given, try to stockpile essential items. Make a list of all things you normally need each week, then multiply by ten.

Of course, there will be no going out to the supermarket once the pandemic hits, and you may be without power. A sufficient supply of nonperishable foods, water, and prescription medication should be the first things on your list. You should also have a portable, single propane-fueled burner to boil water for drinking and to provide minimal cooking needs.

MINIMUM FOOD ESSENTIALS

The average adult needs 1,800 calories a day. This can be accomplished for three months with the following nonperishable items:

- Twenty pounds of rice for needed carbohydrates.
- Three gallons of canola oil for needed fat.
- One hundred six-ounce cans of tuna fish for protein.

Think of the requirements both for physical well-being and to counteract the psychological effects of long-term isolation. Those who practiced hardening up will be able to deal with a dramatic reduction of normal amenities. To fully prepare your dwelling and stockpile all the necessary supplies, check government lists issued by FEMA and other organizations that itemize the supplies needed for long-term isolation. In such emergencies, those who hesitate will go without.

If you failed to previously stockpile the above items and are forced to venture out to seek supplies, understand that there will be a lot of very scared and desperate people on the streets doing the same thing, some of whom will undoubtedly be infected with the virus or bacterial pathogen. In addition to all of the previous instructions, keep in mind that you may need to fight to get and keep your supplies. Do what you can to maintain distance from those around you. Once you return from your supply run, wipe everything down with bleach wipes and place what you've gathered in the sun. The UV rays will damage the virus's DNA, killing anything still on the surface.

Among the more difficult missions SEALs perform are reconnaissance/surveillance ops. These require tremendous discipline: little sleep, no movement, no noise, eating only MREs (meals ready to eat), and the occasional shit/piss in a container (pack it in, pack it out—we were never here). Five days of this, and you are absolutely wiped out. So imagine three months of a similar existence, and you will come to understand the concept of mental toughness. Practice it now—it will keep you alive.

Your Crew

Now that you are indoors, keep a very close eye on one another. Someone who has been infected may not show symptoms for three to six days but will still be contagious. This group you are with is considered the **safety group.** Until the all-clear has been given, these should be the *only* people you interact with. Anyone outside that group, like a next-door neighbor, has the ability to infect the group. Again, maintain your isolation and social distancing. If someone in your unit is noticeably sick, then they have to be contained for the greater good of the whole. This will be a tough call if your crew is your family, even though expulsion of the sickened individual from the sheltered environment would, in reality, be the best call. You could, instead, try creating a secondary isolation room within the shelter for those loved ones or members of your team you find impossible to send off.

When You're the Sick One

If you are sick with symptoms of the pandemic, isolate yourself for at least twenty-four hours, especially if you have a fever. The World Health Organization recommends having the drugs Tamiflu and Relenza on hand, which are used to treat many flulike illnesses; these antiviral drugs could kick in to offer some resistance. If you put on a respirator, trying to protect those around you, make sure it's a mask without a valve, because otherwise it will not filter the infected air you exhale. Don't let anyone use your utensils or linens. In the event the pandemic has reached monumental portions and your chances of recovery are nil, make a decision about whether or not you should leave the safe shelter. If you're grouped with family, for example, they will likely protest your departure. However, bravery comes in many forms; if you stay, not only will you die, but you'll likely infect those you love.

Sickroom

When someone gets sick, it's important to isolate them from the rest of the group. The best thing to do is to choose a corner room that will be the designated **sickroom.** If you have power, place a box fan in a window facing outward so that it pushes the air out of the room. This will create a negative-pressure room that will pull good air in from the house and push the contaminated air outside. Next, seal all of the other windows and doors in the room. Use precut plastic for each window and seal with tape. Don't forget the gaps at thresholds. Cover air-conditioner and heater vents. Finally, you will still need to care for the sick, so create a double barrier at the entry of this room, enabling you to enter and exit while maintaining isolation. This can be done by hanging two sets of trash bags or shower curtains from the ceiling above the door, which will drape down all the way to the floor. You want to fasten these plastics sheets or trash bags so that the door, doorframe gaps, and threshold are all covered. When entering or leaving the room, you will travel through only one set of barriers at a time.

Homemade Protective Gear

When you must have contact with the sick, make sure you limit your exposure. Additionally, you need to wear a protective suit that can be made from items in the house. Start by putting on long sleeves and long pants. Place a rain poncho or several trash bags over the top. A shower cap will protect the head and hair, and the use of dishwashing gloves will protect the hands. Wear a mask or a rag that has been sprinkled or minimally dipped in bleach before you slowly enter the room. Don't drench the mask in bleach because concentrated chlorine fumes could be harmful. Yet, this will offer a good barrier from inhaling contagions. Again, minimize the exposure time, and just prior to leaving the room, wipe down with bleach wipes anything that could have touched the victim.

SIX FEET UNDER

The colloquialism for burial "six feet under" refers to the measurement of depth that is supposed to be ideal for properly burying a body, though six feet is actually excessive. Covering a body with three feet of earth is sufficient to halt the spread of disease, even if, at this shallower depth, there is a chance that scavenger dogs or animals might reexpose the corpse. The Vikings and a number of Native Americans placed the dead on raised platforms and then covered them with soil, primarily for religious beliefs. Nevertheless, the contagions emitted by a decaying body on a raised platform are less harmful than merely covering the body with a heap of stones, for example. During a pandemic, it would take too much time exposed to the environment to dispose of bodies in deep graves. In any regard, the site for the burial should be at the farthest point from the dwelling or safe house, and not near wells or potential water supplies. Determining the farthest point would be dependent on where you lived, and how safe it was to venture from your safe house. If you lived in a Brooklyn row house with a backyard, for example, it would still be better to bury the body at the farthest point from the house than to dig a grave in the basement.

Handling the Dead

Unfortunately, with a disaster as widespread as future pandemics are predicted to be, there will be a very high mortality rate. Morgues will be maxed out, and places like ice rinks and refrigerated warehouses will be used for dead body storage. If your sick friend has passed away, you are going to have to deal with the body. A dead body can't be left to decompose, because the bacteria can cause health problems for everyone else. Wrap the body in plastic and move it to a location far away from you. Wear as much protective gear as you have available before doing so. Bury the body at a depth of six feet if you can, but at least three feet if that's not possible. Mark the grave site for possible future identification and/or services. As mentioned above, if the victim was killed by a disease as contagious as the Ebola virus, cremation would be the only option to halt the spread of the infection.

RIOTS AND STAMPEDES

Riots are any unruly acts of civil unrest caused by an assembled group that result in violence against people and property. Riots can start with an organized call to assemble to protest perceived grievances or to express opinions, though they can suddenly turn disorderly for any number of reasons. Sometimes riots begin as a seemingly spontaneous outpouring of people onto the streets, though signs of potential trouble simmer for some time before it boils over into violence. However, once an organized march, for example, transforms into a violent and uncontrollable mob, another dynamic takes over, which some refer to as "herd mentality." A mob creates its own whirlpool and rapidly draws others into acting aggressively or rebelliously.

Leadership can get bystanders to step up in a positive way, but negative behavior is even more contagious. One person throws a garbage can through a plate-glass window, and like a match dropped into a crate of ammunition, the situation explodes as others follow and a riot is born. There are no rules in a riot; it is an example of humanity without laws, where robbery, assault, and manslaughter are committed openly.

Situational Awareness
As mentioned, civil unrest does not spring up overnight. Be alert to social issues that are creating a ripple of controversy in your community, especially ones that seem to stir up emotions.

BOSTON MASSACRE

An event that had a significant impact on America's formation was the result of a riot. The colonists felt unfairly treated for many years, but this resentment came to a head in March 1770. A crowd of sixty had gathered around a customs house. After someone in the crowd threw a snowball at British soldiers on guard duty, the sentries pointed their rifles at the protesters and fired. Eleven Americans were wounded and five killed.

In the age of instantaneous news coverage, topics that could cause massive civil disobedience are widely broadcast. Don't ignore bad news. Although you may think it less stressful to focus on the latest happenings among celebrities or spend most of your time chatting electronically with friends, survival in the modern world requires a measure of due diligence. Keep informed of organized rallies, especially those designed for protest. Make a note of locations where these activities are planned. Remember, the site of a protest might be the epicenter of a riot, although once anarchy sets in, there is no limit to how far it could spread.

- Be alert to social issues.

- Stay informed and note the location of protest rallies.

- Know if the roads or streets you plan to travel will intersect with areas ripe for a potential civil disturbance.

- Check to see if commuter lines, subways, or bus routes you use will put you in contact with these areas.

- Avoid these areas and know alternate evacuation routes that will get you away from the places where disturbances are most likely to occur. But remember, anarchy has no defined boundaries, so also study evacuation routes that encompass a large radius from the areas in which trouble is likely to brew.

SOME AMERICAN RIOTS

In 1863, President Lincoln passed the nation's first draft law, yet allowed a person to be excluded if he made a payment of $300 or hired a replacement, both of which were something only the rich could afford. What was called the Draft Riots ensued, leaving a thousand dead. The worst labor riot was the Great Railroad Strike of 1877, when hundreds of thousands of workers went on strike in twenty-six states, seeking better wages. In Philadelphia and Baltimore, these protests turned into riots, which left a death toll of nearly eighty. In 1937, a protest by striking Republic Steel workers killed ten and wounded 211. Race riots took place in 1965, when six days of rioting in the Watts section of Los Angeles left at least thirty-four people dead and more than a thousand injured. In 1966, in Chicago, two were killed and sixty-five injured in rioting. In 1967, Newark's riots resulted in twenty-three dead and 725 injured. Simultaneously, five days of violence in Detroit killed forty-three and injured 324. Seven thousand people were arrested, thirteen hundred buildings were destroyed, and twenty-seven hundred businesses were looted. In April of 1968, again in Chicago, rioting left nine dead. In 1992, when four Los Angeles police officers were acquitted of using excessive force against a black motorist, the Police Protest Riot erupted. Riots surged, killing fifty-three people and injuring two thousand. Three thousand six hundred fires erupted, bringing four thousand National Guardsmen. There was $1 billion in damages.

If You Are in a Riot

One of our constitutional freedoms is the right to peacefully assemble, and you could be part of a rally or march, for example, to voice your opinion. However, be exceptionally alert to the mood among the crowd. Riots stem from emotional responses, whether they're based on ethnic, political, or financial unrest. If you are part of a rally or march, try to limit your participation by remaining on the flanks or at the perimeter of the crowd. If the situation turns riotous, you want to have evacuation routes. Check a map of where the planned protest or rally will occur and be familiar with landmarks, streets, and environmental factors; know potential spots where you could get boxed in.

Riot police often use tear gas to break up crowds. Tear gas is made of chemical compounds called lachrymatory agents, which aren't actually gases but solids or liquids that are dispersed by aerosolized pressure. Riot police deliver it via grenades or with the chemicals loaded into blank shotgun cartridges. It causes painful irritation to the mucus membranes of the eyes, nose, mouth, and lungs. It produces tears, temporary blindness, and gagging in those exposed to it. The stuff works! I had the opportunity to be reminded of this several times during training. The odd thing is that each time I got doused, it hurt a little less. Either I was building up a resistance to it, which can happen, or I was prepared for what it would feel like. Flushing your eyes with salted water dilutes the effects, in addition to washing exposed skin with soap and water. Those with asthmatic conditions may need immediate medical attention and the administration of oxygen.

Get Off the X

It doesn't take much to start a riot, and one violent action, or an action perceived to be such by the police, could happen at any time. If you find yourself in the front and see a wall of riot police ahead, know the situation has escalated to one of high danger. Immediately move in the opposite direction. Stay on your feet and crouch low. Expect tear gas, rubber bullets, and any number of tools used by law enforcement to disperse crowds.

- Don't get boxed in; stay at the perimeter of crowds.
- Be alert to emotional levels in the crowd.
- Watch for signs of violence.
- If confronted by police, raise your arms; open your hands to demonstrate you have no weapons or threatening objects.
- Gain distance from the unrest.
- Stay on your feet and crouch low, and move in the opposite direction.

If You Live in an Area Where Riots Are Occurring

As mentioned, rioting has no boundaries. You could find that your house is in the path of this unrest. The best way to avoid getting caught up is to shelter in. Use the following checklist to know what to do in a riot or during the aftermath of any catastrophe when lawlessness prevails.

1. Stay indoors.

2. Paint on the front door or on the outside of your house a warning that the occupant is armed, even if you are not. Simply write: "Occupant is armed." This will usually deter the opportunists who take advantage of riots for purposes of looting.

3. Do not expose yourself, such as by sitting on your front porch with a shotgun in your lap.

4. Barricade doors and windows using plywood or heavy furniture.

5. When sufficiently barricaded indoors, move to an upper floor, if possible. If your house is breached, you want to be

in a position where the intruders have only one way to get to you. This is called creating a choke point. This will give you an advantage in defending yourself against a larger number of intruders.

6. Stay put. Wait for order to return before venturing out.

Stampedes

During a riot, getting trapped in a stampede and being killed by a fleeing crowd is very possible. The actual cause of death during a stampede is frequently **asphyxiation,** when those trapped in the melee are literally smothered under a sea of humans. Others are crushed or suffer broken necks.

If a fire breaks out at a theater, or if some emergency ensues at a stadium event, you will not have much time to act. Upon entering the stadium, practice your situational awareness exercises, knowing where all exits are located and the most likely passageways where human congestion could occur. In such a scenario, the marked exits may not be the best choice for evacuation. Once again, the herd mentality takes over in a stampede. Even though you might be among a crowd, panic sets off the "every man for himself" mindset. You need to distance yourself and not get swept up in the very powerful force that a crowd of human beings can create.

Immediate Actions

1. Do everything in your power to stay on your feet.

2. Don't immediately head for exits; find a safe spot and try to buy some time. The initial rush of people will be like a tidal wave hitting these small exits. Too many bodies, not enough space.

3. Avoid aisles and hallways. For example, in a stadium, finding a path by climbing from seat row to seat row could be a better route.

4. Do not try to fight against the forward motion or the direction of the stampede. You have a better chance heading toward the perimeter by working to break through the crowd diagonally.

5. Gain distance from the crowd.

6. Find a barricade that will not be overturned and wait behind it or under it until the crowd passes.

7. Try to get to the high ground. On the streets, this could be standing on a car roof, or in a stadium, make your way to the higher levels.

The worst U.S. stampede happened on December 30, 1903, at Chicago's Iroquois Theater, when smoke was spotted onstage. With only one exit, 602 died in the stampede to flee. Another stampede stemming from a fire took 492 lives at Boston's Cocoanut Grove Night Club in 1942. The most recent U.S. stampede occurred in February 2003, when 21 people died in Chicago at the E2 nightclub trying to exit from the second floor. Security guards allegedly used pepper spray on a patron, which resulted in a rush for the stairwell. Abroad, death by stampede occurs more frequently, oftentimes at sporting events. For example, in 2003, 125 people died when 70,000 soccer fans tried to flee a Ghana stadium. Someone threw a bottle onto the field, and the police fired tear gas into the stands.

ROAD RAGE: DEFENSIVE AND EVASIVE DRIVING

Road rage is a relatively new phenomenon; the term was coined in the 1980s to describe aggressive confrontations among motorists. Attribute it to factors of the modern world, including previously unheard-of levels of traffic congestion, more miles driven, and the daily stress of multitasking. In addition, there is the human tendency to fight for territorial rights—although most of the "tough guys" doing this would react quite differently if they weren't in the safety of their cars.

Drivers have been assaulted with everything from guns to water bottles, hamburgers, and used diapers. Aggressive drivers frequently tailgate as a means to get the car ahead of them to speed up or get out of their way. They will move into your lane and the very lane space you occupy, weaving in with only an inch to spare. Such drivers like to yell, smash their steering wheels with their fists, swear, use hand gestures, and honk their horns.

During the last seven years, out of all 290,000 people who died in traffic accidents, 45,200 of those deaths were directly related to aggressive driving.

Mental Toughness

The automobile is a powerful machine, and a driver's license is a privilege that expects you to be responsible while operating a vehicle. Even small fender benders result in hassles and a loss of time, but a serious car accident could be life-changing, rendering you or someone else disabled or dead. While on the road you have the choice of whether you will control your emotions and let it go or become enraged and possibly take a life. Letting go requires a high degree of mental toughness. Admittedly, the art of letting it go is one that I have not yet entirely mastered. There have been more than a few times when I have implemented combat breathing to bring the agitation meter back down.

Understand that the split-second decisions you make while driving affect not only you but everyone around you. The simple act of tailgating a teenage driver, as a form of retaliation for his cutting you off, could quickly compound into a mass-fatality accident. Inhale four seconds, exhale four seconds . . . let it go.

Defensive Driving: Expect the Worst

Let's face it: There surely seem to be more bad drivers on the road than good ones, which only adds to the necessity of being an extra-diligent driver. Don't forget that car accidents are the number one cause of accidental deaths in America. Defensive driving is the combination of situational awareness and utilizing a set of driving skills. You need to be aware of not only the environment and the road ahead, but what's happening behind you and to your sides. In SEAL team we said that while driving you need to keep your head on a swivel. In addition, you must anticipate dangerous situations and be prepared to respond without hesitation to the carelessness or recklessness of others.

DEFENSIVE DRIVING CHECKLIST

❑ Scan the road ahead and plan for the unexpected.
❑ Have an eye on any and every vehicle's signals, brake lights, and indicators of inattentive drivers, such as cars drifting from lanes.
❑ Keep control of your speed. Don't drive too fast or too slowly.
❑ Expect other drivers to make mistakes, and be prepared to react.
❑ Be aware of special road and weather conditions.
❑ Avoid "car bunches." That's when moving cars are bottle-necked, although going at regular speed and occupying all lanes.
❑ While driving behind larger vehicles, keep your line of sight clear.

❑ Scan the road for any bicycles, motorcycles, pedestrians, potholes, and animals.

❑ Always maintain an exit route by keeping at least a two-second gap from the vehicle in front of you and space on both sides of your vehicle. Never drive in someone's blind spot.

The last tip above is the most important when it comes to defensive driving. By maintaining distance from other vehicles you give yourself time and options in avoiding and reacting to potentially hazardous situations and events.

Being the driver, or "wheelman," was one of my favorite aspects of the work I did overseas. I learned how to drive when I was six years old and have loved it ever since, and I am a terrible passenger. Tactical driver training at several facilities in the U.S. was a requirement for my job. There is no better time than taking someone else's car and driving the wheels off it, only to have another one waiting for you when it breaks. High-speed driving on the tarmac of an airfield or racetrack in a souped-up Ford Crown Victoria was a hell of a good time. It is a whole different deal when you are driving a ten-thousand-pound armored Mercedes in Indian country. Still fun, but different.

Evasive Driving

There could be a time when you need to implement aggressive and high-speed driving techniques because you are being purposefully pursued, and stopping is not an option. Taking flight in a vehicle is a risky scenario. You are attempting to drive a very heavy object at a high rate of speed, which doesn't afford the same time to make decisions, yet each move has serious ramifications if you make the wrong choice. The foundation for evasive driving is to know the vehicle you are driving: how it handles, turns, brakes, and accelerates. Factors such as how the vehicle handles weight transfer, which means how the vehicle responds to a quick turn from left to right, must be known. In this case, will the car "understeer" (front end gives way or skids in a turn) or "oversteer," meaning that the rear end gives way or spins out during a turn. The better you know your vehicle, the more effective you will be behind the wheel.

BASIC TECHNIQUES FOR A HIGH-SPEED CHASE

The one who survives a high-speed car chase isn't usually the fastest; it's the one who doesn't crash. And action is often faster than reaction, so when someone is pursuing you, allow them to get close to you, and then make a last-second turn. This can also be performed on a highway by taking an exit in the same fashion.

❏ Ocular driving: Your eyes need to be focused *ahead* on where you want to go—e.g., not on the turn you finished making, but instead aimed at the next one ahead. Remember that at high speeds, if you are looking at it, you will go there, be it the next turn or into the tree that caught your attention.

❏ Hands need to be at four o'clock and eight o'clock, versus the standard two-and-ten hand position. Shuffle them; never cross.

❏ Immediate avoidance: This is performed by quickly turning the steering wheel ninety degrees, followed by immediately returning it to its original position.

❏ Use maximum effective braking, or what's called "threshold braking." Know how quickly your car will come to a straight-line stop without locking up the wheels. Practice this turn, or any of the above suggestions, in an isolated parking lot or in a safe clearing until you know how get the brakes to the point when they will not lock and you are able to still maintain control of the vehicle. If you have ABS (antilock brakes), this system will do all the work for you. Just keep the pedal pressed. (Don't pump the brakes on an ABS vehicle!)

ADVANCED TECHNIQUES

The following advanced techniques require a very high level of skill. Seek professional instruction before performing any of these.

EMERGENCY BACKING: Y- AND J-TURNS

You have been cut off and have to reverse out. Get off the X.

Y-turn technique

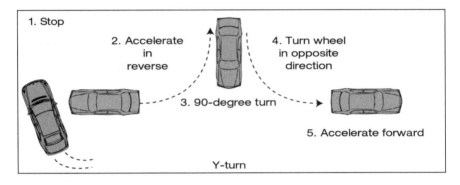

1. With your left hand on the steering wheel at the twelve o'clock position and your right arm over the passenger seat, look over your right shoulder and begin accelerating in reverse.
2. When able, reduce speed and turn the vehicle 90 degrees as you come to a full stop.
3. Turn the steering wheel in the opposite direction and drive forward.

J-turn technique

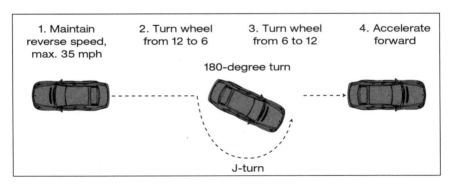

1. Maintain speed in reverse, but do not exceed 35 mph. With your left hand at the twelve o'clock position on the steering wheel, quickly turn the wheel so your hand moves to the six o'clock position.
2. Just before the car has rotated 180 degrees, turn the steering wheel back to its original position.
3. Immediately put the car in Drive or another forward gear and hit the accelerator.
4. If this is done properly the vehicle will, in a fairly smooth transition, have gone from reverse to forward on the same track.

Barricade Breaching

If you are approaching a vehicle barricade consisting of a car or a truck parked broadside to block your path, and reversing out is not an option, then employ this technique:

1. Slowly approach the vehicle barricade. Once you are within fifteen feet, hit the accelerator.

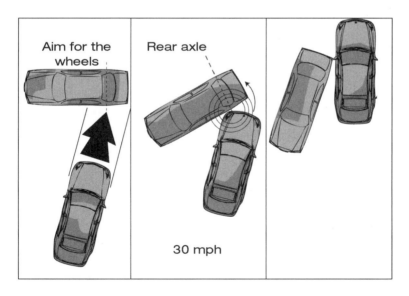

2. Strike the barricade vehicle at the wheels (front or rear). This is where the axles are. Hitting the barricading vehicle

at these spots will cause the vehicle to move and not fold toward you to potentially trap you. Even if you are in a compact car and a truck is barricading you, your 3,500-pound smaller car doing 30 mph and aimed at the wheels will be forceful enough to pivot the truck out of the way.

3. Continue to accelerate, and the vehicle you hit will clear your path to the left or right, depending on which axle you struck.

4. Understand that your air bags may deploy as a result of this technique, so keep your hands at four o'clock and eight o'clock and your head back against the headrest.

Being Rammed

If you find yourself in a situation where you are being struck by a vehicle, understand the most vulnerable place on a car is the side doors. This provides the least amount of protection for driver and passenger. The goal is to keep your car moving longer than that of the person who is chasing or ramming you. Ideally the rear of your car will take the brunt of the impact.

1. Maneuver to try to keep your pursuer directly in the middle of your rearview mirror.

2. Slam on the brakes occasionally to disrupt their attempts at passing you, and thereby getting to your vulnerable driver or passenger doors.

3. Be aware that the pursuer may attempt a PIT maneuver, which is used to spin a car by impacting the quarter panel just behind the rear wheels. Don't let them. If they attempt this, steer in the opposite direction and accelerate.

Passenger-side Driving: "Driver down"

There may be a situation in which you are the passenger in a car, and the driver has for whatever reason become incapacitated and unable to drive. Use the following technique when stopping is not an option.

1. Immediately slide over and take control of the steering wheel and accelerator.
2. Position yourself on the lap of the driver and use your left arm to make yourself stable while steering with the right.
3. If you are in the backseat, the same can be done from over their shoulders. You will, however, need something like a bat, golf club, stick, or rifle to control the accelerator and brake.

SEARCH AND RESCUE

If a major earthquake strikes, it could be three to five days before you see any help. First responders are going to be totally overwhelmed, and it will be up to you and those who survived to do whatever is possible to help.

You may be safe, but there will be people out there fighting for their lives. The clock is ticking, and you have a duty to render aid. Gather as many people as you can. This is a clear-cut case of **strength in numbers,** and your mission is to save lives. Organize the group and tackle one challenge at a time. Don't forget to do a continuous scene size-up. You are operating in a very hazardous and constantly changing environment.

STEP UP!

I have spent most of my life surrounded by excellence, by a group of guys I trust with my life. I have been spoiled by high standards of bravery among men who race into danger whenever they find it. When I see a general lack of courage among bystanders in emergency situations, I have to continuously remind myself of the training and background I come from. That said, you don't have to be a SEAL to have the courage to do the right thing and help those in need.

Gear Up

Wear sturdy, closed-toed shoes to protect your feet from broken glass, and if you have a hard hat or any kind of helmet, put it on. You may think you look ridiculous wearing a football helmet, but if that's all you have, use it. Keep yourself safe from falling rubble and other hazards. Your mission is to save lives, not add to the fatalities.

Search: Going In

As I've mentioned, you should not reenter a structure unless it has been cleared by an engineer, but if there are no professionals of this caliber and you hear survivors trapped, you must take action. Never go in with fewer than two people in your rescue party, following the buddy system used by SEALs.

1. Ensure the gas and power sources to any building you need to search have been turned off.
2. Establish a search pattern: Start right and go counterclockwise. If there are multiple search teams, then direct each group or buddy pair to start at opposite ends, so as to meet in the middle.
3. Use caution while moving through the structure, remembering *not* to move any weight-bearing material. Watch your step; you could go right through the floor.
4. Search six sides to every room—four walls, the floor, and the ceiling, all of which could be places where someone is trapped.
5. Call out and then remain silent. Someone could be wedged in a very small space, or it could take them time to hear you and muster the energy to respond. When you call out, don't merely ask, "Is anyone here?" If there are survivors in the search area, chances are they are dazed. Instruct them in how to respond. Tell them to tap something if they are unable to speak.
6. Be thorough! Do it right the first time.

Mark It

A very important aspect of search and rescue is to mark doors, indicating that the area was already searched or that it is being searched. You don't want to have another team wasting time going over the same areas when they could be searching for survivors in other structures. You can mark the front door or a visible part of the building using anything—spray paint, Magic Markers, chalk, crayons, or even a bottle of mustard.

1. Before entering a room or building, make one diagonal line across the door. This will let anyone know that someone is inside searching.
2. If you don't find anyone inside, place another diagonal line on the door to form an X.
3. At the top of the X write the time and date. At the bottom of the X place a "0." This will let everyone know that the house has been searched and there are no people inside. "0" reaffirms, during a time of major unrest, that the structure has been searched with zero dead. They can move on to the next area and save valuable time.

Search and rescue
in progress

searched:
0 survivors

Extracting Survivors

More than likely you will find someone who is buried under quite a lot of weight. Since there will be no backhoes or cranes available for some time, you must devise ways to get the person out safely. The person could be under rubble that cannot be moved with bare hands. There are two primary methods to use when trying to get them out.

LEVER

Use the longest and sturdiest piece of wood available, such as a long two-by-four or four-by-four, and place one end under the rubble. Then put another object under the lever a few feet from the end. This will serve as a fulcrum. The longer the lever, the more weight it will lift. Choose a place to apply the lever at a portion of the debris closest to where you believe the trapped person to be.

CRIBBING AND SHORING

The second technique you can use is what search-and-rescue crews call cribbing and shoring. This works well if you have a car jack available.

1. Place the jack on top of several pieces of wood to distribute the weight at the base. The width of the wood should be greater than the base of the jack to prevent slippage.

2. Place another piece of wood between the top of the jack and the object to be lifted.
3. Slowly start jacking up the object to a height of about four inches.
4. Place pieces of wood that form a box, or "cribbing," under the object you are lifting. This will shore it up and keep it from dropping back down.
5. Then continue lifting the object another four inches and repeat the cribbing process until the object is high enough that you can pull the victim out.

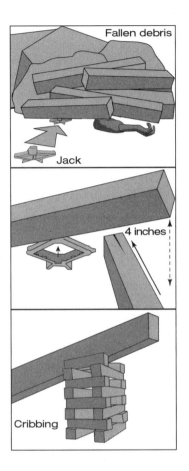

Fallen debris

Jack

4 inches

Cribbing

STALKER AND SURVEILLANCE DETECTION

A person can be stalked or under surveillance for any number of reasons—everything from a spouse wanting to know if their husband or wife is cheating to a criminal preparing to kidnap a wealthy banker, or a would-be robber wishing to learn of your routine prior to committing their crime. In addition, every forty seconds someone is reported missing. Many are found, but a great number end up kidnapped and ultimately as fatality statistics. Learn to detect surveillance and thwart it to help you avoid becoming a victim. Those wishing to do harm follow the rules that all predators do: They watch before they attack and wait for the opportunity to get you alone.

Eight percent of American women will be stalked in their lifetime—
that's 1.4 million American stalking victims every year. The majority
of stalkers have been in relationships with their victims. Women who
are separated from their husbands are three times more likely to be stalked
than women who are divorced outright—and twenty-five times more likely
than married women to be murdered as a result. According the FBI statistics,
during a period of marital separation, stalking and crimes of passion, including
homicide, occur more frequently.

Situational Awareness

We all know what looks normal for a neighborhood. Perhaps we see
the same cars go by, or people walking their dogs, or certain landscap-
ing trucks, or the same well-marked service vans serving an area. Without realizing it, what we have done by observing these normal details is
establish a baseline. Every place, whether it is an urban, suburban, or
rural setting, has its baseline of regular activity. The first step in surveillance detection (SD) is to be alert to changes in this baseline. These
can come in many guises. Sometimes, it could be a person pretending
that his car is broken or someone knocking on your door who just
doesn't seem right, perhaps pretending to try to sell you something.
In the city, someone might be loitering in a doorway, seemingly drinking a cup of coffee, but they still have the same cup in their hand two
hours later. Whenever someone seems out of place, let them know that
you see them. One of the best tools available now is your cell phone
camera. Take the person's picture. Those doing the surveillance don't
want to be caught in the act, or "rolled up."

What to Do If You Are Being Followed

If you are alert and practicing situational awareness, you may see a car
in your rearview mirror that seems to be taking the same route as you.
If walking, you may notice that same person you saw ten blocks ago
is still behind you. Most times, predators, especially if setting up for a
kidnapping or robbery, repeat their observations for days or for weeks.

When I was a SEAL, many of our missions required us to conduct reconnaissance or surveillance. It enables us to collect intelligence on possible targets and plan for follow-up missions. Once, when in the Balkans, my team occupied an abandoned house as our observation point for the surveillance of a particular neighborhood of interest. In that instance, we got rolled because the locals sent in five kids, making believe they came into the house to play hide-and-seek. They immediately reported their findings, and we hauled ass. It was a very effective form of countersurveillance.

1. CHANGE YOUR ROUTINE

If you always leave your house or apartment at eight A.M., for example, leave earlier or later. Enter a highway at a different exit, or take a different road or street to the store you usually go to. There are many ways to alter your routine without changing your life. But this will make you an unpredictable target, and those looking for an easy mark will likely look for another victim.

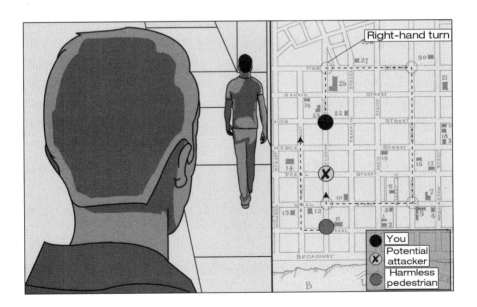

2. LOSE YOUR EYES: SURVEILLANCE DETECTION ROUTE (SDR)

If you want to determine if someone is actually following you, there are a number of ways to do so. If you suspect someone is trailing your car, make a series of right or left turns, or box around a particular area until you return to the same spot. No casual driver would still be behind you at this point. Do the same thing if on foot in a city. If you do this effectively, you could even have the person who is following you now in front of you. You can wave or take their picture. At any rate, you have won by letting them know that you see them.

3. SET UP AN AMBUSH

If those following seem to be more sinister, such as a group of men in a car, you can lead them into a trap. Once you have determined that you're being followed, you can feign that you are still unaware. Use your survival skill of remaining calm under pressure. Continue your route, but call the police and inform them of the situation. You can describe the car or person in detail and coordinate with the police to lead the potential attackers to a specific location.

TORTURE AND BEING HELD HOSTAGE

Torture is any method or means used to inflict extreme pain and suffering for the purposes of punishment, to extract information, or to intimidate a person into total submission. In reality, it's an attempt to kill a person without their dying, through bringing them to the brink of death. The history of torture and the list of devices used to inflict hurt is long; it shows how perversely inventive humankind can be when it comes to devising methods to inflict pain. Torture can be either mental or physical abuse. There are techniques to help you endure it and come out alive, if you should ever find yourself in such a situation. (See also "Tiger Kidnapping," page 187, and "Trouble in a Foreign Country," page 286.) It will test every aspect of your SEAL survival mindset to make it through the torture alive. To survive, you will have to notch up your mental toughness to levels you never thought possible—but it can be done.

One civilian, British consultant Peter Moore, survived an incredible 947 days of continual torture in Iraq. Upon his release, he said he endured by telling himself he would not grovel or beg his captors to spare his life. Instead, he focused on pleasant boyhood memories during the ordeal to help him cope. He counted each escape from death as a little victory and survived.

Torture's Many Forms

It could be argued that the psychological aspect of torture is far more damaging than the specific acts. It's not only being captured and imprisoned or bound but the terror and fear that arises in anticipation of when the next session will begin that creates extreme stress and trauma. In modern times, torture is still widely employed throughout the world. Here are some methods used:

- **Environmental manipulation:** Sleep deprivation, isolation, sensory deprivation, and noise abuse.

- **Pharmacological manipulation:** The use of hallucinatory or muscle-paralyzing drugs.

- **Coercive methods:** Being forced to watch the torture of friends and/or family.

- **Somatic methods:** This is any manner of physical abuse, such as beatings, burning with cigarettes, electric shock treatments, rape, or starvation.

- **Suffocation:** This includes waterboarding and having your head forced into a bucket or container filled with excrement or placed inside an airtight bag.

- **Psychological methods:** This includes mock executions, such as firing at your head a pistol that is perhaps filled with blanks.

Waterboarding is a torture technique used since the Middle Ages. A person is strapped to a board, inclined with the feet raised and the head lowered. The head may be wrapped with cellophane at the forehead and chin or bound in some way. Waves of water are poured on the face and inevitably get in the nose and mouth, which produces the sensation of drowning.

Why Me?

Although the reasons vary, it will become immediately apparent why you happened to have been chosen as a target for torture. You could have a job that gives you access to large amounts of money or to classified and sensitive information. It could be due to your ethnicity or religion if you are in a foreign country. Or you could simply be in the wrong place at the wrong time, such as during a home invasion or even a carjacking. Regardless of the reason, you are now in a situation that will require the greatest degree of physical and mental toughness. Prepare for your comfort zone to be radically challenged.

Accepting Your Situation

Once you have been captured and are controlled by the abductors, it is best not to get too far ahead by imagining what might happen next. In fact, if you accept the present situation, you can then work on making yourself calm. You will need your mind to be in this state to think clearly and look for an opportunity to escape. The goal is to begin working on a survival plan by observing every detail of your situation and the environmental factors in which you find yourself.

Stress Management

Immediately start your combat breathing technique. If you allow yourself to panic, you won't be able to logically address the situation. You need to keep a focused mind and accept that you will probably be beaten and possibly tortured.

Time

This is the one and only element in a torture scenario that your captors have no control over. They can't stop time. So if they can't control this, you must embrace it. This is also your best friend. The longer you are able to stay alive, the greater the chance that you will be rescued or set free. Again think about little victories: *That punch didn't hurt as much as the last one. He must be getting tired because he's starting to sweat from hitting me. Well, I still have two teeth left. I was begging to die five minutes ago but I'm still here.*

Create a ticking clock in your head and constantly say to yourself, "I just survived another second [minute, hour, day]." Do whatever you can to gain time. This may all sound very disturbing, but given the gravity of a torture scenario, you may have only these little victories to cling to.

Escape

Always plan to escape; this is what will keep you alive and able to endure. Make your mental movie of how you will do this. This will also give your mind a positive thing to work on, help you stay numb, and hopefully serve you well. Your captors may see a curled-up, bloody, semiconscious individual strapped to a chair. But the entire time your brain is at work, looking for that window of opportunity to crack and allow you to flee.

Become the Gray Man

In a torture situation, the captors want to prove immediately that they have total dominance and complete control over your fate. It's all about proving that they have the power of determining whether you will live or not. Your goal is to appear as calm and submissive as possible. If, for example, you were abducted in a foreign country, you want to give the impression that you are a face in the crowd and a person of no value. Become the gray man, a term used in intelligence circles that refers to a person who blends into any scene or situation without drawing attention while concealing his survival knowledge and skills. You want to de-escalate this situation by appearing compliant. The worst move at this point would be to aggressively resist. This will only increase the abuse. The more personable and calm you are, the greater the possibility you have of establishing communication with your assailants. It is ideal to attempt to humanize the attackers, such as calling them by name. Again, your goal at this point is to make it to the next minute.

Managing the Pain

This will probably be the worst thing you have ever experienced. Stay strong! You need to dig deep and pull out the maximum mental and physical toughness that you can muster. You must tell yourself that there is nothing they can do that will make you forfeit the will to live. Strategies to employ include:

- **Check out.** Put your brain in neutral and conjure up that mental vacation. Imagine you are floating in a warm ocean or sitting on the side of a mountain, or whatever place offers you interior peace. This is not the time to conjure the image you created in "Creating a Trigger," which will only make enduring the suffering more unbearable. This is not the time for your trigger; this is the time for complete numbness.

- **Guard your eyes.** Your captors are monitoring your reactions to the first round of torture very closely. They want to find your "fear buttons," so they know how and where to press harder. You must remember that our eyes are often giveaways as to how we are really feeling, so make a tremendous effort to present a face of neutrality. If they find anything that can be used to turn you, they will use it.

- **Exaggerate.** If you find that maintaining neutrality and trying not to let the pain show in your eyes has been ineffective, you could instead try to overplay and exaggerate effect the physical abuse is having on you. Make it seem as if you are injured more than you really are. For example, it's okay to moan, groan, and even scream with pain at the slightest touch. This will make them think you have a low threshold for pain and could make them hold back from using greater force. It could also gain you more time and get them to bring you water or food, since at this point they don't want you to die, or they would have already killed you.

- **Let it go.** Urinate, defecate, and vomit on yourself. Your captors will be less likely to physically harm you if they don't want to touch you or even be in the same room with you.

I remember about the third day of being cooped up in my three-foot-by-three-foot luxury concrete box in SERE school, when I was really starting to go stir-crazy. I literally couldn't wait for the interrogations to begin. I said to myself, "Please hit me, you assholes, so at least I'll feel something." Well, it wasn't long before my wish was granted, and I was soon more than ready to get back to my box. This goes under the "be careful what you wish for" column.

Give Something vs. Give Nothing

In many instances you are being subjected to torture for information. They want something from you or they wouldn't be wasting their time. If you give them no information, nothing at all, then you could be considered unbreakable or dispensable, which in this scenario means that they might as well kill you and be done with it. While under torture, it is difficult to make a decision about how much or how little you should talk or what questions you should answer. You must decide what's best based on the specific situation and the captors you are up against.

- Do you give little pieces of information in an effort to prolong the time?
- Do you continue to give nothing?

Giving some information or even the wrong information may have a positive effect in prolonging the time and decreasing the abuse. However, the captors may believe that more torture will produce more information. On the other hand, if you are giving no information, the captors could very well lose patience and kill you. This is one of the lessons we were taught during SERE and is a choice that can be made only based on the particular circumstances of your abduction and torture.

TROUBLE IN A FOREIGN COUNTRY

Travel to a foreign country, whether for business or pleasure, can be an amazing experience. But you should understand first and foremost that as soon as you leave the United States, you are also leaving the rights, laws, customs, language, and culture of America. Do not assume you will be afforded any special privileges because you come from the United States. Quite the opposite—as an American you may be drawing attention to yourself simply because of your nationality. (Many college-age Americans put Canadian flags on backpacks while traveling in Europe to avoid being picked out as an American.) So, when traveling abroad, *please* don't be the "ugly American." Respect and appreciate that you are a visitor in a foreign land, and you will lessen the vast majority of problems you may encounter.

In the 1990s, when American troops went to Somalia on a humani-
tarian aid operation, a one-hour local-culture briefing could have
saved the lives of many U.S. soldiers. When our troops flew around in
helicopters over the local population, they had their legs hanging out, which is
a normal way we sometimes traveled when crammed into these things. We had
no idea that in Somalian culture, showing the bottom of your feet is the same as
flipping someone the bird in the States. It also would have been good to know
that a large portion of the population indulges in a drug called khat, pronounced
"cot," which is a highly addictive drug categorized as a stimulant that creates
feelings of euphoria. They primarily do this drug in the day, so that when night
comes, most of these folks are zoned out and sound asleep. Yep, we stirred
a hornet's nest with day raids against a city of fighters that would have been
otherwise out of commission in the evening—but then again, war is imperfect.

Before You Go

- Know the culture, laws, and customs of the country you
  will visit; that which is considered acceptable in the United
  States may be horribly offensive in other countries. Also
  know some of the language, at least a few key phrases to
  help you ask for directions, for example. Usually making an
  effort to speak some of the native tongue will get people to
  act more hospitable toward you.

- Make sure people at home know your travel plans. Write
  down flight numbers, hotels where you'll be staying, and
  contact numbers, if possible. Also include the names, and the
  stateside contact information, of all persons traveling with
  you. In addition, provide the number for the Office of American Citizens Services division of the U.S. Department of
  State in Washington, D.C. If you get in trouble or lose your
  passport, for example, calls made by relatives in the States
  could help to expedite your situation while you are abroad.

Carry a pictogram guide for the area you're visiting. This will allow you to communicate visually. Learning key phrases such as "Where is the embassy?" and "Can you help me, please?" could be invaluable in any number of situations. In the SEAL team, key phrases we learned before we went to battle in a foreign country included "Drop to your knees! Get down! Hands up!" and "I'm going to shoot you if you don't." We also we found it very useful to have picture cards displaying an IED, an ambush, and a small American flag used to help us interrogate and communicate. Additionally, a one-hundred-dollar bill was universally accepted and overcame all sorts of language barriers.

- Scan a color copy of your passport and attach it to an e-mail, but *don't* send it. It will remain in your "drafts" box, which can be accessed by you at any time should you need to produce a copy. Additionally, bring a certified copy of your birth certificate. Write down your passport number and bring duplicate passport photos, in the event your passport is lost and you need to get a temporary one from the U.S. embassy. Keep this info separated from your cash, in the event you are subjected to theft.

- Make sure you know the location, address, and phone number of the American embassy or consulate, and those of at least three ally nations. Study a map of the country and make note of significant landmarks. Especially include waterways and borderlines, so that you know the direction of "friendly" nations and how to avoid entering countries that are less hospitable.

- Most embassies are open only during business hours, but you may need assistance at any time. Get twenty-four-hour emergency phone numbers for the U.S. State Department. These should be obtained before you leave, but you may find the numbers in local phone directories or at airports.

- Additionally, you can also get numbers of private companies specializing in risk management while abroad, or those that offer chartered-flight extraction services in the event of disasters.

FRIENDLIES

Among the top ten American-loving countries are the Ivory Coast, Kenya (and many sub-Saharan African nations), Israel, Poland, Japan, India, Australia, Mexico, Canada, and England. In numerous European countries and throughout the Middle East, for sure, Americans are not usually afforded any special privileges.

Avoid Trouble

This is a combination of situational awareness and common sense. At the very least, if it's trouble in America, it's probably trouble overseas. An area of town that has "odd-smelling" smoke billowing from its cafés and red-lit windows with partially dressed women dancing behind them might be a hell of a good time for some, but it's also very dangerous, especially to a foreigner. Remember that since you look, dress, and speak differently, you already are a noticeable target. Stay clear of the danger zones.

Additionally, it probably wouldn't hurt to leave the ten-gallon cowboy hat and American-flag sweatshirt in the closet at home. Be the gray man when in a foreign country; enjoy yourself, but try to fly under the radar. Being a low-profile and respectful visitor will not only cause the locals to be more friendly, it will allow you to let your guard down slightly and make for a much more enjoyable vacation.

In Trouble

Every country has its own rules concerning foreigners. If you get arrested, there are **international treaties** in place, which in theory gives permission for embassy officials to communicate with and physically see any of its country's citizens. Arresting authorities will not automatically notify the embassy, and you must ask for this to be done. Also, keep in mind that even if many foreign countries follow this treaty, not all do. Remember that just because it's law in America doesn't mean it's law where you are. And ignorance will not be an excuse.

Soon after you are detained, formally request that the U.S. embassy or the consulate stationed in that country be notified of your situation. If the foreign authorities are reluctant, you could inform them that you have a medical condition, which often makes them more cooperative in notifying embassy officials.

On the Run

For whatever reason, be it a hostile uprising, riot, or incident with a group of locals, you may find yourself on the run in a foreign land. Assume you are on your own and being hunted. You are now in what the military calls **E & E,** or **"escape and evasion."**

When my team was discovered during a reconnaissance/ surveillance mission, all offensive operations were done. We lost the initiative and had to immediately change our focus to the evader mindset. All prior objectives became secondary to E & E.

---

1. Get off the X: First, remove yourself from where you were last seen. Get to an area that is relatively safe and secure to assess your situation. If you have the preplanning map with you, now is the time to pinpoint where you are. If your fleeing was spontaneous, then at least attempt to figure out where you think you are. Your priority is to get to a safe zone, be it a friendly embassy or across the border to an ally country. Making it to an airport or train station might be the fastest way out, although these areas are heavily populated and under a high level of surveillance. A church or religious structure may offer a form of safe house if you are confident their beliefs incorporate offering assistance to a foreigner.

2. Rule of Three: Come up with the three best options and decide on a plan of action. Your possible options could include staying put until night, attempting to contact someone, or moving to another location. Remember, the most direct and shortest distance to your objective is rarely the smartest or safest. Be alert and recognize heavily trafficked areas and possible choke points. Following rivers and waterways can put you in uncomfortable terrain but can possibly provide rapid and undeterred transit to specific locations. Bear in mind, you are in your pursuers' backyard. Those looking for you have a huge advantage. (See also "Stalker and Surveillance Detection," page 277.)

3. Safe Houses: You may need to travel over several nights and hole up during the day. This will require you to take advantage of **hide sites** or safe houses, based on your environment. This could be a drainage ditch or an abandoned building. The more uncomfortable the better, because others will be less likely to explore these areas.

4. Disguise: Do whatever you can to make yourself look like a local, be it a change of clothes or dirt on the hair and face to give a darker complexion, if necessary. You would be amazed how you can disappear in plain sight. In an area rife with homeless, become homeless. Most people will want to avoid you, or even avoid noticing you.

I would be lying if I said that I never wore a burka during my time in the Middle East. No, I'm not a cross-dresser; it was strictly tactical and mission oriented. And you can hide a hell of a lot of guns and gear under those things. It also helped that I learned to say, "Alalalalalalala."

---

5. Cash is king: This is true in any country. Make sure you have it on you in small bills and in three different locations on your person.

6. Cover story: Make sure you are able to come up with something innocuous should you encounter someone who may question you. I found that posing as a salesman or missionary from a neutral English-speaking country like Canada is advantageous.

7. Elicit help from others: Human nature leads us to naturally want to trust and help other individuals—you'll always find some good people, no matter where you go. You may try to engage others to help you, though be cautious about to whom you describe your plight. You may need to make up a plausible, though fictitious, story that gets others to help you. No one likes to deceive decent people, but if your life depends on getting out of a foreign country, this is an option to consider.

I participated in an urban-evasion training exercise in Los Angeles, California, where I was on foot being "hunted" by several members of law enforcement as well as "private sector" folks. I was able to convince a total stranger, after faking a bicycle accident, to allow me to use their cell phone, give me a ride to the hospital, give me $50, and give me their phone number and home address in case I needed anything else. Thanks to that person, BTW, for proving there are still plenty of decent people in the world.

PART THREE

Gear and Improvised Weapons

GEAR

First off, my intention is not to turn anyone into a gear fanatic. I don't want you to carry around a sixty-pound backpack full of survival gear every time you leave the house. You might as well drag around a ball and chain—that's not living. Without question, the right gear and equipment is important, but it is no substitute for knowledge, training, and using your SEAL mindset. Don't depend entirely on gear.

Here are a few phrases we used in SEAL team when it came to gear:

- Two is one and one is none. (If it's that important, pack two.)
- If it takes batteries, it will take a shit exactly when you need it.
- Take care of your gear, and it will take care of you.
- Salt water destroys everything and rust never sleeps.

On the other hand, having the right equipment for a particular survival situation can mean the difference between living and dying. It could be just enough to keep your body that one degree warmer or cooler, provide that vital amount of water or food, or even reach out and get the attention of a search party on the horizon. Obviously, different environments will require different survival equipment. A desert setup will be vastly different from the one that you need on your boat. Nevertheless, there are some basic pieces of gear that you should have within reach at a moment's notice. This collection of gear is called a **go bag.**

Go Bag Checklist

When things start getting bad, you grab this and you go. Please remember it should be in something you can throw over your shoulder and run with. If you add too many items and it starts to weigh too much, it will only slow you down.

It's called a *go bag*—not a drag bag.

Prepare at least one go bag for each person in your family and leave these backpacks or satchels at home. Keep one in your vehicle and one at work. Check the functionality and condition of the items in your go bags every six months. Contents can be modified based on your region or environment, but these are the essentials for every go bag:

- Copy of passport, driver's license, emergency contact list, and any necessary prescriptions in small plastic bag
- Multitool (to include pliers, knife, saw blade, file, screwdrivers)
- Compass, folding mirror type (also used for signaling)
- Marker pen or indelible felt-tip pen and small waterproof notebook
- Flashlight, extra batteries, and a headlamp
- Cyalume chemlights (glow sticks), red and green
- Lighter, waterproof matches, and magnesium fire starter, and cotton balls for tinder
- Candles
- Plastic whistle
- Bottled water and protein or energy bars
- SteriPEN or water-purification tablets and filter (straw type)

- Lightweight water-resistant windbreaker and sun visor
- Emergency/space blanket
- First-aid kit: compressed gauze dressing, tourniquet material, cloth sling, surgical gloves, alcohol wipes, sunscreen
- Trash bag
- Hand sanitizer or bleach wipes
- Zip ties
- Twenty feet of Paracord
- Tape
- Spare socks
- Eye flush/eye drops
- Cash in small bills
- Any medication you are taking or inhaler (three days' worth, which you can add to the bag when ready to go)

Again, the above items are minimal requirements for immediate survival and to serve you during several days on the run. If you want to take your kit to the next level, here are some additional items you could add:

- Increase your water supply to several gallons
- Add food like military MREs (meals ready to eat) or freeze-dried, add-water food
- Gore-Tex coat and pants
- Small sleeping bag and additional ponchos
- Sock hat and gloves; wool is warm even when wet
- Hand-powered radio
- Additional flashlight
- Fishing kit, including line and hooks
- Snare wire
- Extra cell phone with additional batteries
- Larger fixed-blade knife
- Expanded first-aid kit, to include additional dressings, tape, scissors, bandages, antiseptic
- Small monocular

- GPS
- Lock-pick kit and set of jigglers for vehicle entry
- Bear spray (extra-strength pepper spray)
- Folding shovel
- Insect head net
- Seawater desalination kit
- Illumination flares/smoke signals
- Change of clothes
- Firearm (train to get a concealed-weapon permit or check local firearm regulations)
- Last, but not least: *Always carry a copy of this book!*

Go bags available at www.SEALSurvival.com

FIREARMS

I previously discussed this topic, but it's such an important issue that I want to elaborate and make the facts about the handling of firearms extremely clear. If you are going to have a firearm, you must:

1. Know how to use it proficiently. You will achieve this only by taking a course given by an expert. Then you must make a commitment to practice using it, preferably at a designated firing range and in real-world environments. The International Practical Shooting Confederation (IPSC) has lists of where you can get this kind of practice. Every weapon has its own unique characteristics. You need to know the particulars of the weapon you choose to own.

2. Know how to safely store it (especially with children in the home). My recommendation is a fingerprint-recognition safe for handguns and trigger locks for rifles and shotguns.

3. Be willing to use it. Be willing to take a life. You don't want to be the guy who was killed by his own gun.

Here's a statistic to drive home the importance of firearm safety: In 2010, there were six hundred self-inflicted accidental deaths caused by improper use of firearms. And according to the CDC, death by firearms is a significant cause of death among youth—so keep them locked up and out of the reach of children!

What Weapon Is Best?

I am constantly asked, "What kind of gun should I get for self- and home defense?" My first question is, have you satisfied all the requirements in the list above? If so:

1. For home defense I generally recommend a pump shotgun. It is very easy to use and very easy to hit things with. And I don't care who you are; when you hear a pump shotgun ratchet a shell into the chamber, you are going to haul ass.

2. Handguns are also a great option but require more skill to use effectively. Also understand that a bullet has the potential to travel much farther than shotgun ammunition. If you miss what you are aiming at, it may very well penetrate an internal wall and hit a family member, friend, or neighbor. I'm a big fan of the .40-cal for its stopping power and capacity.

3. Occasionally, I get the guy who lives in a residential area asking me about a .50-cal rifle, or if he should get an automatic assault weapon (in the old days called machine guns). I have just two words for him—"Watch list."

REVOLVERS VS. SEMIAUTOMATICS

Handguns come in two varieties: revolvers and semiautomatics. A revolver has a cylinder that holds six rounds and rotates every time the trigger is pulled, causing the hammer to strike the chamber containing the cartridge. A semiautomatic's ammunition is in a magazine that can hold in excess of fifteen rounds. It will fire each time the trigger is pulled, which is why it is called a semiautomatic. A revolver has fewer moving parts and therefore is considered to be more reliable; however, if you clean your weapons on a regular basis, you will minimize malfunctions. Take care of your gear, and it will take care of you.

Basic Firearm Operation and Safety

Each firearm is different in its specific operation, but there are some very basic and general safety rules you can *always* apply:

1. Always assume the firearm is loaded.
2. Never point the firearm at something you don't intend to kill. When handling a firearm, treat it like there is a laser coming out of the end of the barrel. Anything that laser touches, it will slice through, which is why holding the weapon at a high port—meaning that the barrel is pointing straight up—is generally the best nonfiring position for a firearm.
3. Keep the safety on until you are ready to fire. Know how to switch the safety on and off with your eyes closed.
4. Keep your finger off the trigger, and only move it to the trigger when ready to fire.
5. Take a gun- or hunter-safety course. Bring your spouse and children. Education and respect for a firearm are a must. The seriousness with which the courses are taught will impress upon children the seriousness of this weapon.

6. Practice as much as you can, because shooting is a very perishable skill.

CASTLE LAW

The Second Amendment of the U.S. Constitution states that "the right of the people to keep and bear Arms, shall not be infringed." Don't ask a SEAL if he's pro- or antigun—you should know that answer—but I'm definitely pro on learning how to use it and to respect its power. Every state and municipality has different regulations regarding registering weapons or obtaining concealed-weapon permits. It's your responsibility to know the laws on firearm use where you live and wherever you travel with your weapon. If you have a gun in your house for self-defense, become familiar with what's called "the Castle Law." In summary, this law states that you have the right to use deadly force against any intruder who enters your house and presents a threat against your life. However, there are fine points you need to know. For example, if the intruder sees your weapon and flees, you cannot shoot him in the back or chase him down the street.

IMPROVISED WEAPONS

When it comes to choosing what to use as an improvised weapon for defense, you are limited only by your imagination—and your commitment to using it. The true sense of the word "improvised" means you could make just about anything, from the leg of a table to a stalk of celery, into a weapon. The latter probably isn't going to be too helpful, and in a situation where you could get injured or killed, you had better pick the item that has the most potential to be effective.

A former teammate of mine was on a raid in Iraq when not only
did his rifle go down but so did his handgun. He had to perform
an instantaneous assessment of what was within his reach that
he could turn into a weapon. As the enemy charged, he grabbed a toaster oven
and used it with deadly force. In doing so, he became the first American to get
a "confirmed kill" with a small kitchen appliance. True story—and it proves
how improvisation, physical and mental toughness, and utilizing the SEAL
mindset can save your life.

Whatever environment you are in, do a situational-awareness drill
and look around at things that you could use as a weapon. If you are
in an office right now, look at the things on your desk. What do you
think could be used most effectively to disable an attacker? A bit of
creativity can go a long way when thinking of what could be transformed into a weapon. For example, while walking to your car, your
set of keys sticking out between each of your fingers and gripped in
your fist could instantly turn your knuckles into a weapon. A key-
spiked punch with this would do considerable damage to an assailant's
vulnerable points, especially the eyes. In a bar, a stool could be used as
a weapon and a shield. A thick tree branch makes a powerful club, and
even a bench becomes an improvised weapon if thrown at someone.
Remember, whatever you use, you must employ violence of action to
make it work. This, along with your determination to survive, will help
save your life. Here a few of my favorites:

Clothing
- Belts—especially with heavy buckles; wrap part of it
  around your fist and just start swinging
- Coats—always great as a defensive tool against a sharp object
- High heels—ladies, not only can you walk on them, but
  they are a lethal weapon if used as a hammer, or both at
  the same time like a set of cymbals
- Socks—fill with coins or a can of soda

Toiletries (in addition to the obvious uses, you can throw any and all of these items)

- Any aerosol canister sprayed in the eyes will sting like hell
- Nail file
- Straight razor
- Foot powder—same as aerosol

Office supplies

- Laptop computer—can be used as a shield, but even more effective folded up and used to deliver a shot to the throat
- Stapler—use as a striking tool and for smashing in an upward motion against an attacker's nose; could also be used like a vise, opened and closed on an attacker's fingers to bend back and break them
- Scissors
- Ruler (use for slashing)
- Computer power cords, printer cables, and Ethernet cords are thick and excellent for whipping and strangling
- Again, you can throw just about any office supply item

On a plane

- Book—use much like a laptop to strike the throat or throw. And if time permits, feel free to open this book, review the section on hijacking, and then crush the terrorist's windpipe while yelling *"SEAL survival!"* at the top of your lungs.
- Rolled-up magazine—believe me, it will hurt when used with a stabbing motion to the face or throat
- Ball-point pen—can be mightier than the sword if you stab a lot
- Vodka—from the beverage cart to the eyes
- Blanket—throw over the face of an attacker to disorient and blind

Kitchen

- Knives, forks, spoons, rolling pin, pots, pans, lids—need I say more?

- Corkscrew—doubles as a fist pack with protruding point (screw) between knuckles
- Fire extinguisher—throw at an assailant's feet/legs or engage the sprayer to blind

---

HOMEMADE PEPPER SPRAY

1. In a glass, add equal parts cayenne pepper and rubbing alcohol, then stir.
2. Strain the big chunks using cloth and place the liquid in a spray bottle.
3. Spray—effective on attacker for up to thirty minutes.

Garage

- Anything from a toolbox (hammer, screwdriver, box cutter . . .)
- Any sports equipment, not only for use as a weapon but for protection (like a baseball bat and hockey mask)
- Lumber
- Plumbing supplies
- Chain saw (my personal favorite)
- This list could go on and on; you name it, and you have a weapon

---

When I emerge from my garage for a fight, I will be donning a motorcycle helmet, chest protector, and steel-toed boots, with an idling chain saw in my right hand and a sledgehammer in my left, displaying a million-dollar smile. Welcome to my Thunderdome!

In summary, if you find yourself in a situation where someone is trying to harm you, use everything at your disposal to get out of that situation alive. If you can throw it, thrust it, block with it, spray it, crush with it . . . do it.

PART FOUR

Survival Medicine

When tragedy occurs, it always comes down like a hammer. The human body is an incredibly resilient machine capable of withstanding the unthinkable. On the other hand, we are not indestructible, and our bodies can be so unpredictably fragile that a life can be lost within moments. It's almost guaranteed that there will be injuries when unexpected life-threatening situations occur. You may survive an initial ordeal, but if you lack the knowledge of how to stop a wound from bleeding or what to do if bitten by a snake . . . you're done.

Whether you survive a lethal situation will often depend on whether you have some understanding of how to apply basic medical emergency techniques. The information I provide here is designed for educational use only and is not a substitute for specific training or experience. One of the very best pieces of advice I can give regarding survival is that you should go and get some medical training, because when bad things happen, people get hurt.

During an actual emergency you'll have no time to flip through a book and learn—and being ill prepared, regardless of your other strengths or abilities, could be your death knell. Believe me, you do not want to stand by helplessly if someone you care for is in dire need of immediate care. If a dangerous situation were to occur and you were unable to help, it would haunt you and leave a mark for a long time. At a minimum, you should attend a basic first-aid class and get your CPR certification.

Several years ago, when I was considering becoming a firefighter in Los Angeles, I trained and became a nationally certified EMT. I knew how important these skills were as a SEAL. Even though I decided to go a different route, the invaluable knowledge I learned as an EMT enabled me on several occasions to save lives.

Every SEAL platoon has two highly trained medical personnel called corpsmen. When I say "highly trained," I mean they not only perform lifesaving surgical procedures but do so while avoiding bullets and explosions all around them. It's been proven that getting everyone out alive often comes down to how quickly lifesaving techniques are performed at the onset of an injury—and these guys are the best!

STEP UP AND HELP!

In life-or-death situations you must do everything you can to survive and to help others survive. I believe strongly that we as humans have an obligation to provide aid, or a **duty to act.** As I mentioned earlier in this book, I recently came upon the scene of a pedestrian who had been struck by a car. As I approached the lifeless, bleeding body, I was amazed at the group of people who were just standing there and staring. Learning medical techniques makes you a leader and lifesaver in such situations.

Good Samaritan laws were established across the country beginning in 1959 to protect you from liability if, in good faith, you attempt to render emergency care at the scene of an emergency and you are doing so as to not exceed basic lifesaving techniques or beyond your level of training. But don't attempt to conduct certain medical procedures beyond your level of training or "scope of practice," or you may have to deal with legal repercussions. For example: You come across an unconscious person and begin CPR and mouth-to-mouth breathing. Even if this person died, you would be protected by the Good Samaritan Law. However, if you attempted to stop bleeding in the brain by removing the skullcap and plugging the hole with a sock . . . well, that's not in the spirit of the Good Samaritan Law and you might be in some trouble with that call.

I am bringing this up only to further stress the importance of receiving medical training. That said, each situation will be different, and you will decide what you can or will do depending on the survival scenario encountered.

Casualty Assessment

If you arrive at a scene where someone else is injured, the first and most important thing to do is a scene size-up. You must quickly identify possible hazards and decide whether it is safe to enter or stay at this location. The last thing you want to do is rush in to help, only to become one of the injured because of falling debris, an explosion, toxic fumes, or violence, for example. Maintain your situational awareness, because things can change quickly. Continually assess the scene for unusual characteristics such as sounds, smells, or things that seem odd.

As a general rule, you don't want to move an injured person for fear they may have a spinal injury. It is best to attempt to give aid at the location at which you found someone and leave issues of transport to professional medical responders. However, if failing to move someone from a hazardous area means risk of further injury or death, then get them out of there.

A very relevant and disturbing example of the importance of scene size-up is the tactic that the "animals" (insurgents) in Iraq liked to use. This particular brand of despicable individuals would explode an IED or car bomb at a scene. They would then wait for military medics or first responders and ambulances to arrive to give aid to the injured. Ignoring all humane laws established in the Geneva Conventions, and regardless of whether the medics wore the international insignia designating that they were there only to practice medicine, these insurgents would then detonate another bomb, oftentimes a larger explosive device, killing those who were trying to help. Like I said—animals.

Get into Action

If you were injured or involved in the incident, you must evaluate your own condition and treat it before you attempt to help others. In my experience on the SEAL teams, this meant that if we were in a firefight, for instance, and I got wounded, it was expected that I would attend to and work on my own injuries. Everybody else had their hands full with the fight. I didn't want or expect anyone to focus on my injuries when we were in an actively hostile situation. When you see a teammate injured, a guy who is closer to you than a brother, your immediate instinct is to go and help. But the priority must be to win the fight first or instead of one man down, there will be two.

SEALs say: "Self-aid, then buddy aid."
Take care of your own injuries, if possible, because the rest of the guys are taking care of the guys who gave you the injuries.
This is also an example of what is now referred to as CUF ("care under fire").

Practice scene-size up. For example, let's say there has just been an earthquake and you hear someone screaming under the rubble of a large building. Fight the urge to run in and help, because a small after-shock may cause the rest of the building to collapse on you.

Initial Assessment

Once you have decided the area is relatively safe, you may begin the **initial assessment** on your patient, which is a set of procedures used to discover and treat the individual's most immediate and life-threatening conditions. The steps of the initial assessment put in place a systematic approach and help you to make decisions about priorities and the types of care that each of the injured needs. Identify the person with the most life-threatening condition; that person must be treated immediately before you move on to the next portion of the initial assessment. For example, you must restore a person's breathing before you attend to their broken leg or the injuries of any other breathing victim.

If you have surgical gloves (which should be in your go bag and in your vehicle), put them on before you begin treating the injured.

TRIAGE

You may find yourself at an MCI (mass casualty incident) where there are several injured people and you are the only one who can help. How do you decide whom to help first? **Triage** is a system used for sorting patients to determine the order in which they will receive care. This will require you to make some tough decisions, but it will also allow you to provide care for and save the ones that you can.

Triage Categories

Priority 1: The injured who need *immediate* care (major bleeding or very poor vital signs indicative of internal bleeding).

Priority 2: The injured whose care can be *delayed* (minor bleeding).

Priority 3: Those with *minor* injuries who need help less urgently (fracture).

Priority 4: The *"expectant,"* who are beyond help (deceased or fatal injury).

As a platoon commander, I confronted several situations that required difficult decisions. Generally any decision made according to the rule "The greatest good for the greatest number" was the correct one. Stopping and helping one injured man versus continuing on and saving the group from certain death isn't the right move.

IMMEDIATE PRIORITIES FOR TREATING THE INJURED

As I said in Part One, "Whatever you do in training, you will do under stress." It is so important to practice the following skill set because when you arrive on a scene with injuries, it will be extremely stressful. Your immediate priorities will be:

1. Restore breathing and heartbeat if absent.
2. Stop any bleeding.
3. Protect wounds and stabilize fractures or dislocations.
4. Treat for shock.

ABC

When approaching an injured person, call out to them to see if you get a response. This will give you several indications as to their current condition. For example, if a person can answer and talk, you know immediately that he is breathing and conscious. If the victim is unresponsive or unconscious, then begin your ABCs. **ABC** is an acronym you must remember for survival medicine; it stands for **"airway, breathing, circulation."** When you begin to treat an injured person, first check that the Airway is open, that the person is Breathing, and that there is a pulse or other signs of Circulation. Periodically check with the American Red Cross and the American Heart Association for any changes or modifications to the information in this section. Methods and standards are updated annually.

A: AIRWAY

If a victim is facedown, you must carefully roll him over. Place one hand on the back of the victim's neck and the other on his hip, and gently roll the victim over onto his back. If you suspect a back or neck injury, then try to get others to help. Keep the injured's head, neck, and back in alignment as much as possible as you roll the person until faceup.

To open the injured's airway, you must use a head tilt (even if you suspect back or neck injury):

1. Kneel beside the victim and place one of your hands on their forehead while you gently tilt the victim's head back.
2. Place the fingers of your other hand on the cusp, or bony part, of the victim's chin (not on the throat).
3. Carefully lift the chin straight up, keeping the head tilted back. Try to do so without closing the person's mouth. If you think the victim might have a spinal injury, use the jaw thrust method.
4. Check to make sure there is nothing obstructing the victim's throat or interfering with breathing. The tongue may have curled up at the back of the throat. Using what's called a finger sweep, clear the mouth of all obstructions and move the tongue out of the airway if needed.

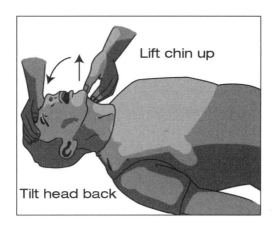

B: BREATHING

Once you determine that the airway is open, listen for any indication of breathing for five to ten seconds. This can be done by placing your ear next to the victim's mouth or pressing your cheek against their lips in an effort to hear or feel breathing. As you are doing this, watch the chest to see if it is rising and falling.

C: CIRCULATION

Then monitor for signs of circulation by placing your index and middle fingers in the groove of the windpipe, which is located just beneath the angle of the jaw. You can also check if there is a pulse by placing two fingers on the inside of the wrist at about one inch above the base of the thumb, or under the armpits.

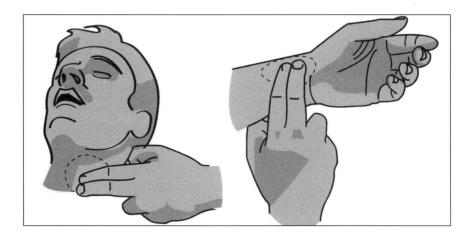

Rescue Breathing

If an **adult** stops breathing but still has signs of circulation, call for EMS (emergency medical services) and then begin rescue breathing. If a **child or infant** stops breathing but has signs of circulation, perform rescue breathing for two minutes before calling for EMS. Then resume rescue breathing. If the victim is not breathing and has no signs of circulation, perform **CPR.**

RESCUE BREATHING ON AN ADULT

1. Pinch victim's nose closed with your fingers, and put your mouth over their mouth.
2. Exhale two full, slow breaths, each for one to one and a half seconds.
3. Then withdraw and wait for the victim's lungs to deflate.

4. If you don't hear air exhaling, then reposition the person's head, mindful of possible spinal cord injury, and try the procedure again.
5. Check for any signs of breathing and circulation, and then continue the method, waiting about ten seconds between each attempt.

RESCUE BREATHING ON AN INFANT

1. Place your mouth over both the infant's nose and mouth.
2. Blow in two gentle puffs.
3. If you feel no exchange of air, reposition infant's head and retry.
4. Observe and listen or feel to see if there is breathing and circulation.

If the person is unconscious, yet there are signs of circulation but still no breathing, then proceed by administering one breath every five seconds for adults and one puff every three seconds for infants.

CPR (Cardiopulmonary Resuscitation)

Upon arrival, if you find an adult not breathing and exhibiting no signs of circulation, call for EMS if this has not already been done. If an **AED,** or **automated external defibrillator,** is available, begin attaching it to the victim. This is a portable electronic device that automatically diagnoses the potentially life-threatening cardiac issues in a patient and is able to treat them through defibrillation by applying electrical therapy that stops the arrhythmia, allowing the heart to reestablish an effective rhythm. If an AED is not available, begin CPR. If a child or infant is not breathing and has no signs of circulation, give CPR for two minutes immediately before calling EMS (if this has not already been done). Then resume CPR.

1. It is best to kneel a few inches to the side of the casualty in a position where you can place your hands directly on the breastbone, the part of the chest midway between the nipples. Put your hands on your ribs right now. Feel how the ends of the ribs curve up? This is where the ribs meet what's called the sternum, or breastbone. This is where you put your hands to perform proper CPR. The idea of doing CPR is to get blood circulating through the heart. If administering to a child, use the heel of just one hand, while placing your other hand on the child's forehead. For adults, put one hand on top of the other, centered at the breastbone.

2. To be effective, align your shoulders above your hands and straighten your elbows. You want to create a chest compression at the very center of the victim's chest, which is best achieved by leveraging and utilizing the weight of your upper body. You press down with the heels of your palms while moving in an upward direction. Again, the point of CPR is to force blood to enter the heart, which makes it involuntarily begin to beat again.

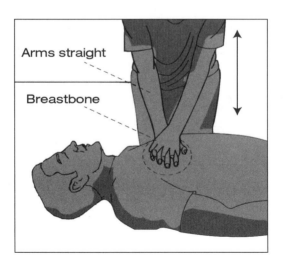

3. Push down and make **thirty compressions** at a rate of approximately two per second. It's recommended to count

aloud, which keeps a steady and regulated pace, as well as keeping your mindset focused on the job. For adults, use both hands to give chest compressions, pushing the chest down about one and a half to two inches each time. For children, use one hand to give chest compressions. Use the same rate, but press less forcibly, compressing the chest down only about one inch each time.

4. Once you have completed thirty compressions, tilt the victim's head, pinch the nose, and place your mouth over the victim's mouth (just as in rescue breathing). Give two breaths for an adult or child.
5. Repeat these steps four or five times.
6. At two-minute intervals assess for signs of circulation and breathing, and continue to perform CPR until breathing begins or until EMS arrives.

CPR, one of the most universally proven emergency lifesaving techniques, was invented by Austrian surgeon Peter Safar in the late 1950s. He dubbed his emergency medical method the ABCs and was nominated for the Nobel Prize three times for this and his other achievements. Unfortunately, although his method saved millions, he was unable to resuscitate his own daughter when she was stricken by a fatal asthma attack.

CPR: INFANT
1. Place two of your fingers on the breastbone.
2. Place your other hand on the infant's forehead to keep the head tilted back and the airway open.
3. Using your two fingers, give thirty chest compressions. Don't do as with adults, though—compress the chest only about half an inch to one inch each time.
4. With the infant's head tilted back, cover the infant's mouth and nose with your mouth and give two gentle breaths.

5. At two-minute intervals assess for signs of circulation and breathing, and continue to perform this method until breathing begins or until EMS arrives.

A good friend of mine went to work for the fire department shortly after leaving the SEAL teams. He had been in the department for only a few weeks when he made the front page of the newspaper for saving an elderly lady from a burning house. There he was, front page, giving CPR. John was just being John, however; you don't have to be a Navy SEAL to do what he did—save a life!

On the flip side, another good friend, also turned firefighter, was given the nickname "Dr. Death" because out of ninety-nine CPR attempts he wasn't able to save anyone. This wasn't his fault. I tell this story to stress the importance of getting to the victim as soon as possible. It's a race against the clock, and every second a person's heart is not beating brings them closer to death. After about a minute without CPR, the chances of resuscitation are greatly reduced.

So, now that your injured person is breathing and has a heartbeat, you must identify other injuries and primarily stop any bleeding. You need to continue to monitor the patient's vital signs (breathing and heart rate), as these can change at any time.

Stopping the Bleeding

You must understand and practice methods to stop bleeding in order to be prepared for an essential element of survival medicine. During catastrophes, accidents, and survival situations, expect to see blood. Whether the result of a bullet, knife, car crash, or fall, bleeding is bleeding and requires immediate attention. As you know, blood is our vital fluid, and if too much is lost, you're dead. Take action, and don't get freaked by the amount of blood you might see. The faster you can focus and remain alert, not panicking over the amount of blood you may or may not see, the more likely it is that you'll be able to take positive actions to save your life or the lives of those around you.

First, examine the body for signs of major bleeding, such as large pools of blood or blood-soaked clothing. Expose the wounded area by cutting away clothing if you have scissors or a knife, or find a way to see where the bleeding is coming from. Blood loss has to be stopped, or the efforts in rescue breathing or CPR will be for naught.

When I was on SEAL Team One, my platoon chief, who had been a SEAL for sixteen years, was a truly tough guy—been there, done that—but he still couldn't stand the sight of blood. We had to wake him up every time he had to get a shot. It was classic.

You can usually detect if there is major bleeding by color, since bright red, spurting bloods comes from arterial wounds, while a darker red bleeding is usually venous, or from smaller veins. Arteries are larger and are a source from which a lot of blood can be lost quickly, causing sudden death. You must be calm and unhesitating. Once you find the source of the bleeding, place your fingers or hand on the wound to apply direct pressure, which frequently helps to stop the more rapid loss of blood. If bleeding continues, and you do not suspect a fracture or a broken bone at the wound area, then try to elevate the arm or leg, for instance, above the level of the heart, while continuing to apply direct pressure.

What looks cool in movies isn't always the right thing to do. So don't dig the bullet out and don't cauterize the wound with a glowing red-hot knife.

Dressing the Wound

As soon as bleeding subsides, try to wrap and cover the wound with what's called a **field dressing,** such as gauze or bandaging. Utilize the dressing to apply continuous pressure to the source of bleeding, wrapping it tightly. If no sterilized field dressing is available, use the cleanest cloth on hand. At this point, the bleeding must be stopped, so use homemade bandages made from T-shirts, socks, or any other garment within reach.

- **Field dressing** is what's applied directly to the wound to control and stop bleeding.
- **Pressure dressing** is added and put over the wound and wrapped very tightly, even using a knot above the wound to create additional pressure on the dressing.

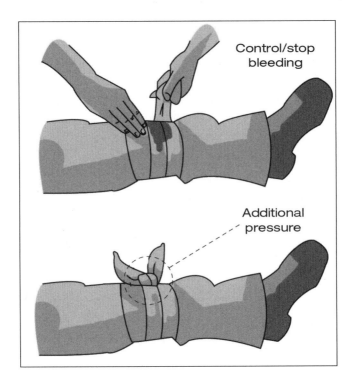

Once you have good pressure applied to the wound, keep it in place and monitor it. The moment it becomes soaked with blood, apply new dressings directly over the old dressings. Remember, the less a bleeding wound is touched and disturbed, the quicker the natural coagulants will have a chance to kick in and help to quell the blood flow.

If all this fails to control bleeding, then work on identifying a nearby **pressure point.** For wounds on arms or hands, pressure points are located on the inside of the wrist, the place where you've seen doctors and nurses feeling for a pulse by using their fingers. Another pressure point is on the inside of the upper arm (called a brachial artery). For wounds of the legs, the pressure point is near the crease of the groin (called a femoral artery). Try to apply pressure to these areas.

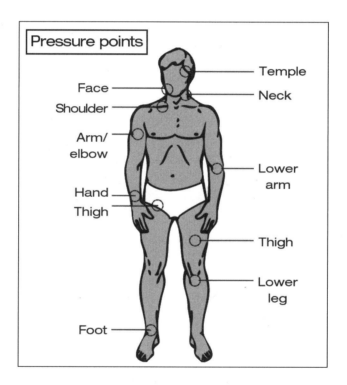

Lastly, if there is broken glass, for example, or something impaled in the wound, and the object is sticking out, don't at first try to remove it in the field. Instead, stabilize the object with bulky dressing made from the cleanest material available. If possible, try to keep the limb that is bleeding elevated. Sometimes, pulling out the impaled object will make the wound larger, and the first course of action is to control blood loss.

When a Tourniquet Is Needed

If none of this works, you then need to resort to fashioning a **tourniquet,** defined as any device that can be twisted and constricted tightly around a limb and above the wound to cut off the blood flow to the area. It can be placed around an upper arm or thigh and then tightened to stop the flow of blood.

With one exception, a tourniquet should be used as a *last resort,* when all other methods have failed, as it stops circulation and, if improperly applied, could kill a person. However, if there is an **amputation** or a loss of any part of the upper arm, forearm, thigh, or lower leg, then a tourniquet is the first course of action and essential. Apply a tourniquet to an amputated limb before attempting to use field or pressure dressings. Incredibly, I've seen that when there is nothing but a stump left for a leg, it oftentimes shows very little bleeding. Nevertheless, apply a tourniquet above the area first and foremost.

Do not apply a tourniquet if there is an amputation to only part of a hand or part of a foot, as this could adversely affect the remaining fingers or toes and cause all the otherwise healthy digits to get cut off from circulation, killing the cells in these areas. Use only a pressure dressing to control bleeding for these types of wounds.

During missions, there was a reason we always had several tourniquets on us when we went outside "the fence." These were tied and placed where you could access them using only your right or left hand, if need be, and brilliantly designed for self-application. You just always hoped that you came back with as many tourniquet straps still unused as when you left.

MAKE A TOURNIQUET

Ideally, tourniquet bands will be made from a cloth or flexible material, cut into two-inch-wide strips. Many other things can operate as tourniquets—belts, ties, headbands, waistbands, towels, duffel bag straps, or dress socks. Keep your wits and improvise with what is at hand. *Do not* use thin wires, electric cords, or shoestrings as tourniquet bands, as these will cut into the flesh.

For best results, apply regulated pressure, wrapping the cloth around a stick and twisting until tight. Also, try to find something to serve as padding to place between the limb and the tourniquet band. Sometimes you can just use the casualty's shirtsleeve, their trouser leg, or the part of the clothing you removed to see the wound.

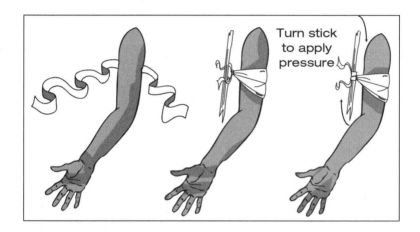

SELECT A TOURNIQUET SITE

The upper arm or high up on the thigh are ideal places to apply tourniquets. Select an area about two to four inches above the edge of the wound or amputation. For maximum tourniquet effectiveness, if the wound is anywhere from the knee down, then apply the band just above the knee. If the wound is on the lower part of the arm, then put the tourniquet slightly above the elbow. Do not apply a tourniquet band directly over a joint where you see a broken bone or suspect a fracture; it will not be effective.

APPLY A TOURNIQUET

1. If the victim is still wearing clothes, simply smooth out the fabric of the sleeve or pants before putting on the tourniquet.

2. Put the tourniquet band above the wound area.
3. Make a half knot, as if beginning to tie a shoelace.
4. Put your stick or other rigid object on top of the half knot and then finish making the knot so the twisting object won't come loose.
5. Then twist the stick or whatever you are using until the tourniquet is tight and you see the bleeding has subsided.

You may still see some darker blood from a vein continue to ooze even after the tourniquet has been properly applied, but the bright red arterial blood should stop. The tourniquet will be so tight as to cut off a pulse to all parts of the body that are below the tourniquet. However, don't be fooled into thinking the blood has stopped and loosen the tourniquet. Doing so could allow the wound to start bleeding again, which could be fatal.

USE WITH CAUTION

A tourniquet stops all circulation below where it is applied. Make sure you keep the tourniquet exposed so that others who might come after you can see it; in survival situations, you may have to leave the victim behind as you continue on with your escape, for example. Hopefully, medical personnel will follow, and you must make it obvious to them that a tourniquet has been applied. You should even draw the letter "T" on the person's forehead and indicate the time the tourniquet was applied. A tourniquet left on too long will kill the cells in the entire limb, even if it is the only way to stop bleeding and save the victim's life.

Protecting Wounds and Stabilizing Fractures or Dislocations

You've done well to this point and stopped bleeding and have your casualty breathing. Now you have the time to do a more thorough physical exam. You want to identify any additional injuries or conditions that may also be life-threatening. Remember to keep monitoring the patient's vital signs (breathing and heart rate), as they can change at any time.

This is not like an annual checkup type of exam. You're under field conditions, and in the lingo of EMTs it's called a rapid trauma assessment. Yet you have to look over the body from head to toe, primarily searching for tenderness. If the person is conscious, they will react if you touch a certain spot. Also, look for swelling or deformities. As if frisking someone, though gently, use both hands and work your way down the body front and back.

FRACTURES

There are more than two hundred bones in the human body, and during accidents and survival situations, chances are some of these are going to break or get fractured. The distinction between a fracture and a break in the bone is really only a measure of how damaged the bone is. Depending on what bone is fractured or broken, however, this can be a life-threatening medical emergency or just a *really* painful inconvenience.

The American Academy of Orthopedic Surgeons defines fractures this way:

Closed or simple fracture: The bone is broken, but the skin is not lacerated.

Open or compound fracture: The skin may be pierced by the bone or by a blow that breaks the skin at the time of the fracture. The bone may or may not be visible in the wound.

Transverse fracture: The fracture is at right angles to the long axis of the bone.

Greenstick fracture: Fracture on one side of the bone, causing a bend on the other side of the bone.

If you have time to identify the fracture and apply a splint before moving the victim, do so. But make a situational assessment, and if you must remove the casualty (and yourself) from immediate danger, such as to escape from a burning vehicle or move out of the line of fire before treatment, then make that call and act accordingly.

Identify the fracture

In all situations, try to expose the area where you suspect the broken bone to be. Try to loosen clothing or anything that might be applying more pressure to the nonbleeding broken bone area. If it is on the arms, remove any jewelry that could limit circulation. Even check the victim's pockets to see if there is anything that will put undue pressure on the break. If the bone is on any part of the legs other than the feet, then make sure you leave the casualty's boots or shoes on. If you must keep moving, he will need them later on.

Stabilize the fracture

Even the smallest broken bone is very painful, because it is causing tissue damage around the area of the break. In the field, you are not going to try to do anything but "immobilize the fracture," which means attempting to relieve pain and prevent additional injury. If an arm or leg is fractured, applying a splint is the most effective way to stabilize the area. In emergency medicine, the general principle is "splint the fracture as it lies." Don't try to snap it back in place; instead, the idea is to try to merely support the limb until you can get proper medical attention.

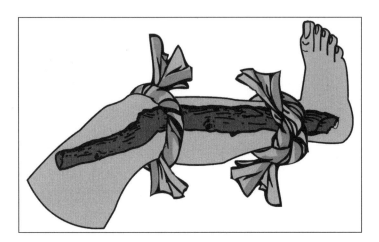

Splints

The purpose of a split is to minimize the movement to the fractured area or bone. A splint may be a special device carried by EMTs, but in survival medicine, you'll likely have to improvise. Look for something rigid, such as a plank of wood, a pole, even a tree branch. Rolled-up newspapers or an unloaded rifle are other things you can possibly use as a splint. You will also need something to tie the splint in place. Strips of cloth or a belt can be used.

1. Apply the splint to the affected area in the position in which you find it. Do not try to set it back in place or realign the bones.
2. When tying the splint in place don't overtighten the strips. This is not a tourniquet. Check to make sure you haven't tied the strips too tight by pinching something like fingers or toes below the splint. The injured should feel this pinch. If they don't, the straps are too tight.
3. It's the inflammation around the injury that is causing pain, so if ice is available, apply liberally, placing an ice pack firmly on the area. You want to try to reduce the swelling, which can be aided by elevating the limb or joint above the heart.

DISLOCATIONS AND SPRAINS

Dislocated bones or sprains are injuries to the musculoskeletal system and are often not an actual fracture. Dislocation means the bone is out of its normal alignment, while a sprain is a twist or injury to the muscles around the bone. All can be very painful and immobilizing. Do not ask the casualty to move the injured area to test to see how much pain it causes. Ice is good for sprains and dislocations, but after twenty-four to forty-eight hours, heat is more effective in reducing pain. A splint can also be used for these types of injuries, depending on the body part. Especially if you must keep moving, a splint can prevent further injury.

TRANSPORTING INJURED

There are a number of ways to help the injured get out of harm's way. The simplest—if you are capable—is called the **fireman carry,** which requires hauling the person over your shoulder. In reality, this will be slow and difficult to do over a long period of time. If there are a few people gathered with you, work as a team. For example, the **two-man carry** is performed when the injured is transported by having one person stand between the legs and grab them while the other person slings the injured's arms over the shoulders. Both rescuers are facing in the same direction and are moving with the injured's legs first. A third form of transportation is the **improvised pull-and-haul,** which is performed by employing a dragline, made from rope, belts, etc. These are placed around the chest and under the armpits to drag the injured from danger. You could also create a **makeshift stretcher** with a blanket or similar item. Place the injured onto it and pull them to safety.

The two words you never wanted to hear the training instructors say were "*Man down.*" It meant that in addition to the 110-degree heat and 100-percent humidity you were performing contact drills in, you now had to carry or drag one of your teammates, who was simulating injury. It was a real dick dragger! But when the real bullets started flying, these drills were invaluable. In SEAL Team we say: "Sweat in training, so you don't bleed in war."

SHOCK

Our circulatory system continuously flows like a river through our veins and arteries, distributing blood to all parts of the body, bringing oxygen and nutrients to the tissues. If that system fails, resulting in an insufficient flow of oxygen to the vital organs, then the body goes into a medical condition known as shock. If a person remains in this state too long, the vital organs will fail, ultimately causing death. Shock is made worse by fear and pain. Prevention and treatment methods for shock are basically the same.

Causes of Shock

If blood isn't flowing properly, then the main pump, the heart, is usually not functioning properly. The most common cause of shock is a heart attack. But it can also be caused by a reduction in the volume of blood and a sudden loss of fluids. Some other causes of shock include: external or internal bleeding and fluid loss from severe diarrhea, vomiting, or burns. What's happening to a person going into shock is that the blood supply is being diverted from the surface of the body, which keeps our bodies at a regulated temperature, and is instead being sent to the core of the body, trying to sustain the vital organs. Sudden redistribution of the circulation can be spotted. Look for the following early warning signs:

- Sweaty but cool (clammy) skin
- Pale skin
- Restlessness, nervousness
- Thirst
- Loss of blood (bleeding)
- Confusion (or loss of awareness)
- Faster-than-normal breathing rate
- Blotchy or bluish skin (especially around the mouth and lips)
- Nausea and/or vomiting

It's a tough thing to witness when you come upon a guy who just fell sixty feet from a helicopter while rappelling and has two broken legs with bones sticking out of the skin. This requires incredible focus to get into action and help. As horrified as I was to see such a thing happen to a fellow SEAL, I had a job to do. You owe it to the person who needs your help to remain calm and go to work, reassuring him by your demeanor that he is in good hands. If a victim of trauma sees fear in your eyes, it will only accelerate the fear in him and bring on life-threatening panic. Your fear could actually make it worse. If a person is injured and he sees that you are panicking, this, in fact, can cause him to go into shock.

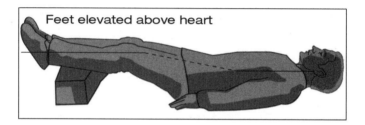

Feet elevated above heart

Treatment/Prevention

If you see these early warning signs, you can prevent shock by having the person lie down on their back. Elevate the feet higher than the heart, and loosen clothing, such as a tight belt or the collar of a shirt. Remember: Do not move the casualty if you suspect fractures, and do not elevate the legs if there is a head injury or abdominal injury. If you are in a cold climate, do what you can to warm them up and keep them warm. Use a blanket or extra coats; you can even warm them with your body heat. If in a warm environment do what you can to keep them cool by placing them in shade, but closely monitor this person. Don't let them cool off too much, which can happen easily with someone who is in or going into shock. *Do not* give the person any food or drinks. Also, if the person is unconscious, turn their head to the side, as this will prevent the possibility of choking if vomiting occurs. In all instances, you must reassure the person that you are in control and show no fear or panic.

Be authoritative by showing self-confidence, because you are now the key to this person's survival. Commit to this as if the roles were reversed and your life depended on them. Your mental and physical toughness is being shared and your only mission is now this person's survival.

HEAT INJURIES

Someone can die from heat when they engage in physical activity when the heat production within their body exceeds the body's ability to lower its own temperature adequately. This results in a rise in inner body temperature to levels that interfere with normal body functions. There are many environmental factors that contribute to this condition, such as air temperature, humidity, wind speed, and sun exposure. Additionally there are individual factors that increase your chance of a heat injury, like fitness level, dehydration, preactivity hydration, higher body fat levels, and the use of some medications. It's important to understand that a heat injury can occur after walking for 5 minutes in 120-degree weather as well as exercising for 60 minutes in 80-degree weather; it all depends on the factors above.

I'll never forget desert warfare training in the midsummer heat at the Special Warfare Center facility near Yuma, Arizona. It was so hot that we had to keep our rifles high ported (pointing to the sky) because rounds in the chamber were cooking off on their own. There was no way to drink enough water. My brain and body were in a constant state of "drunken" delusion. My piss looked like orange juice. Unfortunately, when we go to war it's never at a Club Med. The desert is without a doubt one of the harshest environments on the earth. Like I said, they never send you to war where they serve drinks with little umbrellas in them.

The primary goal in treating a heat injury is to cool down the human body and get it closer to the baseline norm of 98.6 degrees.

Artificially re-regulating an individual's body temperature until their body can once again self-regulate is what we'll be doing here.

Dehydration

Dehydration stems from a sudden loss of body fluids. If not enough water is consumed, or there is severe diarrhea, vomiting, or sweating, dehydration can occur. The body can go weeks without eating but only a few days without water. In the short term, you will feel thirsty and hot. In the long term, the best indicator that you are becoming dehydrated will be the color and frequency of urination: Less frequent and darker in color is *bad*.

TREATMENT AND PREVENTION

Prevention is simple: *Drink water constantly and not occasionally.* Additionally, avoid beverages that are high in sugar when hydrating. **Electrolyte**-enhanced waters are great, or if unavailable you can make your own by adding a teaspoon of salt and some fresh-squeezed orange, lemon, or lime juice to a liter of water.

Pickles (and pickle juice) are higher in electrolytes than beverages like Gatorade or Powerade and have been shown to reduce cramping caused by exertion in high temperatures. The acetic acid in pickles and pickle juice is considered superior to the citric acid found in commercial sports drinks, at least when it comes to rehydration properties.

Fresh produce has a very high water content, so it's a great way to hydrate without having to drink a ton of water. For example, an apple is up to 85 percent water by volume. Again, remember to avoid any food that is high in sugar or contains caffeine.

Heat Cramps

This is when you experience a painful cramping in a large muscle. It could happen in your legs, arms, or abdomen. This stems from a sudden and excessive loss of salt, due to heavy sweating or several hours of nonstop exertion.

Heat Exhaustion

This is displayed by a sudden amount of profuse sweating. You may experience a pounding headache or tingling sensation, or feel light-headed, or vomit. What's happening is that the body temperature has risen to between 99 and 104 degrees, and it's attempting to regulate the surface temperature of your skin.

Heatstroke

If your body temperature reaches more than 105 degrees, then the entire nervous system could malfunction. This is marked by an absence of sweat in a person and can lead to organ damage and death.

TREATMENT

The immediate goal in all three of these cases is to cool down the body by performing as many of the following functions as possible:

1. Get to a shaded environment.
2. Lie down and elevate the legs.
3. Loosen clothing.
4. Take sips of fluid, but don't gulp or guzzle.
5. Remove most clothing.
6. Fan a cold-water mist over the body, which increases evaporation.
7. Wrap the victim in a water-soaked blanket.
8. Put ice packs under the groin or on the back of the neck.

COLD INJURIES

The body doesn't like being exposed for prolonged periods to cold temperatures, since our ability to generate heat, or to limit heat loss, is quite limited. The body works very hard to maintain its core temperature, which means it burns a lot of calories performing this function. Of primary importance is staying dry when facing cold conditions.

A wet layer against your skin, like a sweat-soaked shirt, will greatly reduce your body's ability to stay warm. Whenever possible ensure you have a dry layer that you can put on.

SEALs say: "If you're wet, you're dead."

Cold injuries can also occur with only brief exposure to extremely cold conditions. You must pay close attention to forecasting weather conditions to make for better planning and to know what equipment will be essential. Thorough preplanning can greatly reduce the chances of incurring a cold injury.

Hypothermia

Hypothermia is defined as a decrease in the core body temperature to a level at which normal muscular and cerebral functions are impaired. Many conditions can contribute to hypothermia: cold temperatures, improper clothing and equipment, wetness, fatigue and exhaustion, dehydration, poor food intake, and alcohol consumption. Another huge risk factor can be a lack of knowledge about hypothermia and inability to read the terrain and environment correctly, so practice situational awareness, and always be prepared.

MILD HYPOTHERMIA

When the body temperature drops from the normal 98.6 to 96 degrees, an involuntary shivering occurs. This is the body's only way of trying to generate heat, which is fairly ineffective. However, it still will not interfere with or impair motor functions, so you can still ice climb or ski, for example, and walk and talk coherently.

MODERATE HYPOTHERMIA

When the body temperature dips to between 95 and 93 degrees, you begin to feel dazed and will lose fine motor coordination, particularly in your hands. You'll find that you can't zip up your parka, for example, which is due to restricted peripheral blood flow. You'll experience slurred speech, more violent shivering, and even irrational behavior. I've seen a weird phenomenon take place during such circumstances that I call **paradoxical undressing.** When freezing to death, a person starts to take off clothing, and a strange "I don't care" attitude comes into play.

SEVERE HYPOTHERMIA

If the body goes down to between 92 and 86 degrees or below, death is imminent. Shivering will then occur in waves. It will be extremely violent and then pause. The pauses get longer until shivering finally ceases. The person falls to the ground, can't walk, and curls up into a fetal position. The skin turns pale, pupils dilate, and the pulse rate decreases to a faint beat. The person looks dead, but at this point, they remain alive for an indeterminate amount of time.

As a SEAL, you just come to realize that hypothermia is part of the job. In addition to the constant physical demands of Hell Week, like endless running with a coat on your head, the most physically demanding thing your body goes through is trying to maintain its minimal, functioning core temperature. A couple of doctors did a study on a class going through Hell Week and realized that students were burning more than twenty thousand calories every twenty-four hours, largely due to the body's effort to stay warm. That's the equivalent of eating forty McDonald's Quarter Pounders with Cheese every twenty-four hours. Super-size that!

TREATMENT FOR MILD AND MODERATE HYPOTHERMIA

The basic idea is to get the person warmed up, conserve the heat they have left, and find a way to replace the fuel they are burning up.

1. If the person is in wet clothes, get them off and replace them with dry layers. At this early stage, physical activity

will generate heat, so keep the victim moving at least minimally. Attempt to find shelter or build one.

2. It is essential to stop and forestall hypothermia by eating and drinking hot liquids, if available. Carbohydrate-rich foods are best, and even candy can add a quick release of needed fuel into the bloodstream for a sudden brief heat surge. Avoid alcohol, caffeine, and tobacco.

3. Generate heat from an exterior source, such as a fire. Get into a sleeping bag and create a heat cocoon generated by your own heat. You can do like the penguins do and huddle up, because body-to-body contact also generates heat.

TREATMENT FOR SEVERE HYPOTHERMIA

Even at this point, the body can warm itself more effectively than can warmth from an exterior heat source. This method involves creating a **hypothermia wrap.**

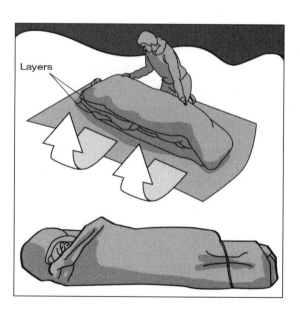

Layers

1. Wrap the person in as many warm layers of blankets or sleeping bags as are available, forming a shell of total insulation at least four inches thick. If possible, once the person

is encased, also try to raise the person off the cold ground or create some barrier between them and the ground, so as not to lose heat or have more cold come in from below.

2. Get fuel into the victim. When experiencing severe hypothermia, the stomach shuts down and will not digest solid foods. The best way to give them energy is by heating water and adding sugar to it. Feed a cup of this mixture to the hypothermic every fifteen minutes.

3. Get the person to urinate. This may sound odd, but the body spends a lot of its heat resources to keep urine warm while it's in the bladder. The more they can urinate, the quicker the body's resources can be used to heat other vital organs.

4. Try to transfer heat to the person by placing hot stones, wrapped in towels or cloth, at major arteries, such as at the neck or under the armpits. Remember, there is also another artery near the groin, called the femoral artery, which can quickly distribute heat to the vital organs.

5. If no external sources of heat are available, transfer heat to the person by pressing your own, warmer hands to these points. Do not rub the victim's skin, as they may also be suffering from frostbite and you might injure them further.

6. A person with severe hypothermia needs to be handled with care (gently) because they are very susceptible to cardiac issues.

Frostbite

Frostbite occurs when body tissue actually freezes. Typically affecting the hands, feet, nose, ears, and cheeks—though other areas of the body may also be affected—frostbite can lead to death or necrosis of tissue, requiring amputation or removal.

You know if frostbite is setting in if you feel a dull pain or tingling sensation. Oftentimes the area feels itchy and will turn colors. At first, it could be red, but then the frostbitten area becomes white or grayish-yellow. The skin will look waxy until it goes numb. When lost to frostbite, the area affected turns black and hard, as the skin tissue has died.

TREATMENT

1. Get the person warmed up with external means (fire) or personal means (cocooning the frostbitten areas). But unless absolutely necessary, do not make the person walk on frostbitten toes or feet.

2. Submerge the extremities in warm water (105 to 110 degrees—no hotter).

3. Try to use a heated, moist towel and gently apply to the skin until the red color returns.

4. If you have no water, then your warm breath can be used. Make a cup with your hands over the area and breathe into it. Also, you can place your hands under the armpits or on the stomach.

5. Do not place anything hot, such as heating pads, directly on the area.

6. Don't add heat and then remove it from the frostbitten area, as this warming and then reexposure to cold air can worsen the damage.

7. Don't rub at the frostbitten area, as the skin will blister and more damage will be caused.

8. When dealing with severe frostbite, the goal is a gradual rewarming process in 100-degree water over a period of twenty-five to forty minutes.

9. As the affected areas warm, there will be some severe burning sensations, change of skin color, and maybe blistering/swelling. Do not try to treat/burst the blisters. Severe frostbite will remain black in color.

10. Dress fingers and toes individually; use cotton balls or other spacers to keep digits from touching and give acetaminophen or ibuprofen, not aspirin, to reduce the pain.

TRENCH FOOT

It's been said that one reason Napoleon had to retreat from his 1812 invasion of Russia was due to footwear—the ultimate wardrobe malfunction. His soldiers became immobilized by what later came to be called trench foot. Soldiers in World War I, World War II, and even Vietnam suffered from this condition. When boots are constricted, get wet, or become soaked with the wearer's own perspiration, a fungal infection forms on the feet. The condition can appear in as few as eighteen hours. The foot will turn red, then blue, and itch like mad. The skin begins to actually smell and die. Trench foot leads to gangrene, and amputation is the only cure if it's left unattended.

Treatment
The best way to prevent trench foot is to take off wet socks, air out footwear, and be attentive to your feet by examining them regularly.

In the movie *Forrest Gump,* the character Lieutenant Dan summed it up: "Change those socks every chance you get."

CHOKING

Choking is one of the top causes of accidental death in America. Anything, though it's usually food, can get stuck in the airway and cut off breathing. It happens so fast that trying to self-administer first aid is nearly impossible, though it can be done. When an airway is obstructed, the person cannot speak or call out for help. Without first aid, brain damage and death by asphyxiation are the end results of choking.

Treating a Choking Victim

1. Make sure the person is actually choking. By this I mean you must determine if it's complete airway obstruction. If the person is able to speak or is making actual coughing sounds, then they have only a partial airway blockage. You want to monitor it, but allow them to try to cough up the item causing the problem.
2. If you are able to look into the mouth and see the obstruction, then manually remove the obstruction with your fingers for an immediate resolution.
3. If the obstruction remains, use the Heimlich maneuver.
   a. Get behind the person and grab them at their stomach, just below the rib cage and above the navel.
   b. Apply pressure by delivering inward and upward thrusts until the blockage is cleared.

If you are alone and begin to choke, find a chair or hard surface and ram your stomach, below the rib cage, at the hard surface multiple times until the blockage is clear. You have only moments of consciousness, so if you are alone and choking, act quickly but with purpose.

If the victim is unconscious, lay them on their back. Straddle their legs and put the heel of your interlaced hands just above the navel and thrust inward and upward five times. Sweep the mouth to remove the obstruction and repeat until successful.

Alternately, if they are in a position where you can do so, give the unconscious victim five hard blows to the back between the person's shoulder blades using the bottom part or heel of your hand. Sweep the mouth to remove the obstruction and deliver an additional five separate forceful strikes.

BURNS

Burns occur frequently during survival situations. A burn is damage to your body's tissues caused by heat, chemicals, electricity, sunlight, or radiation. Scalds from hot liquids and steam, building fires, and flammable liquids and gases are the most common causes of burns. Burns can cause swelling, blistering, scarring, and, in serious cases, shock and even death. It's important to note the distinction in the severity of burns in order to administer the proper care.

First degree: This is the least serious and affects only the outer layer of skin. The skin is usually red, often accompanied by swelling.

Second degree: This is when the burn has affected the second layer of skin, called the dermis. Blisters develop, and the skin becomes reddened and splotchy in appearance.

Third degree: In these most serious burns, all layers of the skin are damaged. The burn destroys skin tissue, fat, and muscle, and may even reach the bone. Third-degree burns can appear charred black or sometimes dry and white.

Short-term Treatment

1. Stop the continued destruction of tissue by running cool water at low pressure over the wound.

2. Remove jewelry and clothes from areas that have been burned.
3. Cover the burn with a sterile dressing or clean and dry improvised dressing.
4. Don't put any ointment on the wound just yet.
5. Try to have the person drink fluids.
6. Electrical burns often cause serious injury to organs inside the body. This injury may not show on the skin.
7. A chemical burn should be flushed with large amounts of cool water. Take off any clothing or jewelry that has the chemical on it. Don't put anything on the burned area, such as antibiotic ointment. This might start a chemical reaction that could make the burn worse.
8. Get ready to treat for shock, if necessary.

Long-term Treatment

It's important to get immediate medical attention if:

- A first- or second-degree burn covers an area larger than two to three inches in diameter
- The burn is on your face, over a major joint (such as the knee or shoulder), or on the hands, feet, or genitals
- The burn is a third-degree burn

Burns also can lead to infections, because they damage your skin's protective barrier. Antibiotic creams can prevent or treat infections. After a third-degree burn, you need skin or synthetic grafts to cover exposed tissue and encourage new skin to grow. First- and second-degree burns usually heal without grafts.

How Long Does It Take For Burns To Heal?

- First-degree burns usually heal in three to six days.
- Second-degree burns usually heal in two to three weeks.
- Third-degree burns usually take a very long time to heal.

BITES AND STINGS

Bites and stings are not often fatal, but they certainly can be. For some people, a bite or a sting can simply cause an irritation, bring about disease, or even send the body into shock. Certain insects and snakes, however, have venom that can cause death.

In all cases, if you get bitten or stung, do not scratch the site because you will further aggravate and potentially infect it.

Bee and Wasp Stings

For most people, bee and wasp stings will be an irritation, albeit a potentially painful one. At the first sign of a bee or wasp attack, the primary goal should be to get off the X and make sure you aren't near a hive or other area with the potential for swarm activity.

While not everyone is susceptible to **anaphylactic shock,** or **anaphylaxis,** from the venom of certain bites and stings, it is such a serious condition that getting yourself and your family tested to see if you're at risk is prudent. If you have been bitten or stung and have experienced anything more than a local swelling/irritation at the point of damage, then you are at a higher risk for this to occur to you. Still, many people who have had no previous adverse reactions suddenly find themselves under the threat of anaphylactic shock. The tests aren't perfect and can't determine everything, but the information they yield might just save your life someday.

1. Remove the stinger by scraping with a sharp edge, the same way you would sharpen a knife on a flat stone or use a spatula to flip a pancake.
2. Determine if victim carried epinephrine or some other treatment that needs to be immediately administered.
3. Wash site with soap and water.
4. Relieve discomfort with cold water.
5. Use antibiotics, depending on the type of wound, or with the advice of a physician.

To clear up a common myth, sucking out venom using your mouth is only a last resort.

Make incisions to a wound only if treatment is more than an hour away, and make the incisions no larger than twice the size of the original punctures. See how many puncture wounds the snake has made in the skin and judge how many incisions to make accordingly. Anything more, and you are merely adding to the injury and increasing the trauma.

Spider and Scorpion Bites

1. Clean and dress the bite area.
2. Treat for shock and be prepared to give CPR.
3. Obtain antivenin if available.
4. Take antibiotics if necessary.

Snakebites

1. Keep the victim calm and still, with as low a heart rate as possible, to reduce the spread of venom throughout the circulatory system.
2. Immobilize the bitten extremity and prepare for immediate transportation to a medical facility.
3. Treat for shock and force them to drink fluids.
4. Remove all jewelry and other constricting items.
5. Clean the bite area.
6. Prepare to give rescue breathing and CPR.
7. Use a constricting band (*not a tourniquet*) between bite site and heart that two fingers can easily slip under.
8. Attempt to remove poison with mechanical suction or by squeezing.
9. Obtain antivenin if available.

Acknowledgments

I would like to thank first and foremost my co-writer and pointman on this project, Michael Largo. This book doesn't exist without you. Thank you for your patience, hard work, writing ability, and navigating me through my first book without allowing me to hit any IED's.

I'd also like to thank Adam Wilson and all the folks at Simon & Schuster. Jesse Peterson for the outstanding illustrations. The paramedics at the Westminster, Colorado, Fire Department for keeping it current and accurate. And lastly my pit bull/agent in New York, Frank Wiemann.